Haven, Harbor & Heritage:
The Holland, Michigan, Story
is dedicated to
Louis Hallacy, II
in recognition of his many
years of selfless service as
mayor, Holland Area Chamber
of Commerce president
and citizen.

**During one of Holland's first Tulip Time Festivals
this pair posed in Centennial Park.**
(courtesy State of Michigan Archives)

Haven, Harbor and Heritage: The Holland, Michigan, Story

by
Larry B. Massie

Foreword by
Mayor Albert H. McGeehan

The Priscilla Press
Allegan Forest, Michigan

Cover and dedication page photography by
Vito Palmisano.

ISBN: 1-886167-05-2

Table of Contents

Foreword

There is an old American tale centered in the New World Dutch colony of New Netherlands. Along the banks of New York's Hudson River a Dutchman awakes after twenty years of sleep only to be astonished over how his locale had changed. This familiar story of Rip Van Winkle has been repeated around the shores of Lake Macatawa in Ottawa and Allegan Counties of West Michigan.

If the reader recalls Holland, Michigan, around the time of our nation's Bicentennial you will probably remember "that nice sleepy little Dutch community where citizens work hard, raise families, attend church regularly and let the rest of the world go by."

The term "sleepy little Dutch town" is history! All the Vans and Vanders have arisen from their slumber only to be joined by the Garcias, Rodriguezs, Washingtons, and Khouns. In the last twenty years Holland's economic and population growth has been fast and furious. Between 1980 and 1996 the population has grown by 16%. The community that was solely identified by tulips and wooden shoes (there are plenty of both still there) now traces one-third of its public school students from minority families.

Industrially and commercially Holland can only be described as a "boom town." Under the able leadership of the Holland Economic Development Corporation (HEDCOR) Holland, Michigan, has redefined the term "industrial site." Founded in 1962 by a group of local business leaders, the corporation's purpose is to "provide land and services for business growth and expansion in the Holland area."

This private, nonprofit organization has developed two industrial parks over 35 years. HEDCOR's first development, the 650 acre Southside Industrial Park, is home to more than 52 companies employing some 15,000 workers. HEDCOR's second project, the 535 acre Northside Industrial Center, is presently home to 17 businesses which employ 8,000 area citizens as well as those who commute daily from Muskegon, Grand Rapids and South Haven.

At the 1996 Tulip Time Governor's Luncheon, Governor John Engler boldly stated that "Michigan's newly invigorated economy was leading the nation and Holland is leading Michigan." While that is quite a tribute to Holland's success, the statement is valid. An unemployment rate of under 3% is proof positive. Holland's industrial sites led by the Prince Corporation with its 5,000 employees and the Haworth Corporation with its 3,200 employees look more like a college campus than an industrial operation. There are no ugly smokestacks piercing the sky; no tall paper covered steel fences; only grass-covered, landscaped vistas of "Dutch Clean."

While the ongoing national phenomenon of suburban malls has hit Holland, again local public and private leaders were prepared. Becoming a "Main Street" community in 1984, Holland's downtown evolution has been a remarkable success. First led by now Holland Assistant City Manager Greg Robinson and currently under the guidance of Ms. Patty Seiter, Holland's downtown storefronts are filled to capacity. New specialty shops replaced the national chains who moved to suburban mall settings. New restaurants have taken root. People of all ages now frequent downtown coffee and bagel shops.

A 1988 restoration project that rebuilt 8th Street's sidewalks, curbs, gutters and street surface and installed hot water pipes from Holland's electric generating plant was a financial gamble for both the public and private sectors. That gamble has paid off handsomely. People walk under new streetlights along brick pavers, and window shop along a mainstreet that boasts "No Vacancy."

The rate of construction has not diminished in 1995 or 1996 with two additional major downtown streets being totally rebuilt. This construction will respond to the reality that we need to get people both "to" and "through" downtown. The good news is that once again we have a "parking problem." People want to be downtown.

With all of this infrastructure improvement coupled with Michigan's newest and most beautiful railroad depot, the Padnos Transportation Center, as well as Hope College's now-under-construction Haworth Center linking the college's 3,000 students physically with downtown, the future looks bright indeed for downtown Holland. But the story continues. Currently a 6.5 million-dollar renovation of Holland's 85-year-old city hall is underway. City Hall's neighbor, the Herrick Public Library, is ready to launch a major building project scheduled to increase its size to 65,000 square feet. Also, a five year study has brought a new "Holland Area Sports, Convention and Fine Arts" facility to the brink of reality. This project, if supported by area voters, will bring a much-needed multi-purpose facility to the community and will ensure the future of the east end of downtown.

Holland is a community where traditions and "roots" are important. Nowhere are old memories better kept alive than in the shadow of Holland's symbol, the windmill De Zwaan. Since 1965 Holland's Windmill Island has been a tourist destination. Over two million visitors have "stepped back into time" and walked the steps of this 250-year old structure.

With roots firmly set in the past Holland is looking to the future as well. Windmill Island is a major piece of Holland's future. Standing on the balcony of the windmill one can see acres of open land. Partnering with the Netherlands city of Groningen, as well as the Dutch firm of Foorthhuis, Bulder, Van Dijk and DeVries, Holland is moving toward the creation of an entirely new commercial and residential neighborhood which will reflect a typical northern Netherlands village. Transporting centuries-old buildings from Europe and adding new construction as well, the vision is to entice homeowners, condo dwellers, and shopkeepers to this new village of 70-90 buildings clustered around the windmill along the shores of the Macatawa River. It is a vision that will be nurtured into reality.

The final piece, as Holland plans to enter the 21st century, is to build a trade facility which will assist in the development of trade between Holland/West Michigan and the Northern Provinces of the Netherlands. Representatives of the Michigan Jobs Commission, Netherlands Foreign Investment Agency, the cities of Holland and Groningen, and the Queen's Royal Commissioners of Groningen and Drenthe Provinces have all committed to this vision.

So, if there is a West Michigan version of Rip Van Winkle out there somewhere, and if there is that someone who has not seen the new Holland, Michigan, I invite you to return to Holland. I guarantee that you will like what you see. Here in Holland our success is not a dream; it is a reality.

Happy 150th birthday Holland.

Albert H. McGeehan
Mayor

Preface

The Holland area beckoned as a haven of freedom in 1847 when the Rev. Albertus Van Raalte led a rag-tag band of Dutch colonists to found a Zion in the wilderness. As thousands of fellow countrymen joined those vanguards the sandbar that choked the harbor's mouth threatened economic success. When pleas for government assistance fell on deaf ears, the Hollanders rolled up their sleeves and solved the harbor dilemma themselves, converting a liability into a glorious asset that would soon lure great floating palaces crammed with vacationers. The resort industry buttressed a diverse local economy fueled by the entrepreneurial daring of men with better ideas and a labor force that cultivated the virtues of hard work and a job well done. Changing times brought industrial evolution as some companies fell by the wayside only to be replaced by vibrant young others.

The haven and the harbor were key but the pulse of Holland's past also beats with Ottawa chiefs and French fur traders, with the get-rich-quick schemes of frontier "paper city" promoters and doughty Yankee pioneer families who tackled the wilderness with little more than an axe and a dream. It rings with Dutch tenacity, a core of religious conviction, the ethnic pride that continues to draw legions of spectators each May and with the 20th century contribution of Hispanic citizens and southeast Asian refugees.

The crackle of the flames that devastated the community in 1871 but steeled its citizen's resolve as a better Holland rose from the ashes. All too often came the tramp of volunteer armies as the city's young men went forth to protect freedom. They battled Confederate cavalrymen, kamikaze planes and Viet Kong snipers — and four of Holland's heros won the Congressional Medal of Honor. The faint rustle of turning pages also marks Holland's annals as its educational institutions sent into the world scientists and pastors while a local literary tradition embraces *Microbes and Men* as well as the *Wizard of Oz*.

Yes, Holland's history comprises a colorful tapestry of stirring events and flamboyant personalities — a heritage matched by few other American places. It's a story worth the telling, a saga that inspires the justifiable pride that permeates the well-kept community as it prepares for the sesquicentennial celebration of its origins.

We were deeply honored when the Holland Area Chamber of Commerce contacted us in December, 1995, with a prospect to publish a pictorial history of Holland in commemoration of its sesquicentennial. We also appreciated the endorsement for this project by the Holland Sesquicentennial Committee, which we know is planning some gala events for 1997. But this book would not be possible were it not for the participation of the heritage firms whose stories are also told here. We thank each of them for recognizing the importance of preserving and celebrating their respective roles in making Holland the great place to work, live, raise a family and retire, that it is.

Some others who deserve special thanks for their contributions to this book are Louis Hallacy, II, and the excellent staff of the Holland Area Chamber of Commerce, Larry Wagenaar and staff at the Joint Archives of Holland, Bob Sherwood and the staff of the Herrick Public Library, John Curry and LeRoy Barnett of the State of Michigan Archives, Marguerite Miller of the Allegan County Historical Society, the Zeeland Historical Society, Loren McKinstry for his photographic processing and Judy Barz for her lay-out skills. Special thanks go to Myron Van Ark for generously making available his fine postcard collection.

We thank June Anstiss and Kim Ratulowski for the excellent care and love for our daughter Maureen Danielle while we worked on the book. We could not have done it without you.

Thanks do not seem enough for our long time friend Don van Reken, Holland's premier historian, for his support throughout this project, but we give them anyway.

We hope that you who read this story of Holland's heritage enjoy it as much as we have treasured the opportunity to assemble it.

Larry B. Massie & Priscilla Massie
Allegan Forest, Michigan

IX

Skilled Ottawa paddlers glided along Michigan's watery thoroughfares.

Wigwam Tales & Paper Cities

The breath of Kabebonicca, the Ottawa god of the North, had stilled the shores of Lake Macatawa. Snow plastered the trunks of the great hardwoods and bent low the branches of the towering white pines. To the west the setting sun tinged crimson the white muffled wilderness and the frozen wind-swept surface of the big lake. The only manmade features in sight were a huddle of half-barrel shaped bark covered wigwams that stood where many years later the H.J. Heinz pickle plant would rise.

An Ottawa woman swished through the snow, bearing a heavy load of firewood. Bending low, she parted the rush mat hanging at the doorway and entered the lodge. Within the smoke filled interior blazed a cheery fire, casting dancing shadows on the wall of the dozen men, women and children who sat cross legged on fur robes. It was the season of storytelling and a wrinkled

elder began in his melodious Indian voice to tell the exploits of Manabozho, the Hiawatha-like demigod of the Algonquin tribes:

"Manabozho was the most remarkable, wonderful and supernatural being that ever trod upon the earth. He could transfigure himself into the shape of all animals and live with them for a great length of time. He has done much mischief and also many benefits to the inhabitants of the earth whom he called his nephews; and he shaped almost everything, teaching his nephews what materials they should take for their future utensils."

"The legends say, that once upon a time the sugar trees did produce sap at certain seasons of the year that was almost like a pure syrup; but when mischievous Manabozho had tasted it, he said to himself, 'Oh that is too cheap. It will not do. My nephews will

Attracted to torchlights, many fish fell victim to Indian spears.

11

obtain this sugar too easily in future time and the sugar will be worthless.' And therefore he diluted the syrup until he could not taste any sweetness therein. Then he said, 'Now my nephews will have to labor hard to make sugar out of this sap, and the sugar will be much more valuable to them in the future time.'"

The elder paused, staring into the dancing flames, while the dark eyes of the family were upon him, eager to hear more of these stories that passed on from generation to generation the core of the Ottawa religion, ethics, humor and character. And then the old man began again, to tell of the great flood that once swept over the entire world. He told of Manabozho's hunting companion, a great black wolf, and that the god of the deep water became jealous of the wolf, killed and feasted on it. He told of how Manabozho disguised himself as a stump on the beach and when the god of deep and his host lay dozing on the hot sand Manabozho unmasked himself and slew the evil god with an arrow through his heart.

"Then all the host started to pursue the slayer of their master. Manabozho fled for his life, but he was pursued by the host with mountains of water. He ran all over the earth, still pursued with the mountains of water. So when he could not find any more dry land to run to he commanded a great canoe to be formed in which he and the animals who were fleeing before the water were saved. After they floated, Manabozho wondered very much how deep was the water. Therefore, he ordered one of the beavers to go down to the bottom of the deep and bring up some earth if he could, as evidence that he did go to the bottom. So the beaver obeyed, and he went down, but the water was so deep the beaver died before he reached the bottom, and therefore, he came up floating as a dead beaver. Manabozho drew him up into his canoe and resuscitated the beaver by blowing into his nostrils."

"So he waited a little while longer, and afterwards he ordered the muskrat to go down; but the muskrat did not like the idea, for he had seen the beaver coming up lifeless. So he had to flatter him a little in order to induce him to go down, by telling him, 'Now, muskrat, I know that thou art one of the best divers of all the animal creation; will you please go down and ascertain the depth of the water, and bring up some earth in your little paws, if you can, with which I shall try to make another world? Now go my little brother' - the legend says that he called all the animal creation his little brothers, - 'for we cannot always live on the waters.' At last the muskrat obeyed. He went down, and descended clear to the bottom of the water, and grabbed the earth and returned. But the water was yet so deep that before he reached the surface of the water, he expired."

"As Manabozho drew him up into his great canoe to resuscitate him, he observed the muskrat still grasping something in his little paws, and behold, it was a piece of earth. Then Manabozho knew that the muskrat went clear to the bottom of the deep. He took this piece of earth and fixed it into a small parcel; which he fastened to the neck of the raven which was with him. Now, with this parcel, Manabozho told the raven to fly to and fro all over the face of the waters; then the waters began to recede very fast, and soon the earth came back to its natural shape, just as it was before."

How the Ottawa would come to have within their mythology an episode with so many parallels to the Biblical story of Noah and the flood is open to conjecture. Some early ethnologists saw it as proof that the American Indians had descended from the lost tribes of Israel. Others would explain it as a cultural adaption of the Biblical teaching introduced by the early Jesuit fathers in the 17th century. Actually, stories of a deluge, of which the Ottawa version is an interesting variation, occur in the mythology of diverse races scattered across the globe. Indian artist and ethnologist George Catlin found stories of a great flood as part of the oral tradition of at least 120 North American tribes. Given the watery environment of the Ottawa, a domain lapped by great inland seas, it would be a greater anomaly had they not a legend of a deluge. And perhaps, also, the Ottawa realized through the fossil record they saw around them, the shifting sand dunes and other remnants of ancient beaches and the glacial outwash spawned terrain of morains, eskers, drumlins and kames, physical evidence that great floods had indeed swept over the Michigan peninsulas.

Elements of Michigan's geologic record that date back more than a billion years still baffle scientists. Volcanic rocks, among the oldest on the earth, underlay and thrust up through successive layers of sedimentary strata, thousands of feet deep. Deposits of sandstone, shale, limestone, salt and gypsum were laid down during the 30 or more times that prehistoric seas washed over and retreated from Michigan. Relatively late in the geologic time frame came a series of four glaciers, ice sheets more than a mile high, that inched down from the north, scouring the bedrock, scooping out the Great Lakes basins and successively leaving their mark on the land in the form of glacial outwash features and the more than 15,000 inland lakes that dot the peninsulas.

By the time the last glacier began to recede around 11,000 years ago man had arrived in the Lower Peninsula. Shadowy unnamed cultures came and went, leaving little but distinctive burial sites, mastodon kills and scattered stone artifacts to mark their presence. As early as 7,000 B.C. Paleo Indians utilized red-ocher stained grave offerings and leaf shaped projectile points. By 5,000 B.C. mysterious tribes known only as Old Copper Indians pocked the surface of the Keweenaw Peninsula in their quest for red metal. From 5,000 B.C. to 500 B.C. Indians of the Boreal culture left their presence in the form of turkey tail projectile points, banner stones and duck decoy shaped bird stones whose function remains a mystery. Next came representatives of the Early Woodland culture who reared conical earthen burial

The function of bird stones, such as this example in granite porphyry dating from 3,000 B.C. to 5,000 B.C., remains a mystery.

mounds and fashioned broad mouthed pottery jars. About 100 B.C. the Hopewell Indians arrived in the Lower Peninsula, bringing elaborate ceremonial motifs, finely wrought grave offerings, mysterious garden beds and the first agricultural traditions. The late Woodland period began by 800 A.D., a time of great cultural diversity that produced effigy mounds, stone pipes and distinctive pottery.

And then in the 17th century the swirling mists of prehistory parted with the arrival of the first French explorers. No longer would Michigan's past need to be puzzled together solely by archaeologists, for with the Europeans came recorded history. And what did those pale-faced intruders – French noblemen in quest of a northwest passage to the Orient, black robed priests carrying the cross to the wilderness and steel sinewed voyageurs who paddled their birch bark bateaux in quest of furs – encounter when first they reached what would become Ottawa County?

They found the forest primeval. Dense stands of virgin timber blanketed every feature of the terrain. The better soil supported hardwoods – five or six varieties of oak, shag-bark hickory, walnut, butternut, wild cherry, sugar maple, gigantic tulip poplars, and muscular beech. Here and there, the bone-white trunk of a sycamore relieved the monotony of green. White pine claimed the sandy uplands. Forest giants, 200 years old and six feet through at the base, rose straight as an arrow for 150 feet and more to their craggy tops.

The forest floor was dark and dank. In the growing season, sunlight never penetrated the leafy canopy, so that it was practically bare of underbrush. But in the many swamps, cranberry bogs, and flood plains where the trees grew less dense, impenetrable thickets of bushes, vines and briars flourished. Rivers and creeks flowed in tunnels through the woods, shielded from above by the over arching branches of the massive trees crowding their banks. The forest stretched seemingly forever in every direction except west, where Lake Michigan checked its dominion with shifting sand dunes.

White-tailed deer bounded over fallen trunks. Black bear, bobcats, panthers, packs of wolves, and fox roamed in search of prey. The smaller forest mammals—raccoons, skunks, rabbits, squirrels, chipmunks, and groundhogs—led their secretive lives. Wild turkeys strutted and gobbled, owls hooted, and enormous pileated woodpeckers beat fist-sized holes into dead wood. Mink, marten, fisher, otter, and other choice fur-bearing animals abounded. Broad tailed beaver toppled trees with their teeth and fashioned dams that transformed the terrain. The water teemed with whitefish, trout, muskellunge, pike and prehistoric–looking sturgeon ten feet long and more. Mussels lined the bottom of clear flowing streams. Mud turtles sunned on logs in the rivers. Ancient snapping turtles the size of washtubs wallowed out of the swamp in the spring to burrow holes and lay broods of eggs in the sun-warmed sand. Long blue racers climbed trees as fast as lightning. Harmless blow snakes pretended to be bad in imitation of massasaugas, the nasty-tempered little Michigan rattlesnake.

The land that lay between the Grand and Kalamazoo rivers was the home of the Ottawa. Their legends say they emigrated from northeast of the Great Lakes to wrest it from another tribe some time before contact with the whites. However, historical sources record that bands of Ottawa were driven by the Iroquois from the region of Manitoulin Island in Lake Huron during the seventeenth century. By the early eighteenth century a portion of the tribe had established its seat at L'Arbre Croche, near Harbor Springs, from whence they spread along the east shore of Lake Michigan as far south as the Kalamazoo River. South of the Kalamazoo lived the Potawatomi and north into the Upper Peninsula and on the eastern side of the Lower Peninsula lay the domain of the Chippewa. Known as the "people of the three fires" and the "three brothers," the Ottawa, Chippewa, and Potawatomi belonged to the Algonquian linguistic stock. They also shared similar traditions, life-styles, and general appearance. The three tribes lived in peace, sometimes intermarrying, and banded together to fight their common enemies, the Iroquois to the east and the Sioux to the west.

The Ottawa, whose name comes from the Algonquian term for trade, were noted among their neighbors as intertribal barterers, dealing mainly in cornmeal, sunflower oil, furs, woven mats, tobacco, and medicinal plants. They practiced a migratory existence, hunting, fishing, and trapping in the winter and making maple sugar in the spring. In the heat of the summer, the Ottawa of the Grand River Valley journeyed by canoes along the shore of Lake Michigan to the Leelanau Peninsula, a region still coveted by vacationers for its cool breezes. In the fall, the bands returned to their respective villages to harvest the corn, beans, squash and other crops planted in the spring.

Villages were invariably located on the banks of streams. Known settlements occurred at the present sites of Allegan, Grand Rapids, Ada, Grand Haven,

Great Lakes Indians torture a prisoner with fire in this plate from Joseph Lafitau's book, Moeurs des Sauvages Ameriquains, published in 1724.

14

Ottawa bands dwelt in movable wigwams covered with bark during the warm seasons.

and Holland. In warm weather the Ottawa lived in conical wigwams—usually a simply constructed framework of poles, lashed together and covered with sheets of birchbark or with woven mats for better ventilation. A small aperture at the top allowed some smoke from the cooking fire to escape, but wigwams were notoriously smoky. A family of three or four persons inhabited the small summer dwelling, sleeping on benches made of brush and covered with skins, furs, and mats. Larger wigwams, sometimes domed long houses, that accommodated several families were erected for winter habitation.

The Ottawa observed a sharp division of labor between men and women. Braves hunted, fished, made war, and in general performed tasks that required sudden bursts of energy. To the squaws fell the tedious and more menial tasks. They grew corn, brought in firewood, lugged buckets of water, picked berries, made maple sugar, tanned hides, and fashioned moccasins, in addition to the usual domestic duties.

Despite the seeming unfairness of work duties, Algonquian cultures maintained a close-knit family life. White observers recorded many instances of deep affection between husband and wife. Both doted on papooses, and children, given the run of the camp, rarely suffered corporal punishment. Males furnished leadership in most areas, but within the wigwam the squaw was unequivocally in command.

Far from a life of subsistence farming, the Ottawa harvested from nature a surplus that allowed extensive trading for the luxuries of life. Early white settlements profited from substantial quantities of smoked fish, venison hams, Indian corn, cranberries, huckleberries, and mococks of maple sugar, as well as leather, sweetgrass, and birchbark artifacts beautifully decorated with porcupine quills. At Grand Rapids, for example, entrepreneurs shipped large quantities of Indian cranberries and maple sugar to eastern markets.

The major article of Indian commerce, however, was fur. The quest for furs had dominated Michigan's history from the days of the seventeenth century French *coureurs de bois*, the unlicensed traders who first explored much of the peninsulas. The great rivalry for Michigan's fur riches pitted European armies against each other as the Hudson's Bay Company of England succeeded the French at the close of the French and Indian Wars and in turn was replaced by John Jacob Astor's American Fur Company following the War of 1812. Sault Ste. Marie and Mackinac Island became the hubs of the Great Lakes fur trade, where thousands of Indian trappers and European traders made their annual rendezvous. Competition drove ambitious entrepreneurs, not content to await Indian delivery to these depots, to establish small

To the lot of Ottawa women fell the more tedious chores as shown in a 1724 copper engraving from Lafitau's Indian book.

Voyageurs hefted their canoes and one or more 90 pound packs to traverse portages.

16

Beaver, whose pelts became the medium of exchange on the frontier, transformed the terrain with their teeth.

trading posts throughout the Michigan wilderness. Indeed, the shrewdest of the traders often traveled directly to Indian camps to get a jump on rivals.

The workhorses of the Great Lakes fur trade were known as voyageurs, devil-may-care French/Canadians, often with Indian blood. Clad in bright sashes and jaunty plumed hats, their steel-sinew arms paddled the big birch bark bateaux. They were the men of which legends are made — short by modern standards — averaging five feet four inches, but with great broad shoulders and barrel chests — capable of almost superhuman feats of strength and endurance. Dipping their red-painted paddles at the rate of 50 strokes a minute from dawn to dusk, they stopped but once each hour for a few puffs of their clay pipes and for a hasty midday meal and then returned to their task.

The canoe became their home. In it all day, they slept under the craft at night. When they encountered rapids where sharp rocks might pierce its fragile birch bark bottom, they quickly unloaded the cargo — three tons or more of trade good, furs and supplies — then two men ran with the canoe above their heads and the other six to ten voyageurs hefted 90 pound packs to their backs. Aided by a tumpline across their fore-

heads, they slung two, three, four — celebrated voyageurs carried as many as five bundles at a time – and away they trotted along the portage.

By the 1820s prices for the furs that inspired such Herculean efforts had become standardized. It was an era when "beaver was king" in Michigan. Beaver pelts that went into the making of fashionable and expensive beaver hats were the medium of exchange on the frontier by which the value of other goods was reckoned. Officially, prime beaver pelts were valued at $1.25 per pound. Traders, however, rarely carried scales into the woods; instead, they hefted each fur and guessed at its weight. Needless to say the furs always proved heavier when officially weighed at the warehouse, to the traders' benefit. Other furs were evaluated by the piece: mink at 50 cents to $1.00, marten and lynx $1.00 to $1.25, muskrat five cents, and deer hides $1.00 each. These sums were translated into trade goods such as blankets, copper kettles, iron hatchets, knives, guns, ammunition, pocket mirrors and gaudy baubles. Unfortunately, few traders remained in business without stocking a good supply of liquor as well.

In violation of federal laws against the trading of

Rix Robinson's Ottawa wife of many years was River Woman, the daughter of a Grand Haven area chief.

their trading stock.

Returning from Mackinac in 1809, a sudden storm blew their canoe ashore somewhere between present-day Muskegon and Grand Haven. When they chanced upon a party of Potawatomi a young brave named White Ox demanded whiskey of Laframboise. When he refused, the angry brave ambushed and murdered him. Despite her grief, Magdelaine pushed on to winter quarters where she managed the business alone. At the end of the season she dutifully conveyed the remains of her husband back to Mackinac Island for proper burial.

During her subsequent career as a successful fur trader, Madame Laframboise won fame for her fairness. When John Jacob Astor's American Fur Company squeezed out the independent traders following the War of 1812, she shrewdly joined him. She continued to trade each winter in the Grand River Valley until she retired in 1821 and sold her trading post to Rix Robinson.

Robinson, one of Michigan's most respected traders, was born in Massachusetts in 1789. His family migrated to western New York around 1800. Robinson initially prepared for a career in law, but when the War of 1812 broke out he moved to Detroit where he became a sutler for the army. Following the war, he met Astor, who hired him as an Indian trader. Robinson gained experience in the Illinois country and then took over Laframboise's post at the confluence of the Thornapple and Grand rivers near present day Ada. He also established a post at the mouth of the Grand River. From those locations he roved throughout the Grand, Black and Kalamazoo river valleys. Robinson married an Ottawa woman in 1821 and when she died he remarried Se-be-quay (River Woman), the granddaughter of a chief from the Grand Haven area. After his colorful career in the fur trade Robinson became a prominent citizen of Michigan, serving as state senator for four terms.

Gurdon Hubbard, a contemporary of Robinson, also carved out a notable career in the Great Lakes fur trade. An extremely powerful man who the Indians named Pa-Ma-Ta-be, the Swift Walker, in recognition of his ability to travel by foot as many as 75 miles a day, Hubbard had signed on as a clerk at Mackinac Island when only 15-years-old. He also spent his first trading season in the Illinois country. En route back to Mackinac Island in the spring of 1819 with his canoe heaped high with bales of glistening furs, Hubbard and a party of fellow traders camped near the mouth of the Grand River to observe the Ottawa "Feast of the Dead." Normally this major religious

ardent spirits, in 1832 alone nearly 9,000 gallons of whiskey were shipped to Mackinac Island for distribution throughout the peninsulas. Some traders further stretched their liquor supply by watering it down and bolstering it with pepper and chewing tobacco for an extra kick. The aptly named firewater, for which tribesmen might swap their entire winter's catch, was a recognized evil of the fur trade.

Little is known about the early fur traders who worked the Grand, Black and Kalamazoo river valleys, but a few names have survived. Joseph Laframboise, an independent French trader, established the first recorded post in the Grand River Valley some time in the 1790s. In 1796 he married a beautiful 16-year-old Metis woman named Magdelaine Marcot, and together they operated posts at Muskegon Lake, Crockery Creek in northern Ottawa County, and near Ada on the Grand River. They passed the winters trading at those sites and in the late spring paddled up the coast of Lake Michigan in heavily laden bateaux to Mackinac Island to sell their harvest of furs and replenish

Ottawa Chief Okee-Makee-Quid posed in ceremonial finery
for artist Charles Bird King ca.1830.

Great Lakes Indians performed a Discovery Dance for Thomas McKenney
during his trip to the lakes in 1826.

During the winter months Ottawa families erected more substantial dwellings such as this
wigwam sketched by McKenney in 1826.

Lafitau included a fanciful engraving of the Feast of the Dead in his 1724 book about Indians.

celebration, held at three to 12 year intervals, occurred in the fall, but Hubbard is explicit in his chronology and observations. The ceremony began when the bodies of those who had died during the previous cycle were disinterred and stripped of remaining flesh by the female relatives. The bones were lovingly placed in birchbark bundles, conveyed to the feast and reburied in a large communal grave. The ritual included two days of fasting followed by an elaborate feast, orations by the chiefs, athletic games and socializing.

At the close of the feast, Hubbard witnessed an example of Indian justice which he recorded in his published autobiography as "the grandest and most thrilling incident of my life." A Canadian Indian had stabbed to death the son of a local chief during a drunken quarrel. Ottawa law required his life to be forfeited unless he could satisfy the honor of the kin of the slain with a sufficient ransom. A poor man with a large family, he had spent an unsuccessful season in the Muskegon Marsh attempting to trap a supply of valuable furs to meet the ransom. Knowing that Ottawa custom decreed revenge be taken on another member of his family in his absence, he appeared at the festival to accept his punishment.

The execution took place in a bowl-shaped hollow amid the towering sand dunes near the future site of Grand Haven. The white traders and Indians watched from the surrounding heights. Accompanied by his family, the accused solemnly walked to the offended chief while thumping a drum and singing his death song, confessed his guilt, and handed him the knife with which he had committed the crime. The chief presented the blade to his oldest son and said, simply, "Kill him." The son advanced to his victim, made a couple of feints with the weapon to test the man's courage and then plunged the knife to the hilt into his heart. Justice having been accomplished, the chief adopted the dead man's family into his own.

By the time Hubbard witnessed the scene that was so "indelibly stamped" on his mind, the days of the Indian in Ottawa County were already numbered. The People of the Three Fires had brought much of the trouble on themselves by consistently picking the loosing side in the warfare that periodically bloodied the frontier. Michigan warriors backed their long time French allies against the British and their allies, the

Pioneers lived in primitive conditions as they gradually hacked away the wilderness.

Iroquois, during the French and Indian Wars. Following the defeat of the French in 1760 and their loss of New France, the Michigan tribes switched loyalty to the British, fighting against the Americans during the Revolutionary War and the War of 1812.

While the French and British had been content to trade with the tribes and leave them in possession of their domain, the ever westward moving American nation sought to extinguish Indian land titles via treaties. And treaty makers who often had fought against the Indians were not above such tactics as stupefying the signers with whiskey, outright bribery and the recognition of lesser chiefs in favor of more legitimate leaders not inclined to sign.

Beginning with a treaty made in 1785 the Michigan tribes found themselves divested of increasingly larger blocks of their homeland. In 1807, Gen. William Hull negotiated a treaty at Detroit which ceded most of the southeastern Lower Peninsula to the United States. Michigan Territorial Governor Lewis Cass supervised the signing of the Treaty of Saginaw in 1819 which swallowed up another multi-million acre tract to the north and west. Two years later the Treaty of Chicago cost the Indians their land south of the Grand River, with the exception of several small reservations.

By the provisions of that 1821 treaty, however, the Ottawa were to be paid $1,000 annually forever, and for 10 years $15,000 was to be appropriated for the support of a blacksmith, teacher, and agricultural agent in an effort to acculturate the Indians to the white man's ways.

The Indians signed away their land north of the Grand River in 1836. That treaty also carried elaborate provisions for annual payments and additional sums for teachers, agricultural implements, and livestock. An amusing incident, illustrative of the male–female dichotomy in Ottawa culture, occurred at the treaty signing held at the Grand Rapids mission house. The local Baptist missionary, the Reverend Leonard Slater, had been chosen to interpret the treaty provisions to the Indians. Slater, who had translated a number of books into Ottawa, considered himself an expert linguist. He translated paragraph by paragraph in his best oratorical ability, intending to impress the chiefs with the words of the "great white father" in Washington.

When Slater finished, the council sat silent. Finally, after a long period of solemn stillness, a chief arose and said, "If the Great Father sends words to men, why does he use a woman's tongue?" Slater, it seems, had learned Ottawa from the females in his household and had insulted the assembly by employing certain words and accents used only by women. Needless to say, another interpreter skilled in masculine pronunciation soon replaced Slater, and the chiefs were satisfied.

The period between the treaties of 1821 and 1836, which effectively stripped the Michigan Indians of their tribal lands with the exception of several thousand acres of reservations in northern Michigan, had witnessed tremendous growth for the Michigan Territory. Due in part to U.S. Surveyor General and former Ohio Governor Edward Tiffin's erroneous report in 1817 which labeled Michigan a vast swamp, filled with malarial mosquitoes, savage beasts and unfriendly natives, the territory had been largely bypassed by the westward migration. But when government surveyors laid out the first road across the Lower Peninsula, the Chicago Military Road, roughly the present route of U.S. 12, and the Erie Canal opened in 1825 to form a watery highway linking the Hudson River with Detroit, news of the lush land found by early arrivals soon circulated back east. A mass migration to "Michigania" began. Homesteaders quickly staked out the fertile prairies and oak openings found in the southern tiers of counties, and then pushed the frontier northward.

To accommodate the torrent of pioneers, the Federal Land Office, where claimants registered and paid for their land, was relocated from Monroe to White Pigeon in 1831 and to Bronson, soon renamed Kalamazoo, in 1834. Two years later more land was registered in Kalamazoo than at any other land office in the nation. Following the Treaty of 1836, another federal land office opened to the north in Ionia.

The hordes of New Englanders and the sons and daughters of those who had pioneered western New York the generation before rushed for the Michigan bonanza. The land hungry hordes included genuine settlers anxious to start a new life in the territory but also numerous speculators who had no intention of settling. They planned to acquire large tracts of prime land at the standard $1.25 per acre government price and when the best acreage was gone resell to later arrivals at a large profit. Entire six mile square townships in Ottawa and Allegan counties were grabbed up by wealthy speculators, and this ultimately retarded genuine settlement.

Other investors sought sites that they could plat out, develop into towns, and sell in lots for hundreds of times their original cost. Chief among the attractions desired for a townsite was a stream of water,

23

which could be dammed to power the wheels of saw-mills, gristmills, and early factories. A harbor on one of the Great Lakes or central location in a county which might bring county seat status were also considerations. Having acquired title to what they deemed a prime location, townsite developers typically promoted their holdings with ornate printed maps depicting nicely graded roads, grand structures and other civic improvements, usually only in the planning stage. Ottawa County sported more than its share of these "paper cities." Warren City, platted on the Grand River near the mouth of Bass River, never amounted to more than a few log cabins. Nevertheless, it won title as the Ottawa County seat. Pioneers, however, had the good sense to continue to hold court in Grand Haven which emerged as the county's first real center of population. Charleston, located near present-day Lamont, also enjoyed an early reputation on paper far in excess of the few log structures ever erected there. Macatawa, depicted as a thriving community at the mouth of the Black River, failed to attract even one settler.

Port Sheldon, among the most illustrious of Michigan's paper cities, sprang into existence on the northeast bank of Pigeon Lake, located approximately seven miles north of present Holland. A syndicate of New York and Philadelphia capitalists first selected the mouth of the Grand River as the site for their venture. But when they found that location already in possession of the rival Grand Haven Company, the Port Sheldon Company settled for an inferior site 10 miles to the south. They planned to overcome its geographical deficiencies through the intensity of their efforts.

In the fall of 1836, a ship loaded with supplies and pre-cut lumber for structures dropped anchor at the mouth of Pigeon Creek. Some 40 company employees proceeded to lay out roads, survey lots, and construct buildings. They improved the harbor, extended piers into Lake Michigan, and built a short railroad into the woods. A $20,000 steam powered mill, the finest in the area, went into operation. Visitors to the busy commu-

The Subscriber, late of the MARSHALL HOUSE, Philadelphia, begs leave to inform the Public and Travellers generally, that he has taken that LARGE and COMMODIOUS HOTEL lately erected at PORT SHELDON, Michigan, known as the

OTTAWA HOUSE,

Which he intends opening about the 1st of June next. The House will be furnished in a style not surpassed by any House in the Country, his Furniture will be entirely new, selected from the EASTERN CITIES, his BAR will be furnished with WINES and LIQUORS of superior quality and choice brands, all selected in NEW YORK and PHILADELPHIA. The Subscriber from his long experience in the business, and unremitting attention, hopes to share a portion of public patronage.

CHARLES T. BADGER, Proprietor.

Charles Badger's luxurious Ottawa House was the pride of Port Sheldon in 1836.

nity enjoyed the hospitality of a large Greek Revival hotel, resembling a southern plantation in its opulence. Unfortunately, guests, particularly those interested in settling there, proved few and far between. Nevertheless, by 1838 the city numbered 300 inhabitants — nearly all company employees.

The panic of 1837, in part caused by similar reckless speculation nationwide, brought about the downfall of Port Sheldon as well as most of Michigan's other "wildcat cities." Bankrupt, the Port Sheldon Company abandoned its settlement, leaving one watchman in charge. A few years later, he sold the magnificent Ottawa House hotel and 30 lots for less than the original cost of its paint and glass.

About the same time that the Port Sheldon investors were plowing their funds into that ill fated enterprise another group of speculators were following their dreams of reaping riches from a community they platted near the mouth of the Kalamazoo River. Oshea Wilder, an entrepreneur from Rochester, New York, had succumbed to the Michigan land fever in 1831. Five years later he had convinced a group of investors to join him in establishing what he was convinced was destined to be the site of a major metropolis. Wilder bestowed an alluring Oriental name on the sandy, wind swept site - Singapore - why, nobody knows for sure. He erected a steam powered sawmill there and a brick bank that printed its own "wildcat" currency. Residences, a general store, and a three story hotel soon lined Singapore's waterfront. The settlement barely survived the depression brought on by the Panic of 1837. Then it prospered as a lumber town with as many as 600 ships a year trafficking there until the Kalamazoo River Valley's supply of white pine was depleted in the mid 1870s. The sawmill was moved farther north, the residents followed and shifting sand covered the site. In the winter of 1894, two boys returning from an outing in Holland, warmed themselves by setting fire to the last remaining vestige of Singapore, the tip of the three story hotel's roof protruding through the sand.

Another "wildcat city" with more direct impact on the development of Holland, lived its brief existence on the shores of Macatawa Lake. The major part of a vil-

In 1869, before the shifting sand buried it, Singapore was a bustling lumber town near the mouth of the Kalamazoo River.

lage called Superior was located at present-day Waukazoo and a smaller plat lay on the opposite side of the lake. Edward Macy, captain of a Great Lakes steamer, had visited the harbor previous to 1835. Impressed by the grandeur of what was then called Black Lake, he convinced Kalamazoo entrepreneurs Cyrus Burdick, Elisha Belcher, and Caleb Sherman to join him in platting out a village containing 587 lots. By 1837 the community boasted a sawmill, blacksmith shop, and seven dwellings. Macy stopped at Superior that summer to repair the engine of his ship, the *Governor Mason*. As the vessel steamed over the sandbar at the mouth of the harbor, all on board reportedly marveled at the beauty of the site.

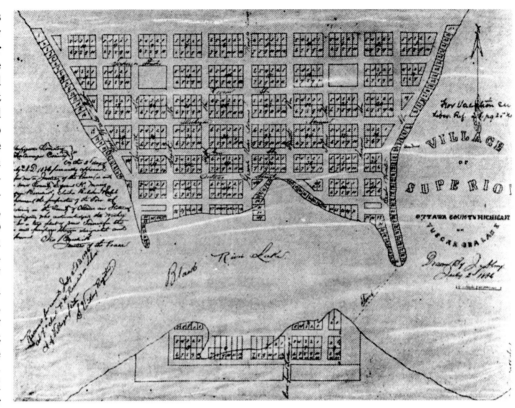

Platted in 1836, the ghost town of Superior lay on both sides of Lake Macatawa.

Soon, Henry Knox placed a tannery in operation at Superior. A ship maker from Massachusetts arrived and constructed a vessel called the *A.C. Mitchell*. With its hold loaded with leather and lumber the ship sailed for Chicago. The city received a post office in October 1837. It was designated Tuscarora because a Washtenaw County village had already received the name Superior. A year later the Ottawa County Board of Supervisors authorized Macy to operate a ferry across the lake, thus connecting north and south Superior. The tax assessor that year placed a valuation of $38,950 on the site.

But things soon went sour for the promising settlement. The nationwide depression that began to smother economic activity in Michigan by 1838 hurt the sale of the settlement's products. Macy informed Alexander Walsh of other bad news in October 1839: "Our company, Black River Harbor Association, is not doing much, for the harbor is blocked with sandbanks so that our schooner cannot get out. Our mill is idle. We have four families here." Soon after, Macy was accidentally killed during a visit to Kalamazoo, and Superior went the way of most other paper cities.

In the meantime, Michigan had finally won its hard fought battle to enter the Union. When the territory

adopted a constitution in 1835, its population numbered well beyond the 60,000 necessary for statehood. But Ohio, a state since 1803, blocked Michigan's bid in Congress because of a dispute over a tract of boundary land known as the Toledo Strip. Michigan and Ohio, in fact, dispatched militia forces to the contested land in 1835 and nearly went to battle over the affair. President Andrew Jackson defused the hostilities by temporarily removing from office Michigan's hot-tempered young governor, Stephens T. Mason. Michigan finally agreed to Ohio's version of the boundary, receiving title to the western two-thirds of the Upper Peninsula as compensation, and entered the Union as the 26th state on January 26, 1837.

Eleven months later, Ottawa County was officially laid out to contain two townships: Ottawa, now all of Ottawa County, and Muskegon, to the north. Over the next two decades, as more townships evolved, the total area of Ottawa County grew to encompass part of Muskegon, Oceana, and Mason counties as well. Finally, in 1859, the county assumed its present dimensions.

Ottawa County townships, much larger originally than now, also gradually attained their present dimensions. Most, with the exception of those bordering on Lake Michigan, are now six miles square, contain-

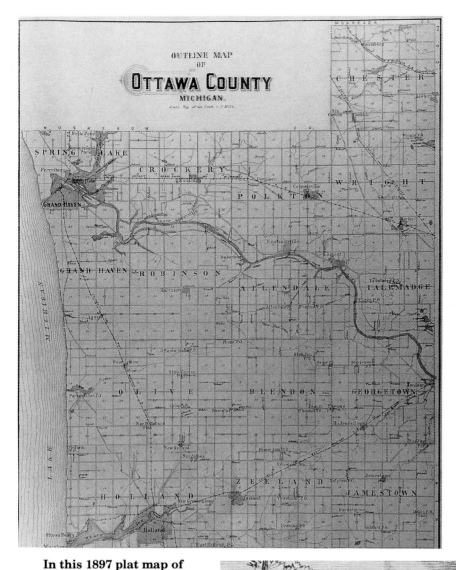

In this 1897 plat map of Ottawa county, Holland Township still encompassed present day Park Township.
(courtesy Holland Historical Trust Collection of the Joint Archives of Holland)

ing 36 one-mile square sections. In the early days, however, township boundaries often proved a bone of contention. Michigan pioneers, in fact, were quite adept at their own brand of backwoods gerrymandering.

In 1838, for example, the state legislature created Georgetown Township. It encompassed the present townships of Georgetown, Blendon, Zeeland, and Jamestown – the entire southeast section of the county. Talmadge Township to the north included what are now Talmadge, Polktown, Wright, and Allendale townships. At a time before a single bridge had been constructed the legislature maintained the surveyed township lines, but the Grand River, a natural obstacle, would have made a more satisfactory boundary in the early days.

Georgetown Township had been purchased largely by speculators, and the taxes levied against the lands of those absentee owners resulted in a tidy sum to be allocated for road-building purposes. Talmadge Township, on the other hand, located predominantly north of the Grand River, had not been put on the market until after the Indian Treaty of 1836, and most of the land

Log cabin living proved particularly hard on women because of the lack of society.

Passenger pigeons, as shown in this 19th century print, were beautiful birds resembling mourning doves.

still belonged to the federal government. Nevertheless, it had more bona fide settlers, and they were anxious to get control of the highway funds raised on non-resident lands south of the river.

In 1842, the state legislature granted a petition by Georgetown residents to reestablish the Grand River as the township boundary. But because of an error in the newspaper account, Talmadge Township settlers thought the land south of the river was to be annexed to their district. Georgetown voters were not about to correct that misconception until after the township election had legally allocated the nonresident taxes to their own road-building accounts. The situation became a comedy of errors when the Talmadge voters assembled at the wrong voting place some 15 miles to the east. Cagey Georgetown advocates detained them by engaging in debate until the afternoon of election day, too late, they thought, for them to get to their proper polling place in time to decide the election. The Talmadge voters somehow learned of the ruse and set off on a mad dash by horseback, foot, and canoe to reach the legal polls in time. A few made it, but not enough to carry the election, and Georgetown rejoiced, for that year anyway, over its bonus revenues.

Such shenanigans offered a welcome diversion from the difficult task of converting a trackless wilderness into farmland. It was a lonely and dangerous livelihood. More than one pioneer suffered the fate of Lemuel Jenison, founder of the village of Jenison, who was killed by a falling tree in 1837.

Beyond the dangers of such "widowmakers," as dead tree branches ready to fall were known, the Ottawa County wilderness harbored hordes of blood sucking insects, poisonous snakes, predatory beasts that might attack unattended children and the ever present prospect of getting lost in the trackless forest. For pioneer wives, in particular, log cabin living and the loss of creature comforts were not nearly as bad as the lack of society – dark loneliness that drove some women insane.

While the men folk labored to clear the land, erect log structures and plant crops among the big stumps, the women kept track of their often large broods of young ones and improvised to try and prepare meals with the primitive resources available. The wild game that abounded in the region proved an important supplement to the limited pioneer fare. A celebrated passenger pigeon nesting ground, where each year during breeding season millions of the colorful mourning dove-like birds broke down entire forests under their weight, lay near the site of Port Sheldon and in Olive Township. When news of a nesting spread throughout the frontier, residents dropped all other concerns to harvest wild pigeons by the thousands. Some "pigeoners"

brought down as many as two dozen with a single muzzle blast. Others knocked the tasty "butterball" squabs out of their nest with long poles and the children gathered up the downed birds by the bushel basket. Professional hunters lured flocks with a captive "stool pigeon" to land in traps strewn with salt, which the pigeons craved, and caught several thousand at a time in huge clap nets. Eaten fresh, stewed, roasted, baked in pies or salted down in barrels for later consumption, passenger pigeons proved one of nature's tastiest treats until man's greed totally obliterated the species.

Some pioneers took advantage of the absence of game laws to slaughter amazing numbers of other wild animals. A Mr. Hermit of Jamestown Township earned a niche in local history by killing 86 deer in one winter alone. Similarly, Daniel Angell, who pioneered in Talmadge Township in 1837, killed 70 wolves for the township, county and state bounties the scalps

The Rev. George Nelson Smith founded Old Wing Mission in Fillmore Township in 1839.

brought. Angell also killed at least one panther in the township. Needless to say the greediness of white hunters rapidly depleted the game upon which the local Ottawa depended for survival.

Increasingly bereft of their ancestral hunting grounds and often debauched by the traders' "firewater," the Indians' plight moved a group of concerned Presbyterians and Congregationalists to ponder a means for their economic betterment as well as their spiritual welfare. The Reverend George Nelson Smith, a 30-year-old Congregational minister who had immigrated from St. Albans, Vermont, to Richland, Kalamazoo County, with his wife Arvilla in 1833, attended an organizational meeting of the Western Society of Michigan To Benefit the Indians held in Allegan in January 1838. He soon became the leading advocate of the cause. Gaining the sanction of the Presbyterian Synod of Michigan and working in unison with the Congregational Church, Smith preached his first sermon to the Indians in Allegan on December 23, 1838.

Smith also opened an Indian School in a temporary building near Allegan. His first class of seven students had grown to nearly 30 by April. He left with a party of Indians for a month-long exploratory expedition to locate a permanent site for his mission on April 13, 1839. They ranged as far north as Petoskey before choosing an isolated site on the northern edge of Allegan County in what would become Fillmore Township.

Smith and his Indian followers paid $1,600 for a 1,360-acre tract. In August 1839, the missionary, accompanied by two hired men, arrived at the site to construct a log cabin. The following month Captain Macy conveyed Smith's family and household goods to Superior by sailboat. The Indian colony soon became a reality. It was named Old Wing Mission in honor of a recently deceased chief, Ning-wee-gon, the Wing. The Holland area had begun a new epoch in its development.

Commissioner of Indian Affairs Thomas McKenney included this painting of a Great Lakes Indian mother with papoose in his 1836 History of the tribes.

Ox Yokes & Wooden Shoes

Oxen were king on the Michigan frontier. Yokes of trained steers were indispensable to the pioneers in conveying their covered wagons along the wilderness roads, plowing unbroken land, snaking out tree trunks and many other tasks requiring brute strength. As late as 1854 the state census taker counted 1,278 working cattle in Ottawa County compared to only 381 horses.

Pioneers favored oxen over their equine counterparts for a number of good reasons. They were cheaper to obtain – bull calves converted to steers were worth far less than cows or horses. They were also cheaper to feed since they thrived on pasture and hay while working horses needed grain. Leather work harnesses were expensive and wore out while a simple wooden ox yoke lasted almost indefinitely. Horses were subject to more diseases and easily hurt themselves among the stumps that covered the crop fields. Steers were as "strong as an ox" and easier to manage in tight situations. Last but not least, when they grew old or times got tough oxen could be slaughtered and eaten.

The major disadvantages lay in the facts that most were "slow as an ox," "stubborn as an ox" and "dumb as an ox." Furthermore they could not be ridden and a brace of oxen lacked the prestige of a horse team. It was a rare frontiersman who could not manage a team of horses, but a pioneer maxim held "a man may be able to govern men and guide the state and yet make a poor fist of it in holding a breaking plow behind seven or eight yoke of oxen."

And beginning in 1842, Dr. Osman D. Goodrich would learn full well the wisdom of that maxim. Born in Oneida County, New York, in 1808, Goodrich left his father's farm at the age of 17, studied medicine and received his degree in 1834. Two years later he moved to Allegan, becoming the first doctor to minister to the needs of Allegan County pioneers.

To supplement the meager income brought via his horseback practice, on January 17, 1842, Goodrich accepted appointment as Indian Agricultural Agent at the Old Wing Mission with a yearly stipend of $400. His task was to teach the resident Ottawa the mysteries of white men's farming techniques, including, of course, the art of driving an ox team.

Assembling his students, Goodrich would proceed to demonstrate as, heads down, the oxen pawed the ground, straining against their wooden yoke. The cast-iron share of the ponderous breaking plow bit deep into the virgin Fillmore Township soil. "Haw! Haw!" Goodrich would shout as the team began to wander to the right. Resisting the urge to curse the recalcitrant brutes, the doctor struggled to show the proper way to run a straight furrow. His Ottawa students would watch the white man's exertions in solemn silence until he

Oxen, strong, dependable and which could be eaten when times got rough, were indispensable on the frontier.

handed the goad to one to practice the craft. Then the Indian would talk to the oxen in his own language, with little results, and laughing, hand the whip back to the teacher.

But the problems faced by the agricultural agent were minor compared to the vicissitudes encountered by missionary George Smith and his family. Following their arrival via Capt. Macy's ship at Superior on September 7, 1839, Arvilla Smith and her three small children enjoyed the relative comfort of a cottage there while the Rev. Smith, with the assistance of James Everts and Andrew Herman, worked at grubbing out a clearing and erecting a log cabin at the site of the mission, six miles upstream and three miles into the woods. Two months later the family loaded household goods in a skiff and set out for their new home. They landed late in the night. Smith and a hired man lugged the bedding, while his wife, carrying two babies, stumbled along the dark forest trail. Her five-year-old son bravely trudged behind.

When she reached their new home, to her dismay Arvilla Smith found a miserable hovel, little more than "a pile of logs." Her husband had failed to tell her he had been unable to complete the cabin. It comprised a 16 by 18-foot log room and a 12 by 16-foot lean-to covered by a makeshift, leaky roof. She silently surveyed the dirt floor, vacant window openings, and doorway, and looked in vain for a fireplace. A cold rain fell for days and the family huddled together, shivering, on the damp ground. Three weeks later Smith returned to the Black River where he had cached the remainder of the supplies. By that time the stream had overflowed, soaking everything, including their only barrel of flour. They grimly ate the gummy mess.

As winter set in their situation worsened. The snow fell almost daily and Smith was forced to lug in all provisions 10 miles through the wilderness on snow-

shoes. Potatoes, turnips and rutabagas bought from Captain Macy at Superior were frequently the only food. While Smith was absent, the screams of a wildcat that prowled the clearing terrorized his family. Their only source of illumination was "a rag tied on a button and dipped in a saucer of grease."

Arvilla Smith remembered many years later her "sorest trial was to get sufficient food for the three children." They often knelt in prayer so that "papa would bring home something to eat." Over the course of the following decade, the Smiths buried five of their children near the garden in their yard. Later Smith reburied those sad remains in a common unmarked grave in Pilgrim Home Cemetery. Somehow Arvilla Smith retained her sanity, and the family's plight gradually improved. By the summer of 1840 primitive narrow roads had been hacked out to connect the mission with Richmond (now New Richmond), Allegan and Singapore at the mouth of the Kalamazoo River. The following summer brought a shipment of lumber, shingles, farm equipment, and such luxuries as tea. A 24 by 32-foot schoolhouse stood complete in January 1842, and soon lessons for the Indian children and agricultural training for the adult men began in earnest. In addition to the "three R's," Indian boys studied manual trades and the girls received instruction in spinning, sewing, weaving and the like. Since Smith could not speak the Ottawa language, an interpreter, Miss Mary Willard, arrived from Green Bay in July 1841. She made his primary goal of converting the Ottawa

Arvilla Smith on the right and Rev. Smith posed for the camera with a daughter and granddaughter after moving from Old Wing Mission to Northport.

to Christianity at least feasible.

Understandably, the Ottawa were not eager to forsake their traditional naturalistic beliefs for the austere tenets of Calvinism. Furthermore, Smith was not the only missionary angling for Indian souls in those waters. On March 21, 1841, Father Andreas Viszosky, a gaunt blond priest, visited the Indian camp on Black Lake. Born in Hungary in 1796, Viszosky had journeyed to America in 1833. Two years later, he took over the mission that Father Frederick Baraga had established at Grand Rapids. Many of the Ottawa preferred the ministrations of Baraga, Viszosky and other of the "Black Robes" who for centuries had worked to convert them to Catholicism. The Catholic Church, with its mystique and imagery, offered a more palatable substitute for their native beliefs.

Father Viszosky made frequent appearances at Black Lake to deliver mass and perform baptismal rites, and he won the allegiance of a segment of the band headed by Maksabe. Within a few years a Catholic church and cemetery was in place near the Indian landing at the present site of the H.J. Heinz plant. Unfortunately, rather than working together for the benefit of the Indians, Viszosky and Smith campaigned against one another.

Despite theological discord, Old Wing Mission prospered. The Ottawa may not have cared much for Smith's straitlaced religion, but they valued him as a friend and benefactor. Smith received appointment as official government teacher in 1844, which carried a salary of $400. For the first time he had a dependable income, and he began to improve his living conditions. Francis Mills had replaced Goodrich as agricultural agent to the Indians in 1844 and the following year he was succeeded by Isaac Fairbanks, a 27-year-old native of Massachusetts who had homesteaded in Fillmore Township a few months before. In addition to his other duties, Fairbanks began working on a new frame house to replace Smith's leaky old cabin. By December 1846 the 24 by 38-foot structure in the fashionable Greek Revival style stood substantially complete.

The Smiths had just settled into their comfortable new home when there came a knock on the door that would dramatically affect their lives and the fate of the Holland area. It was New Year's Day 1847, and the Ottawa were celebrating the holiday in the fashion they had learned from the French frontiersmen by firing guns, going from house to house shaking hands, repeating "Boshoo! Boshoo!" to everyone they met and expecting to be treated to food or a drink at each place. Anticipating Indian well-wishers, Smith opened the door. Instead, there stood two white men. He knew one well: it was Judge John R. Kellogg of Allegan, a

The Rev. Van Raalte sat for the camera with his son-in-law Peter J. Oggel ca. 1861.
(photo from Holland Historical Trust Collection of the Joint Archives of Holland)

land speculator and a member of the group that had originated the concept of the Old Wing Mission. Kellogg introduced him to the stranger, a distinguished looking gentleman who spoke a foreign tongue. He was the Rev. Albertus Christiaan Van Raalte from the Netherlands. To Smith's surprise Kellogg told him that Van Raalte and a colony of Dutch immigrants were about to locate in the vicinity.

Born October 17, 1811, in the Netherlands province of Overijsel, Van Raalte was one of 17 offspring sired by his father also named Albertus, a pastor in the Dutch Reformed Church. The younger Van Raalte planned to follow in his father's footprints, studying theology at the University of Leiden in the early 1830s. While there he became friends with Antonie Brummelkamp and Hendrik P. Scholte, members of a student group rebelling against the manner that the official Dutch church sanctioned by King William I was being conducted. The state church, these students felt, had become too liberal, permitting less than a strict interpretation of the Bible, allowing hymns to be sung that had been composed by men rather than found in the Bible and not requiring members to be bound to the concepts of original sin, predestination and other elements of the Calvinist creed. Unlike most university student movements, these so called "Separatists" were conservative, favoring a return to the good old fundamentalist church of yore. Ultimately they and like minded pastors throughout the Netherlands would establish a new Reformed Church.

Through the influence of his friends Van Raalte was converted to this rebellious thinking, and when he took his final exams in 1835, his theology professors found him not in agreement with the accepted dogma and did not ordain him a minister. Van Raalte became more and more convinced of the righteousness of the Separatist movement and began openly preaching its concepts. On March 2, 1836, he was ordained a Separatist minister and three weeks later became pastor of two combined congregations.

Despite the more liberal character of the state sanctioned church, the Holland of this era was not exactly a haven of tolerance. The church in power attempted to quash what it considered a heretical splinter group. The civil authorities ordered soldiers quartered in the homes of Separatists and their pastors and forbade the holding of religious meetings by more than 20 persons. Mobs attacked Separatist's homes, pelting tile roofs and windows with cobblestones. Not surprisingly, this persecution only caused the Separatist's resolve to grow stronger.

In retrospect, those Separatists who ultimately migrated to America, and especially later generations of their descendent, often compared their plight in Holland with that of the Pilgrim fathers who settled New England. Driven by persecution they sought freedom of religion in the new world. But other factors, especially economic causes, were also involved in the Dutch exodus that began in the 1840s. Economic conditions in the Netherlands had worsened when, as a result of increased efficiency brought about by the Industrial Revolution, English manufacturers drove the Dutch out of world markets. The ensuing widespread unemployment coupled with onerous taxes on food, unwisely levied by the Dutch government, brought misery to many. The situation worsened in 1845-1846 when the potato blight that sent hordes of Irish scurrying to America also eliminated that staple foodstuff in Holland.

Dutch immigrants en route to a new life in the wilds of America made quite a spectacle.

In 1876 a group of the original colonists posed for posterity.

Whether it was spiritual needs or those of a hungry belly that motivated individual immigrants is open to conjecture. Clearly, most of those who came to America in the 1840s, only slightly more than 12,000 people as compared to half a million Germans and close to one million Irish during the same period, came not because of religious persecution. That persecution had gradually declined following the abdication of King William I in 1840, and a new liberal constitution eight years later all but eliminated it. But the Dutch immigration did not abate after 1848.

What is more, the Separatists were actually in the minority among immigrants. In 1847, the peak year of the exodus, twice as many members of the state church as Separatists migrated. Those figures are representative of the entire period when emigration was at its zenith. By 1860, Michigan's population numbered 6,335 Dutch born citizens.

Be that as it may, in Van Raalte's case financial considerations were not a concern. From the sale of a tile factory he invested in he had netted $10,000, a sum equivalent in contemporary buying power to more

than $1 million. But by early 1846, concern for the economic and spiritual well being of his flock had convinced him that immigration to America promised relief for both needs.

Van Raalte, Scholte and Brummelcamp were also convinced that willy-nilly immigration was not in the best interests of their congregation - firm rules must be established to keep the potentially wayward in line and those who migrated should be bolstered by the presence of the like minded. Scholte wrote: "If Hollanders are scattered among a foreign populations, they will be too much left to themselves." Being unable to hear sermons preached in their own language to "warn them against the cravings of the flesh that militate against the spirit" was a dangerous risk. Van Raalte and his fellow ministers thought immigrants needed to establish distinct colonies in America.

Accordingly, early in 1846 Van Raalte's congregation formed an association and drew up a constitution to govern the quasi-communal colony they intended to plant in the new land. To insure that the colony was not tainted by the spiritually unregenerate provisions

35

limited membership to those "from whom it may be expected that they will be obedient to the will of God." To further maintain control all land purchased was to "be made in the name of the society."

Having adopted a constitution to govern the colony, the association then funded passage across the Atlantic of several needy families who were to act as scouts reporting back on conditions found in the "New Canaan" The families arrived in Boston in May and June 1846. They soon sent back long letters describing what they had encountered. One woman wrote: "Nearly all people eat meat three times a day... everybody is kind and helps us with everything... Washing hangs out on the line all night, nobody steals them... schools are free here... pubs for drunks one does not find here." Another who made his way to Milwaukee wrote that "he ate pork and beef three times a day." And still another wrote from Decatur, Illinois, "the poor here are as good as the rich, no one needs to doff his hat to anyone, as in Holland."

Convinced by those glowing accounts, Van Raalte's group made final preparations for their exodus. On September 24, 1846, he, his wife and five children, including a baby girl still in the cradle, a maid, and 101 practically destitute followers embarked from Rotterdam on the English three masted brig the *Southerner.* En route, the captain of the vessel, Tully Crosby, assisted Van Raalte in learning the rudiments of English. None of his other countrymen on board had yet mastered the language when the immigrant ship docked in New York Harbor 54 days later. The Hollanders must have created quite a spectacle as they clumped down the gangplank in wooden shoes, clad in their traditional peasant costumes.

Van Raalte intended to establish his colony somewhere in Wisconsin, then still a territory with plenty of available land at the government price of $1.25 an acre. The Hollanders traveled to Albany, stopping briefly to visit with the Rev. I.N. Wyckoff, a pastor of Dutch descent with whom Van Raalte had corresponded. But the season was growing late and if the colonists were to reach their destination before winter set in they needed to hasten westward.

Boarding a train in Albany for Buffalo, there they booked passage on a steamship. A storm held them up in Buffalo for a few days - not until November 27th could they proceed. Upon reaching Detroit, Van Raalte learned the disheartening news that the early onset of winter had prematurely ended the shipping season. Unable to steam to Milwaukee via the Straits of Mackinac, a relatively inexpensive voyage, the immigrants faced the option of traveling by train and stage which would have drained their limited funds. They attempted to bolster their resources by finding

The Rev. George Duffield befriended Van Raalte's people in Detroit.

jobs in Detroit, but as Van Raalte wrote in a letter to Brummelkamp: "The uncouth manners and ignorance of our people make it difficult for them to get work."

The captain of the steamship, Eber Brock Ward, took pity on the confused immigrants and offered employment to ten families at his shipyard in St. Clair. The Rev. George Duffield, a Presbyterian minister at Detroit, also befriended the fellow Calvinists and a member of his congregation, a Scotch baker named William Witherspoon, provided temporary housing for the Hollanders in his warehouse. Duffield also gave Van Raalte letters of introduction to Presbyterian elders located in the west, including one in Lockport near Chicago.

Securing an apartment for his wife and family, Van Raalte determined to push on alone on a scouting expedition to the west. His planned itinerary was to travel by rail to Kalamazoo, at that time the terminus of the Michigan Central Railroad, by stage coach to St. Joseph and by coach or steamship to Chicago. From there he hoped to reach Milwaukee, then "to travel straight across Wisconsin and from there along the Mississippi or through Iowa to St. Louis."

Christiana Catharina Van Raalte shared her husbands trials and tribulations in founding Holland.
(photo from Holland Historical Trust Collection of the Joint Archives of Holland)

But when Van Raalte reached the end of the railroad tracks in Kalamazoo he met two men who would change the destiny of southwest Michigan. One, referred to by Van Raalte only as Mr. Colt was most likely Dr. Edwin N. Colt, a physician who had settled in Kalamazoo in the 1830s. The other, Rev. Ava Phelps Hoyt, had been pastor of the Kalamazoo Presbyterian Church since 1840. Eager to secure for southwest Michigan a better share of the settlers who had been bypassing the region for western lands, Colt and Hoyt promoted local advantages. Western Michigan, the boosters assured Van Raalte, with its established villages and transportation facilities and its "better educated, more religious and more enterprising people," would make a better location for his colony than Wisconsin or Iowa.

Those arguments caught Van Raalte's fancy. He sent a letter to his wife in Detroit on December 24th stating "more and more I am coming to believe that Michigan will become the state in which we shall establish our home." Colt and Hoyt next introduced

Van Raalte to Judge Kellogg, a New Yorker who had pioneered in Allegan in 1837. An intimate friend of Michigan Territorial Governor Lewis Cass, Kellogg had served in the state legislature in 1838. Van Raalte thought him "a good man, intelligent and well informed." Kellogg took the Dutch pastor under his wing and recommended what he considered suitable tracts of land at Ada in Kent County, farther east on the Grand River near Ionia and in northern Allegan County, where land could still be purchased from the government at $1.25 per acre.

That latter site appealed most to Van Raalte as the best value for his limited funds. On New Year's Day, 1847, Kellogg and an Indian guide led Van Raalte on a land-looking expedition from Allegan north along the narrow trail that wound through the dense virgin pine forest. Their destination was the Rev. Smith's home. Smith, no doubt, welcomed the prospect of additional Protestants, Dutch or otherwise, to assist him in his feud with Father Viszosky. Smith showed them what he thought would be a prime site for the headquarters of the colony, a tract near the Catholic mission. That location was destined to become the nucleus of the colony Van Raalte named Holland.

Van Raalte stayed at Smith's home for ten days as he surveyed the surrounding region in detail. Unused to the rigors of snowshoe travel in the wilderness, he often relied on his guides to break trail through the waist high snow that covered the ground. At times he could make no more than 50 paces before stopping to catch his breath - but even as he rested he scooped through the snow to examine the quality of the soil. Once, completely exhausted, the 35-year-old Van Raalte collapsed on the snow, crying in his broken English "I can no more! I can no more!" But his guides helped him to his feet and he plowed on.

Despite those ordeals, the Dutch pastor liked what he found. The terrain bordering Lake Michigan was too sandy for agriculture, but the thick growth of virgin hardwood that blanketed much of the inland region promised fertile soil. The timber itself would prove ideal for the manufacture of fine furniture. The tempering influence of the big lake would allow fruit culture. The land near the mouth of the Black River and along its banks, unsettled save for the resident Ottawa, could be purchased cheaply. Perhaps, most importantly for Van Raalte's goals, the river lay halfway between the more developed Kalamazoo and Grand River valleys which

Ottawa County sawmills such as Timmers' Mill located at the corner of 56th and Baldwin were part of the region's first economic base. Note the acrobatic lumberjack on the roof.

Big wheels, invented by Silas Overpack from Manistee, made logging possible year round.

By the turn-of-the-century logging operations such as this in the Marigold Woods had become more sophisticated. (courtesy Myron Van Ark)

offered markets. Yet the site was isolated enough to allow a theocratic Dutch colony to mature without undue interference by the ungodly.

Van Raalte trudged back to Allegan on January 12th and then made further investigations about available acreage in Grand Haven. Satisfied that he had found his people's promised land, the latter day Moses returned to Detroit with Hoyt, Kellogg and the Rev. Andrew B. Taylor, minister of the Grand Rapids Reformed Church, to convince his followers.

He also acted quickly to secure the "keys of the region." His congregation was practically penniless and appeals to the association in the Netherlands founded to finance the expedition brought next to nothing in the way of cash. Ultimately he resorted to spending his own fortune with some additional loans from New Yorkers proud of their "Old Dutch" heritage. He purchased tracts from the government at the standard $1.25 per acre and additional plats for as little as 600 acres for $11.68 and back taxes. He also acquired 3,000 acres for $7,000 from disappointed real estate investors in New York City.

In early February, Van Raalte dispatched an advance party to prepare the Holland site for later arrivals. Those six families arrived in Allegan where the women and children remained while the men made their way to temporary headquarters at the old Wing Mission. By February 23, the colonists, with the assistance of Smith, Fairbanks and some Ottawa, had chopped out a narrow roadway and raised their first primitive log cabin. The family members waiting in Allegan soon rejoined them, bringing news that additional parties of Hollanders were en route.

Smith and Fairbanks obligingly opened their own houses to the immigrants until additional structures could be readied. But the travail of accommodating 15 strangers who spoke no English in her small home, already crowded with her numerous children, pushed Arvilla Smith to the limits of her endurance. She designated her parlor as their sleeping quarters and insisted that the Hollanders prepare their own meals. Except for the Van Raaltes and the pastor's assistant, Bernardus Grootenhuis, the bulk of the colonists were peasants with bizarre European customs. Smith's daughter, Etta, for example, recalled with disgust half a century later how "in the morning the good vrouws (housewives) would empty out their night vessels, wash them and stir up their pancake batter in them." Needless to say, such "thunder mug" cookery would not be perpetuated in the numerous Holland area recipe books later produced by housewives proud of their culinary skills.

In early March an additional contingent of 15 Hollanders arrived, bringing the colony's population to 43. But the Europeans were unfamiliar with frontier building techniques and ill equipped with tools and supplies. Construction of much needed dwellings proceeded slowly. Until they grew more adept at lumberjack skills, the Dutch pioneers also had an unfortunate tendency to fell trees on top of newly completed cabins. Van Raalte sent a group of men to the mouth of the Black River to construct a shanty for the use of new arrivals. They salvaged planks and boards that drifted up on the beach, but the project stalled through lack of nails.

Food for the increasing numbers of colonists that arrived through the winter became increasingly difficult to obtain. Some Hollanders lugged sacks of flour on their backs from Singapore, Grand Haven, and Grand Rapids. Others bought corn and game from the Indians. An enterprising, albeit unscrupulous, merchant from Allegan capitalized on their plight by rafting a load of potatoes down the Kalamazoo River and up the lake to the colony where he disposed of them at a dollar a bushel, twice the going rate.

The lack of proper nourishment and shelter coupled with the rigors of pioneer life rendered the Hollanders easy prey to disease. By the summer of 1847 few had escaped a bout with the ague, known variously as the "Fev-Nag," the "Ag-an-Fev," the "Shakin Ager," and simply the "Shakes." Its intermittent fever and chills made life miserable. Though normally not fatal, many in their weakened condition succumbed. Pioneers theorized the disease came from rotting vegetation, newly turned soil or the miasma that arose from the marshes. That latter hunch proved the most nearly accurate but not until the turn-of-the-century would doctors discover the true cause of the affliction we now know as malaria — the anopheles mosquito — which bred in incredible quantities in the stagnant water of the area's many swamps. Privies located too close to open wells, lack of screens to keep out flies, and other unsanitary conditions resulted in many cases of diphtheria.

As if the native diseases were not enough, incoming colonists imported smallpox, which raced through the colony in an epidemic. Van Raalte later remembered that the entire settlement became a "sickbed" during that first summer. No doctor of any type accompanied the original party of colonists who arrived in the winter of 1847. Had Van Raalte suspected what lay in store for his followers in the American wilderness he undoubtedly would have made better medical provisions. The saddlebag doctors who served Allegan, Newark, Grand Haven and other nearby settlements made emergency housecalls to the Holland colony. Dr. Goodrich, however, had become ill and left the region

Left to right G.J. Diekema, J.T. Kanters, A. Visscher, G. Van Schelven, I. Cappon and G.J. Kollen posed before the replica of the first Dutch cabin built for the 1897 Semi-Centennial of the Holland celebration.
(photo from Hope College Collection of the Joint Archives of Holland)

to recoup his health for ten years beginning in 1845.

In July 1847, Dr. J.J. M.C. Van Nus arrived with a party of emigrants from Zeeland. When Van Nus, who was a trained soldier as well as a physician, spotted the local Ottawa, he yanked out his sabre to make a show of military force as he marched back and forth guarding his fellow colonists. The brave doctor offered his services to the Holland community only briefly, however, and he soon departed for the Dutch settlement in Iowa.

Van Raalte and the Rev. Cornelius Van Der Meulen, leader of the colonists who settled Zeeland, made a rudimentary study of medicine, supplied themselves with a few common remedies and did the best they could for their flocks. Van Raalte, in fact, held regular office hours in his home each morning where he doled out medicine to a steady stream of patients. In 1849, Dr. C.D. Shenick, migrated from western New York to settle in the Groningen colony between Holland and Zeeland. Prior to moving west five years later, he not only plied his medical skills but served as Holland Township clerk, justice of the peace and director of the poor.

In part owing to the limited health care available, so many parents died the first year that the colonists erected an orphanage. Happily, the orphans were speedily adopted and the building was never used as such. Instead it served as the city's first schoolhouse.

The adventures some Hollanders experienced en route to their new homes in Michigan rivaled the rigors of life once they reached the colony. John and Minnie Wilterdink, for example, took their children by the hand in 1846 and left Holland for the United States on the sailing vessel *William Tell*. The ship was wrecked by running upon a rock. Fortunately, all aboard were rescued by passing ships. Diverted from their original port of entry, Baltimore, the family languished on shipboard for 90 days before being landed in Florida. Proceeding up the Mississippi River to St. Louis, they finally reached Holland in May 1847, where, like many other new arrivals, they found temporary lodging with the Indians in their village until they built their log cabin.

The Wilterdink family survived their ordeal and ultimately prospered on their homestead in Holland Township. Not so fortunate was John Wilterdink's brother Hiram and ten other relatives who were among the approximately 450 passengers, including more than 125 Dutch immigrants, who perished when the overloaded steamer *Phoenix* caught fire off the coast of Sheboygan, Wisconsin, on November 21, 1847.

Despite such tragedies and the many adversities they faced once in Holland, the colonists made substantial progress over the first few seasons. By August 1847 the population of Holland and the surrounding settlements had reached 1,500. Allegan County surveyor E.B. Bassett platted out the town of Holland that summer. From the beginning downtown centered around the intersection of the two main arteries, River Avenue and Eighth Street. Jan Binnekant moved an abandoned building, the remaining structure from ill-fated Superior, on skids over the frozen lake to the northwest corner of River and Eighth streets. It opened as the city's first hotel. By August 1848 approximately 50 dwellings dotted Holland's sandy streets.

The construction of a log church began during the summer of 1847, and it was completed the following year. The 35 by 60-foot structure stood at the southwest corner of the Pilgrim Home Cemetery. That first fall, colonists devised plans for a cooperative store.

The Orphanage built because so many parents died during the harsh first year was used instead as the city's first schoolhouse.

Goods were to be imported from Chicago by schooner and sold at their wholesale cost plus expenses. The vessel would also convey tanbark and cordwood to market. The colonists purchased a 100-ton vessel appropriately named the *A.E. Knickerbocker* and launched the ambitious enterprise. Unfortunately, a lack of sufficient capital and the additional expense of painstakingly hauling the cargo over the sandbar that blocked the mouth of Holland Harbor to the vessel doomed the venture. Within a few months, the store went bankrupt and the *A.E. Knickerbocker* was sold.

An initial project to establish a water-powered sawmill in 1847 failed but by the spring of 1848 Dutch entrepreneurs had

Holland's second church was constructed by the colonists of logs in 1847 and 1848. The first church was a Catholic Mission House.

The Rev. Cornelius Van der Meulen founded Zeeland in 1847.

constructed a wind powered sawmill similar to those they were familiar with in the old country. The 70-foot-tall octagonal structure sported sails with a spread of 64 feet. But wind proved undependable for reliable power and that venture also failed within a year. Oswald Van der Sluis, however, erected a steam-powered sawmill at the foot of Fourth Street and it operated successfully. Van der Sluis also installed a set of millstones in his mill in 1849.

Meanwhile, hundreds of land-hungry refugees from Holland had arrived to fan out across southern Ottawa and northern Allegan counties, carving homesteads out of the dense forest. Some Hollanders banded together to establish separate communities that bid to rival Holland as social and economic centers. The Rev. Cornelius Van der Meulen led a contingent of his congregation from Zeeland in 1847 to organize a community they named after their old country province. One of that number, wealthy farmer Jannes Van de Luyster, made the settlement possible through his generous loans to his countrymen and lost his fortune in the process. Originally laid out in one acre lots, by the fall of 1848 Zeeland comprised a log schoolhouse, a 40 by 60–foot church of square hewn cedar timbers and 65 to 100 residences.

Other groups pioneered communities named after their home provinces including Graafschap and Overisel in northern Allegan County and Drenthe which was settled by 57 families who emigrated from that province in 1847. Noordeloos was named in hon-

42

or of a resident pastor's home province in the Netherlands and nearby Norde Holland was founded by Jan Van Tongeren in the spring of 1848.

Those communities all began their existence as agricultural centers. But Groningen, the namesake of another Dutch province, was intended to have a manufacturing focus. The brainchild of Dutch entrepreneur Jan Rabbers, Groningen came into existence between Holland and Zeeland in 1847 when he opened a store there and constructed a dam and sawmill on nearby Frenchman's Creek. Rabbers' manufacturing attempts failed but during the early 1850s others placed grist mills, a tannery and a furniture factory at Groningen. In 1851, a big boost came when Jan Hendrick Veneklasen went into production of bricks. Soon that enterprise was turning out bricks by the millions. But Groningen's bid for industrial success came to an end in 1856 when the road linking Holland with Zeeland was relocated and most of the community's enterprises shifted to New Groningen about 3/4 mile to the north.

Trouble arose in the Dutch settlements when some

One of Van Raalte's apostles, Rev. Seine Bolks, led a group of his followers from the province of Overijsel to found the northern Allegan County namesake community in 1847.

The 1880 Allegan County History contained this view of the first structure in Zeeland.

Pioneers constructed fences out of uprooted pine stumps. Some of these hardy fences survive in isolated parts of the Allegan Forest. (courtesy Myron Van Ark)

colonists, in their eagerness to establish new lives for themselves, failed to respect the rights of the resident Ottawa. Indian venison found hanging in the woods was considered the gift of providence and carried home. Others burned hundreds of Indian sugar-making troughs and sap buckets as cordwood and appropriated caches of axes. Springs the Indians relied on for water were dammed up or polluted. During the spring, the Indians planted corn and bean fields before leaving for their traditional hunting grounds in Berrien County and to the north. Assuming that they had deserted for good, new arrivals grabbed the choice, cleared fields. The bands returned in the fall for harvest only to find log cabins and grazing animals on their croplands.

Van Raalte earnestly sought to resolve the growing hostility and some settlers paid restitution to the Indians. Unsatisfied, the Ottawa realized they could not live in harmony with their neighbors. Fairbanks' son Austin later remembered some Indians saying: "The Bad Spirit says; shoot every Dutchman but the Good Spirit says; go away, let Dutchman be." On May 18, 1848, the Rev. Smith led a party of Ottawa on an exploratory trip to the north to locate land for a new mission site. The settlers bought some of the Indians' lands and the Catholic Church was purchased for $26 and used as a receiving center for new arrivals. In 1849 the last of the local Indians moved with Smith and his family to the new mission site they had selected near Northport in Leelanau County.

That year Isaac N. Wyckoff, of Albany, New York, visited the Dutch colony. He found the region booming. He reported, "The city of Holland with its environs contains 236 houses; Groningen, 30; Zeeland, 175; Drenthe, 45; Vriesland, 69; Overisel, 36; Graafschap, 50. In all about 630 houses which, at an average of five souls to a house, will make the population over 3,000 souls." A few years later another visitor marveled at the perseverance with which these "very industrious and frugal people" were subduing the wilderness.

Some accounts of pioneer determination seem incredible by modern standards. John S. Kronemeyer, for example, pioneered in Fillmore Township near the Old Wing Mission. He reached the site with his wife and four children during the winter of 1847 and immediately set to work clearing the ground. Three days later he misjudged a falling tree and it broke his arm. Down but not out, he continued to chop one-handed for four months until his arm healed. Falling trees, in fact, posed one of the biggest dangers to life in the woods. Dead limbs called "widow makers," killed many a pioneer traveling through the forest. In 1850 alone, three settlers lost their lives to falling trees in Polkton Township.

Other less deadly but certainly aggravating conditions confronted the Dutch pioneers. Mosquitoes were a constant annoyance throughout the summer, and could only be held back through the use of lung choking smudge fires. The incessant buzzing around their heads of deerflies thirsty for blood drove some settlers temporarily insane. Poisonous snakes, bears, wild cats, and an occasional panther still lurked in the woods. Wolf packs posed a threat to livestock. The young daughter of Fillmore Township pioneer H. Bonselaar killed a marauding wolf in her yard with a pitchfork. Rats, mice, chipmunks, raccoons, wood-

44

Pioneer era felines like this were highly sought after among the Dutch settlers.

develop its potential until commercial vessels could gain passage through the harbor. As agricultural goods and products manufactured from wood stacked up in the city, Van Raalte explored ways to eliminate the bottleneck. He repeatedly petitioned state and national officials for assistance. In 1852 the U.S. Congress responded with an $8,000 appropriation, but President Franklin Pierce vetoed the entire River and Harbor Bill as an economy measure.

Instead the colonists had to solve their problem on a local level. They hand-dug a channel two feet deep through the sand bar that allowed access to flatboats. This helped, but still the task of loading and reloading cut into profits. In 1857 Van Raalte devised a plan to allocate one percent of tax revenues from the surrounding communities for harbor improvement. A referendum vote passed overwhelmingly. In 1858 the townships of Holland, Zeeland, Overisel, and Fillmore bonded $19,000 for the harbor.

chucks, and other destructive mammals nibbled away at crops and provisions. House cats were so valuable that one itinerant merchant regularly called out "Katten te Koop" ("cats for sale") as he made his rounds. Settlers long remembered 1851 as the "year of the squirrel." That spring an enormous migration of squirrels and other small animals swept over the croplands and gardens, eating everything in its path.

The most perplexing problem faced by the colony, however, was the lack of a decent harbor. The sand bar at the mouth of the Black River had hastened the demise of Superior. Holland, too, would be unable to

By the fall of 1859, Holland Harbor could accommodate even the largest of the Great Lakes ships. That year the passenger steamer *Huron* began weekly runs between Holland and Chicago. The Hollanders also built and launched a fleet of their own vessels. The annual trade volume doubled after the harbor improvements and increased steadily each year. Holland had become a major distribution center for the settlements of western Michigan, and its economic success seemed assured.

Schooners such as this transported Holland's commodities to market after the harbor was improved in 1859.

Fire Fights & Fighting Fire

They were "strangers in a strange land." Bad enough that their old country customs and differing technology little suited them to life on the raw frontier, scarcely one among the thousands of Dutch immigrants who settled in Holland and the surrounding townships prior to 1850 understood the rudiments of English. Differences in dialects between the various Netherlands provinces and between city and rural folk made it difficult for many of the Dutch speaking immigrants to even communicate with each other. And despite the fact that the Hollanders vastly outnumbered the few Americans who resided in southern Ottawa and northern Allegan counties, they remained disenfranchised until they qualified for naturalization.

The Michigan legislature created Holland Township on March 16, 1847. As originally laid out it included all of present day Holland, Zeeland and Park townships. Not until April 2, 1849, was the first township meeting held at the Van Raalte home. But since nei-

ther Van Raalte nor any of his countrymen could vote in the election held at that meeting, only 10 votes were cast. Those 10 American voters proceeded to elect seven from their number as the first township officers. The following year's election brought out only three voters.

Michigan's 1837 constitution specified that only white, male American citizens who had resided in the state for six months would vote. Under the U.S. Constitution aliens had to reside in the country for five years prior to becoming naturalized citizens. But the various states could determine their individual requirements for state citizenship. Michigan's Constitution of 1850 granted state suffrage to all males 21 years of age who had resided in the state prior to January, 1850, and had declared their intentions of becoming citizens of the United States. In July, 1848, Van Raalte had invited Ottawa County Circuit Court Clerk Henry Griffin to visit the colony to receive appli-

Van Vleck Hall, the first building on Hope College's campus, was built in 1858.
Waverly sandstone was first quarried for the foundation.

46

cations for naturalization papers. Griffin walked 22 miles from Grand Haven on a Sunday morning and attended a sermon preached by Van Raalte in which he exhorted his followers to seek citizenship. The next day the clerk registered the intentions of about 440 males. The 1851 township election, the first in which Holland immigrants could participate, brought out 260 voters in Holland Township.

While no longer politically powerless, the period when the Hollanders had been at the mercy of their American neighbors evidently left a lasting impression of distrust. Van Raalte, for example, seems to have held the Americans in low esteem. In a letter dated January 9, 1851, to Paulus Den Blyker, a wealthy Dutch immigrant who chose Kalamazoo as his home rather than Holland as he had urged him, Van Raalte wrote: "I consider your association and involvements with the Americans as definitely unsafe and destructive for you for the following reasons: You find in them none of the Hollander's open heartedness and mutual good understanding; between you and them there is in language, character, customs an insuperable chasm. You will find yourself among them as a babe in arms, and they will bear you whither they want you and you will not understand what they are doing. You will constantly find yourself in the most painful dilemmas; each fresh entanglement will carry you into a new maze. My guiding principle is: do not enter into affairs in which you cannot secure full knowledge, and assuredly you will not be able to raise yourself to the plane where you can safely move among the Americans; that can take place only with your children after you. Should you scorn this rule,

then your life will be one of painful uncertainty and full of corroding suspicion. Also you will be compelled to give that blind confidence which corrupts people. Remember, opportunity begets desire. Moreover, the Americans as a rule despise the Hollanders, and we Hollanders become embittered by their cold selfishness. With bold compliments they seek our money and our influence but really hold us in contempt as an uncultured, dull, and sluggish folk, and they are bold in their knowledge. Never will you be able to mingle with them as a friend among friends in free and cordial relationship. Much of this have I observed and experienced at first hand. I cannot bear this contempt, and I thank God that I live in the midst of my own people though beset with many troubles."

While a distrust of American outsiders would unfortunately continue too long as a tradition among some elements of the Holland area community, one institution that drew in outsiders and worked to ultimately break down the city's ethnic insularity was Hope College. Among the early classmates, for example, are sprinkled the names Gilmore, Brown, Jones, Steele, Simonson, etc.

Hope College traces its origins to 1850, when Van Raalte donated a tract of land, later known as "The Five Acres," as a site for an academy to prepare the young men of the community for advanced study. There in October 1851 "The Pioneer School" opened under the management of Walter T. Taylor of Geneva, New York, and a teaching staff consisting of his son and two daughters. Four years later the institution was renamed the Holland Academy and in 1858 Van Vleck Hall, the first major structure on the campus,

By the turn-of-the-century Van Vleck Hall was one of six major structures that comprised Hope College's tree lined campus. (courtesy Myron Van Ark)

was constructed in the fashionable Italianate style. In 1859 the campus was enlarged to 16 acres.

Henry J. Brown, a young theology student who arrived to study at the academy that year, never forgot his first impressions of the colony. He had hitched a ride on a surveyor's wagon at Allegan, and as the heavy vehicle lurched along the rough logging road that wound northwest to Holland, he saw little but vast beech, pine, and hemlock forests interspersed with cedar swamps. At Rabbit River, the future site of Hamilton, lay a lumber camp, and beyond, toward Overisel, stump-covered openings in the woods appeared. The crosscut saw had yet to make its appearance in Michigan and for miles he heard the distant thud of axes as Dutch settlers laboriously hacked away at clearing their land.

Told he was nearing Holland, Brown eagerly strained his eyes through the trees for his first view. Suddenly, as the wagon rounded a sandy knoll, a panoramic vista of the town appeared. Charred trunks and tangled piles of hemlock branches bounded the settlement. No shade trees had been spared; all was bleak, desolate sand and forest debris. Rows of one-story cottages, discordantly painted dark red, orange, and green, flanked sawdust-covered Eighth Street. A long white church and the Academy's new Van Vleck Hall were the most conspicuous structures in the entire community.

No horses were to be seen, only stolid ox teams. Many of the inhabitants wore costumes in the style of the old country peasantry, including wooden shoes called "klompen." The wilderness still hugged the outskirts of the town and within a week after his arrival Brown learned that a bear had lumbered in and dragged a 200-pound hog away. Deer and the smaller forest creatures, too, still occasionally wandered into town, and on clear, moonlit nights, the spine tingling howls of wolves serenaded the inhabitants.

Brown recalled the winter of 1859-60 as particularly cold. Macatawa Lake froze across all the way to Lake Michigan and for miles upstream. True to their native culture, the Dutch settlers strapped on quaint ice skates with "the blades turned up in a great circle over the toes" and skated across the bay, a la Hans Brinker. Arend van der Veen, Brown remembered in particular, "used to glide over the bay with a short stemmed pipe, puffing away, his hands in his pockets and bundled in short jacket."

Despite Holland's primitive appearance, much progress in terms of culture and education had already been made. Printing, an art in which Hollanders had excelled since the days of the famous Elzeviers, early made its appearance in the colony. The first newspaper in Ottawa County, the Dutch-language *De Hollan-*

der, had been published since September 1850. Seven years later two religious newspapers, *De Paarl* and *De Wekker*, sprang into existence in Holland. By 1861, E. Meijer and C. Vorst, publishers of *De Paarl*, had begun the ambitious undertaking of printing books. Their 346-page church history in the Dutch language became the first book published in Ottawa County. Jan Binnekant, an industrious entrepreneur who in addition to opening the city's first general store and the first hotel, had been involved in the publication of *De Hollander*. In 1862, Binnekant launched the first of a lengthy series of theological tomes that were published throughout the 1860s. Set in close minute type, some were over 800 pages long. In 1862, Binnekant also published the first issue of a religious weekly, *De Verzamelaar,* which four years later evolved into *De Hope.* The official paper of the Dutch speaking citizens of western Michigan, it was published in "The Printing House," a frame structure on 12th Street near the Hope College campus.

The first English newspaper, the *Ottawa County Register*, began in 1859 under a Democrat-oriented editorship. The following year John Roost and M. Hoogesteger established *De Grondwet*, a Dutch-language newspaper that supported the infant Republican party which had been born in Jackson, Michigan, six years before. *De Grondwet* was also the first paper published in Ottawa County to be printed on a steam-powered press. The other papers and books had been laboriously printed page by page on a hand press.

The great wave of Hollanders which immigrated to Michigan during the late 1840s and 1850s tended to support the American Whig party at first. However, many turned to the Democratic party in the 1850s. Until the publication of *De Grondwet*, there were no Dutch language Republican-oriented newspapers. But the Republican party's stand against the extension of slavery, with which the Dutch were strongly in agreement, caused an overwhelming swing to that party during the election of 1860. Abraham Lincoln's victory, which brought the slavery controversy to a head, was followed by South Carolina's secession, the bombardment of Fort Sumter, and the states found themselves at civil war.

Lincoln issued a call for volunteers to resist the "insurrection," and Michigan's young men rushed to join the colors. Van Raalte actively campaigned to get the single men of the colony to enlist. Eighteen-year-old Joos Ver Planke was working as a cobbler in Grand Haven when Van Raalte gave an impassioned speech there. Ver Planke later recalled, "On the evening that Van Raalte was speaking, I was sitting at my shoemaker's bench. My thoughts were with my companions who had decided to enlist. At last I could stand it no longer. I threw down my apron, rushed to the Hall and declared my desire to enlist." Some 60 men from Holland enlisted shortly after the war began, and in the summer of 1862 another 61 joined the army. Van Raalte wrote that there "was a clean sweep of all the boys." Ultimately over 400 Dutch volunteers from Ottawa County served in the Union army.

Forty of that number served in the Twenty-First Michigan Infantry, 26 in the Second Michigan Cavalry and 45 in the Michigan Engineers and Mechanics. Ninety-two Ottawa County men enlisted in the Twenty-fifth Michigan Infantry. Company I, in particular, was composed primarily of volunteers from the Holland environs. The first day of recruitment, 53 local youths enlisted. Van Raalte's oldest son Benjamin joined the unit as a sergeant on August 14, 1862 and a week later his 18-year-old brother Dirk followed him.

When the regiment was mustered into service in Kalamazoo the following month the women of Holland presented Company I with a silk flag bearing the inscription "God is Our Refuge." For four weeks Col. Orlando Moore drilled his ten companies of raw

A brave young 18-year-old, Dirk Van Raalte posed in an ill fitting uniform after he enlisting in the 25th Michigan Infantry in 1862.
(photo from Western Seminary Collection of the
Joint Archives of Holland)

recruits. On September 29, 1862, the 25th left for Louisville, Kentucky. For nine months, the 25th performed routine scouting and guard duty in the region south of Louisville. July 2, 1863, found Moore with only 200 of his normal strength of nearly 900 men stationed at a small fortress that guarded a bridge over the Green River, approximately 10 miles north of Columbia, Kentucky. That afternoon he received a scouting report - Gen. John Hunt Morgan's force of three to four thousand cavalrymen had crossed the Cumberland River to invade Kentucky.

Moore determined to attempt to retard the progress of the overwhelming force of Confederate raiders. He located an ideal site to make a stand where an open

Col. Orlando Moore led his infantrymen from Holland to a glorious victory on July 4, 1863.

five-acre field was bordered by the steep bank of the Green River on the north and deep ravines on the south. The men of the 25th hurriedly constructed earthworks in the middle of the field and chopped down trees in the woods to the rear and along the side of the field to provide cover and hold back a cavalry charge.

At dawn on the Fourth of July Morgan sent a couple of cannonballs crashing into the Michigan position. Then ordering a cease fire, he sent forward a flag of truce. Moore rode out to meet the Confederate delegation which handed him a written demand to surrender. Moore smiled as he replied, "Present my compliments to Gen. Morgan, and say to him that this being the Fourth of July I cannot entertain the proposition to surrender."

The officers wheeled their mounts, galloped back and the Confederate cannoneers opened fire. The infantrymen who had grown up among the woods of southwestern Michigan where squirrel shooting was a way of life, began picking off Morgan's gunners with unerring accuracy. With hideous rebel yells, the Confederate cavalrymen charged, but they could not withstand the murderous fire of the Michiganders. Eight times they charged and eight times they were driven back.

Meanwhile, another of Morgan's regiments had cut its way though the fallen trees and opened fire on the Michigan right flank. Moore had held Company I in reserve and when he blew a bugle, giving the impression that a large relief force was advancing, the Hollanders fired on the rebels with such deadly marksmanship that they retreated.

For three and a half hours, the battle raged. Then,

suddenly, Morgan retreated. The Confederates succeeded in crossing the river at another point but the 12 hours he lost caused Morgan to abandon his plan to

Flamboyant Confederate cavalry leader Gen. John Hunt Morgan got more fight than he bargained for at the Battle of Tebb's Bend.

By 1889 the ranks of Civil War veterans were already growing thinner when these old soldiers posed at the corner of 8th Street and River Avenue during a GAR reunion. (photo from Holland Historical Trust Collection of the Joint Archives of Holland)

sack Louisville. The 25th Michigan's casualties numbered 22 wounded and six dead, while Morgan lost 50 men killed, including some of his finest officers, and 200 wounded during the engagement that came to be known as The Battle of Tebb's Bend. The heroic stand by the Michigan soldiers at Tebb's Bend received scant publicity as the nation's newspapers focused on the bloody events at Gettysburg and the surrender of Vicksburg, Mississippi, that occurred on the same day.

John A. Wilterdink, who had experienced the perilous journey across the sea to the colony with his family in 1846 and 1847, participated in that glorious victory. One of his letters home to family describing the battle records the poignant death of his companion Pieter Ver Schure, the only casualty from Company I during the engagement: "Four of us carried him from the battlefield. The first he asked was, 'Oh John, give me water.' I had a full canteen. Then he said, 'Just keep it for yourself,' He kept his eyes fixed on me and said, 'John, can you pray for me' My answer was, 'Yes, Piet, with my whole heart.' And that was it. 'I will die before I reach camp.' He was afraid to die but I had to let him rest."

The men of Company I continued to serve bravely until the end of the war. Van Raalte's sons distinguished themselves. Dirk lost his right arm at the shoulder after receiving a severe wound while carrying a message to headquarters during the Battle of Atlanta in August 1864. Despite that loss, he continued to serve as a hospital steward. Benjamin heroically recaptured his regiment's colors following a Union retreat on August 8, 1864. The men of the Twenty-fifth Michigan were discharged in July 1865, and the Holland veterans returned to the city for a hero's welcome held in the public square.

The drain on the local labor force brought about by enlistments, the rapid rise in commodity prices, the successful fund-raising campaigns organized to benefit Union soldiers, and, of course, news from the battlefields had preoccupied the Holland home front during the war years. But the period 1861–1865 also witnessed the beginnings of evangelical efforts that would later have a dramatic influence. Van Raalte had long cherished dreams of missionary activity. Prior to his decision to immigrate to America he had advocated the establishment of a mission in Java. The pioneer school that evolved into Hope College had been founded in part to train children "to become light bearers of the Gospel to the dark places of the earth." The spring of 1864 witnessed a revival of evangelical zeal. On June 24, 1864, Hollanders laid the keel for a missionary ship intended to carry a group of pious families to establish a colony in some "heathen land." Those ambitious plans stalled through lack of funds, and the ship was never launched.

During the Civil War the Holland Academy continued to experience the shortage of funds that plagued its early years. A number of its students, like Dirk Van Raalte, enlisted in the Union army. In December 1863, Van Raalte wrote his sons asking them to donate money to support the college or the students attending. Dirk responded with a letter revealing his bitterness about those who stayed behind: "As far as I am concerned, I do not want to pay one penny for that purpose... I think that the students had better come here and take up a gun and knapsack. I think we need them more here than anywhere else. We have to bleed and suffer while they stay at home and live at our expense. And they make fun of us... It would be better if half of the students would join our ranks instead of staying home like cowards and waiting to be drafted.

Following his discharge in 1865, Van Raalte returned to the Academy. He graduated two years lat-

Hope College's first gymnasium, constructed by students in 1862, also served as a chapel.
(courtesy Myron Van Ark)

The original Cappon and Bertsch Tannery was located along the shore of Macatawa Lake in 1857.
(courtesy Holland Historical Trust Collection of the Joint Archives of Holland)

er. In the meantime the institution had received a much needed financial boost in 1865 in the form of a subscribed endowment of $40,000 raised by the principal, Philip Phelps, from churches in the East. Additional subscriptions came from churches in the West and in 1866 Hope College was incorporated under the Michigan General College Law. On July 17, 1866, the first class of eight students graduated at the commencement exercises held in the college gymnasium. Each of the graduates delivered an oration in either Dutch, English or Latin.

The student body, under the leadership of Principal Phelps, had constructed the gymnasium themselves in 1862. They felled trees in the nearby forest, rolled the logs to the Black River, and floated them to the Plug-

ger Sawmill, where they were sawed into 11,000 feet of lumber. The gymnasium also served as a chapel and general purpose meeting hall. The building the students constructed served the college well until it was replaced in 1906 through funds donated by Andrew Carnegie.

The year following Hope College's incorporation brought Holland its first city charter, despite the opposition of Van Raalte, who apparently did not want to pay additional taxes on the lots he owned within the village. Isaac Cappon ran on the Republican ticket and narrowly defeated Democratic contender Dr. Bernardus Ledeboer, a former township supervisor, in the first mayoral election that year. Cappon had been active in civic affairs, especially through his work on the Holland Harbor Commission. In partnership with Grand Rapids entrepreneur John Bertsch, he had established a tannery on Black Lake in 1857. Bertsch had his doubts about Holland as a site because so many of the inhabitants still wore wooden shoes, not a promising market for shoe leather. The enterprise did receive a severe setback during its first year due to the financial panic of 1857. But Cappon and Bertsch persevered and the Civil War brought profitable government contracts. By 1864 the firm had erected a large new tannery at the present site of the Holland Civic Center at a cost of $13,000, financed entirely out of one year's profits. The Cappon and Bertsch Tannery became one

The engineer, brakeman, porter and other officials proudly posed with Pere Marquette Railroad Engine Number 69 in this turn-of-the-century view.
(courtesy Myron Van Ark)

of the area's most prosperous businesses and stimulated collateral enterprises, such as the local tanbark industry.

Holland received another major economic boost when the first train chugged into the city on June 9, 1870. The Michigan Lake Shore Railroad linked Holland with Allegan and by July 1, 1870, it had reached Muskegon. Its first depot stood at the intersection of Seventh and Fish (now Columbia) streets. By the end of the following year, a second railroad line, the Chicago and Michigan Lake Shore, connected Holland with Grand Rapids. The C&MLS erected a depot on the south side of Ninth Street just west of Land (now Lincoln) Street.

Those railroad systems reduced the Holland area's economic isolation, but the residents themselves continued to resist the assimilation process. Dutch remained the predominant language and many residents knew only a few words of English. The tendency to retain Old World customs and language was reinforced by the local Dutch language newspapers and by the numerous church services in their native tongue. Van Raalte's original goal to found a theocratic colony isolated from the spiritual and moral temptations of society at large was being eroded, but very slowly.

Gilbert Haan, who grew up in the Vriesland area and graduated from Hope College in 1893, remem-

One of Holland's architectural treasures, the Pillar Church, was constructed in 1856.
(courtesy State of Michigan Archives)

bered the Dutch colonists of the 1860s and 1870s as "on the whole, good, sober, quiet religious people." Lengthy prayers and Bible readings were always practiced before each meal. But, as Haan admitted, religion was so dominant a part of the culture that no reading of a secular nature was even available. Consequently the Hollanders were "extremely ignorant" of worldly affairs. As for the reading material that did circulate in the colony, Haan thought it to be "of value as spiritual food," but added "though they might have a wagon load of it and read themselves blind, it would not enrich their minds with general knowledge."

Those who failed to attend church regularly risked social ostracization. For most, the Sabbath was the highlight of the weekly cycle. The monumental church dedicated by Van Raalte as the People's Church in 1856, and long known as the Pillar Church because of its graceful, Doric-pillared facade, the Third Reformed Church organized in 1867 and the Market Street Christian Reformed Church were, in many respects, the focal point of the social life of the entire community. Sermons in Dutch that might last two hours or longer were varied by traditional hymns sung without musical accompaniment as a "voorsinger" set the note, pitch and speed. The congregation kept itself awake through the lengthy services by sucking on hard mint candy. Ladies carried little silver boxes called "snuifdoosie" containing a pungent perfume. Like smelling salts they were periodically passed to revive drowsy family members.

Members supported the church with annual pew rents, which in 1880, for example, netted the Pillar Church $800. A weekly offering was also collected through the use of tasseled velvet bags attached to long poles. An interesting funeral custom decreed that church bells toll the age of the deceased en route to the cemetery. Of its many religious scruples, the community would have occasion to lament one in particular, an aversion to fire insurance. To carry insurance was to doubt the benevolent will of Providence.

The spring and summer of 1871 had been among the driest on record. Throughout the Midwest, farmers had watched their seedlings shrivel in the parched soil. The woods were bone-dry and Michigan's vast stretches of cut-over pine land, covered with tangled piles of tops and branches left by the lumbermen, lay like tinder on the land. For months, forest fires raged throughout northern Wisconsin and Michigan. Billowing clouds of yellow smoke burned eyes as far east as Philadelphia and caused Chicago's street lamps to be lit an hour earlier than usual.

The situation worsened that fall. Nine-year-old Gilbert Haan of Vriesland remembered that "the world seemed to be on fire." At night through a window facing west he watched the "whole sky aglow from all the fires of barns, houses and dry cut down wood lots." He asked his sister, "Is the Judgement Day here?" Many adult residents of Holland probably thought that it was.

On October 8, 1871, the Great Chicago Fire nearly leveled that city, and a forest fire fanned by hurricane strength winds swept over Peshtigo, Wisconsin, where more than 1,000 people died within hours. These disasters eclipsed Holland's fiery holocaust in the national press, but not in the minds of the 2,400 Dutch residents living there.

The forest fires that burned millions of acres of Michigan woodlands all but wiped out Holland in 1871.

with several wild fires that burned out of control in the woods, and residents had beaten back a fire that threatened the city from the south. The afternoon of Sunday, October 8, seemed particularly hot and sultry as fine wood ash sifted down on the city. At about 2 p.m. the wind shifted and began to blow harder from the southwest. The Third Reformed Church's bells tolled the fire alarm, and men armed with shovels and other tools hastened to fight the fire that licked at the city's southern limits. A story, probably false, was reprint-

Forest fires had flared up for weeks prior to October 8. The previous week the Holland City Council had castigated Holland Township officials for not dealing

ed in popular books about the Chicago fire: "Mr. George Howard, at the commencement of the fire, took fourteen spades and handed them each to Hollanders, who were standing around, and requested them to use them in throwing sand on the fire, so as to prevent it from spreading to the destruction of the city. They actually refused to work, giving as a reason that it was Sunday, and it would be wrong to do any work on that day."

That evening, gale force winds pushed the fire into the city. The recently constructed Third Reformed Church caught fire about midnight, followed by the Cappon and Bertsch Tannery. The wind, now of hurricane strength, swept flaming shingles from the church and chunks of bark from the tannery into the Eighth Street business district. By 3 a.m., practically the entire city lay in ruins, "mowed clean as with a reaper."

Charles F. Post, whose home was on the south part of the city, had taken the precaution to fill every available bucket and tub with water. As the forest fire approached he climbed to the top of his roof and thoroughly soaked the wooden shingles which saved the

After its 1871 fiery devastation Holland developed a professional fire department. This turn-of-the-century rig posed before the City Hall-Fire Station on East 8th Street. (courtesy Myron Van Ark)

In the days when a fire engine's horsepower meant just that, firemen took excellent care of their prize animals. (courtesy Myron Van Ark)

boy and his wheelbarrow clear from the ground and carried them some little distance; still Walter would not let go of the handles, though his hat was gone and his eyes full of sand." The Post family all survived the ordeal.

Miraculously, only one person died in the flames, Mrs. J. Tolk, an aged widow who lived alone. A few residents buried their choice possessions in the sand or lowered them into wells but to little avail. Some took to the lake in boats and hundreds of refugees thronged the roads leading out of Holland.

Van Raalte, who had been in Muskegon preaching during the conflagration, returned to find his home had been spared, but was now packed with refugees. Hope College, the two railroad depots, the Pillar Church, the

structure. When he saw the fire leaping from roof top to roof top he sent his wife, their 18-month-old baby and five-year-old son fleeing to a safer part of the city. The wind was so strong that several times his wife had to throw herself on the ground with the baby. The five-year-old, Walter, had refused to leave behind a nice little wheelbarrow his uncle had given. As he valiantly wheeled the toy, "once the wind took both the

Market Street Christian Reformed Church, the Plugger Mills, the residential section comprising the southeast part of the city, and a few other structures were all that survived. Two hundred and ten homes, 75 stores, 15 factories, 5 churches, 3 hotels and 50 other structures, totaling $900,000 worth of property, went up in smoke. Owners carried only $35,000 worth of insurance. Fortunately, Hope College, the Pillar and

J. Van 'T Lindenhout, who visited Holland in the 1880s, included an engraving of the city as seen from the Hope College campus in his travel narrative published in the Netherlands.

Employees at the huge Cappon and Bertsch Tannery worked long ten hour days while performing tasks such as scraping the remaining flesh from the hides.

that of the first colonists, and Holland made a slow but steady revival. S.L. Morris launched a new weekly publication in English, the *Holland City News*, on February 24, 1872, and his newspaper featured glowing accounts of rebuilding efforts. Much lumber came from the Plugger Sawmill, along with Scott and Schuurman's appropriately renamed Phoenix Planing Mill, which was soon rebuilt on River Avenue. From Jan Henry Veneklasen's brickyard near New Groningen came millions of quality bricks. New brick buildings and scores of brick farmhouses, built in a unique vernacular style of polychromatic patterned brickwork, soon dotted the area.

By the spring of 1872 the rebuilt Cappon and Bertsch Tannery was back in operation. The financial panic of 1873 brought a setback, but by 1875, 50 employees processed 30,000 hides annually. Five years later, business had doubled, and in 1885 the company added another tannery on the north side of Black Lake. With more than 100 workers the leather company was the city's largest employer, and the Cappon family had become the city's wealthiest. Cappon's economic success and his many civic contributions helped to boost Holland's revitalization after the fire

Holland paused amidst its efforts to rebuild to celebrate the 25th anniversary of its founding. On September 17, 1872, approximately 5,000 people gathered

the Christian Reformed churches, the cultural and spiritual centers of the city, offered a foundation on which to rebuild.

Relief assistance soon came from nearby communities. Grand Rapids citizens organized a general relief committee to distribute aid throughout the western part of the state. Friends from Grand Haven delivered wagon loads of food; their generosity in supplying goods from stores and home pantries was long remembered by the Hollanders. Dutch Reformed churches in New York and New Jersey collected a total of $40,000 for the relief of Holland. Hollanders in Wisconsin sent $800 and other funds came from as far away as the Netherlands. A citizens' committee met in the City Hall on October 10 to coordinate relief activities. At the meeting Van Raalte announced "with our Dutch tenacity and with our American experience, Holland will be rebuilt."

Lack of insurance, a rise in building material costs brought about by Chicago's need and the financial depression of 1873 hindered Holland's rebirth. Some businesses were never able to reestablish themselves. But residents set to work with a zeal that rivaled

Tannery workers placed hides in vats containing a tannin solution for their conversion to leather.

for a festive day of parades, music, and orations. Like many descendants would each May beginning in the 1930s, townspeople marched in native costumes. Ox-drawn wagons conveyed surviving pioneers through the city to the site of a speakers' platform in the woods one mile east of Holland. Following lengthy prayers and hymns, Van Raalte delivered a classic speech on the history of the area. Proud of the growth of the colony he had started, Van Raalte said: "The central colony, now at least numbering 15,000, covers more than ten townships... This area is a field covered with farms, villages, 24 churches and all over with school districts taught in the English language, and the central city of Holland is gifted with a college in behalf of the Holland immigration in the western states." Zeeland, Overisel, and Vriesland also held similar historical celebrations in 1872. These events marked the beginnings of a long tradition of honoring the achievements of the pioneers.

Another notable celebration occurred in November 1873, when the Reverend M. Cohen Stuart of the Netherlands toured the region as part of his trip to America to attend the General Meeting of the Evangelical Alliance in New York. Despite a raging snowstorm, Hollanders packed the Pillar Church and the partially reconstructed Third Reformed Church to hear their distinguished visitor's sermons. Stuart penned an interesting description of Van Raalte, who he thought resembled more a pensioned general than a retired minister.

Before traveling to other Dutch settlements in Kalamazoo and the western states, Cohen was given a tour of the Holland vicinity. He noted the scars left by the fire, an "extensive wilderness of scorched trunks, black branches which stuck up ghostlike into the sky." Cohen was also treated to a sailboat ride, past the 450-meter-long clay and stone pier that protected the harbor entrance. His hosts were especially proud of a grape vineyard planted on a hill along the shore. The climax of Stuart's visit, a feast put on by the "well-to-do of the colony," proved particularly memorable. Some 50 guests sat at a long table groaning with "oysters, capon, game dishes, pastries, torts and cakes of all kinds." Perhaps anticipating some of the fruits of the vineyard he had visited, Stuart seemed mildly disappointed to discover that the only beverage served was "crystal clear ice water." But he drank heartily of it, anyway.

Van Raalte's beloved wife of 25 years, Christiana Johanna died in 1871. Renowned as a cook, decades later some of her recipes, including her prize angel food cake, would continue to find their way into cookbooks such as that published by the Ladies of the Pillar Church in 1896. Van Raalte died on November 7, 1876, to be laid to rest next to his wife in Pilgrim Home Cemetery. The summer before his death he had witnessed the creation of a beautiful park, honoring the nation's centennial, on the site of the market

Centennial Park, shown at the turn-of-the-century, sported "Keep off the Grass" signs.
(courtesy State of Michigan Archives)

square he had laid out in 1847. The park site was graded, a central mound shaped, and winding gravel paths laid out. Citizens lined the paths with flowers and shrubbery and planted trees taken from the surrounding woods as well as maple saplings from a local nursery. Beautiful Centennial Park, a shade-covered and immaculately groomed oasis, stands today as a monument to the less hectic Victorian era.

In 1881, the Reverend Roelf T. Kuiper, pastor of the Graafschap Christian Reformed Church, wrote that Holland had not yet recovered from the 1871 fire, but that "improvements and revival is anticipated." The following year, the compiler of the first history of Ottawa County noted a number of thriving commercial establishments. The largest, the Cappon and Bertsch Tannery, was housed in a struc-

Masons erected this enormous chimney at the Cappon and Bertsch Tannery only to see it collapse as it neared completion.
(photo from Holland Historical Trust Collection of the Joint Archives of Holland)

ture more than 400 feet-long on Ninth Street, containing 380 curing vats, a huge bark storage building, and an adjacent 40 by 125-foot five-story drying and processing plant on Eighth Street containing the city's first elevator. Five to six thousand cords of tanbark were used to produce over $500,000 worth of leather annually. A rival tannery, established by George Metz, Jr., in 1870, also turned out $150,000 worth of leather each year.

A variety of manufacturers made use of the abundant timber supply. The Holland Stave Factory on River Avenue, rebuilt in 1880 by Joseph Fixter of Milwaukee, employed 25 laborers to produce barrel staves and butter tubs. Also established in 1880 on River Avenue, J. Van Putten's Butter Tub Factory utilized 900 cords of wood each year in the

(Below) The C.L. King & Co. factory utilized local lumber to produce an enormous output of baskets beginning in 1882.
(courtesy Holland Historical Trust Collection of the Joint Archives of Holland)

manufacture of its product. The Phoenix Planing Mill specialized in doors, sashes, window blinds, and moldings. The Plugger, Howard, and Boone sawmills were together capable of cutting 40,000 feet of lumber each day.

The Veneklasen brickyard in Holland Township marketed an annual output of 5 million bricks statewide. In the 1890s it would relocate to the Zeeland outskirts and boost production to as much as 20 mil-

The Walsh-DeRoo Mill, constructed in 1882, produced nationally famous brand names of flour. (courtesy Holland Historical Trust Collection of the Joint Archives of Holland)

lion bricks a year. Other entrepreneurs had founded specialized manufacturing establishments. The Holland Manufacturing Company began producing "Palmer's Self-regulating Windmills" in 1881. The ten artisans at Flieman's Wagon and Blacksmith Shop turned out a line of wagons, carriages, cutters, and sleighs. The Holland City Foundry, built by W.H. Deming in 1859, and Peter Wilms' Holland Pump Manufacturing, established the year of the fire, planted seeds for a local metalworking industry.

The Holland City and Plugger mills had ground much of the grain grown in the surrounding farmlands. In 1882, however, Isaac Cappon and partners constructed the modern Walsh-De Roo Milling Company, which pioneered in western Michigan with a new "Hungarian Roller Process." Walsh-De Roo's Sunlight, Daisy, Puritan, Idlewild, and Morning Star brand flours soon became nationally known products.

The year 1882 also marked a major development in the evolution of the local religious community. The Dutch Reformed Church had experienced a long history of infighting over dogma; past feuds had led to a number

of secessions by splinter groups. The Christian Reformed Church, for example, sprang into existence in 1857 when four congregations left the Reformed Church because of differing beliefs. A debate, which now seems rather trivial, gripped the Dutch religious community in the early 1880s. The controversy arose over whether or not to allow members of secret fraternal societies, such as the Freemasons, to remain church members. The issue caused the congregation of the Pillar Church to vote to secede from the official Dutch Reformed Church in 1882, and fraternal society members were prohibited from church membership. Two years later the Pillar Church joined the Christian Reformed Church. The schism between the Christian Reformed and Dutch Reformed churches caused by this seemingly minor conflict introduced to Holland an issue that would long remain divisive.

This stalwart citizen seemed ready for anything as he stood before Pete Brown's Saloon on West 8th Street ca. 1885. (courtesy Don Van Reken)

A daredevil Hollander perched atop one of the massive telephone poles that lined
West 8th Street by the turn-of-the-century. (courtesy Myron Van Ark)

Factory Whistles & Tourist Dollars

The team of snow white horses stepped high as it pulled the buckboard piled with ladders and spools of wire down 8th Street on October 27, 1883. A crowd soon gathered to gape as the construction crew climbed trees and slung the first wires across the roadways. Nine days later they had completed the project – all 12 of Holland's first telephone subscribers were hooked up and ready to crank for the operator. Little matter that those 12 could talk only to one another, that they needed to yell into the receiver to be heard and that the operator did not staff the switch board at night – the advent of the mechanical marvel invented by Alexander Graham Bell but seven years before put the city on the cutting edge of technology. Other innovations followed in rapid order. By the end of 1884 "long distance" lines linked Holland with Grand Rapids and folks could call one another even at night. The original operator, a boy, was soon replaced by young women because "boys drank beer, fought, played marbles during working hours and quarrelled with subscribers." In 1888, the telephone company, then managed by Miss Myra McCance, proudly announced it had nearly 100 subscribers.

Yes sir, Holland was no hick town as it prepared for the dawn of the 20th century. It was a thriving industrial mecca with many of the modern conveniences. The final two decades of the 19th century witnessed a burst of civic accomplishments similar in many ways to the fast paced developments that would revolutionize Holland a century later.

The city had constructed its first public water system in 1885. Responsibility to "superintend, maintain and take complete charge of the city's water works system" was given to a three member Water Commission, the forerunner of the present Board of Public Works. By the end of 1886, four-and-a-half miles of water mains had been completed. The first water rates varied with business use. The city set annual fees for dwellings and saloons at three dollars, barber shops paid one dollar for the first chair and 50 cents extra for each additional chair, and liveries paid 50 cents per horse stall.

The city's first electrical service began through the efforts of Alfred Huntley, a young entrepreneur who with his brother James had immigrated to Holland from England in 1871. Huntley worked as an engineer

In 1905 eight telephone operators and a supervisor staffed the city's switchboard.
(photo from Holland Historical Trust Collection of the Joint Archives of Holland)

for the Metz Leather Company before opening a machine shop in partnership with William A. Holley.

When the two constructed a small electric plant for use in their shop, several business urged Huntley and Holley to build a larger plant and furnish their stores with electricity. On July 15, 1890, Huntley and Holley applied to the city for permission to erect poles along streets to distribute electricity. The city granted that request with the provision that if it decided to establish its own electric plant the franchise would be relinquished. The Huntley and Holley Electric Light Company operated for a year and was then replaced by the pair's larger Wolverine Electric Light Company. Then on April 4, 1892, the city electorate overwhelmingly passed a referendum vote to construct a municipally owned light plant. On May 8, 1894, the light plant constructed by the Commercial Electric Engineering Company of Detroit began providing service to the city and the unfortunate Huntley and Holley were soon out of the power business.

Other advances during the "Gay 90's" included the beginnings of the city's first sanitary sewer system that replaced the traditional privies hand emptied by the unenviable members of a profession known as "city scavengers." In 1897 local free delivery of mail was implemented. Prior to that, citizens had to pick up their mail at the post office, which since 1893 had been located on 8th Street just east of Central Avenue. Another major improvement came in 1898 when the Holland Lake Michigan Railroad Company began operating its electric streetcars that ran down 8th Street and south on River Avenue. In 1899 the line was extended to Macatawa Park and Saugatuck. Four years later came the first paved streets. At a cost of $40,000, 8th Street from River Avenue to Lincoln Avenue was covered with bricks, not yellow however.

Electricity, municipal water and sewage, telephones, street cars, brick streets and home delivery of mail — Holland certainly had come a long way since the days of its founding a half century before. Yet some services such as medical care remained remarkably primitive. A variety of quacks continued to gull townspeople with patent medicines or occult healing powers. The so called "Dr." F. McOmber, for example, who in 1899 held periodic office hours at a room in the Hotel Holland, promised to "make the deaf hear, stop ringing noises in head and ears, cure catarrh to stay cured and straighten cross eyes in a minute without pain or chloroform." The good doctor, it was rumored, kept his bags packed in that hotel room for a quick getaway should those eyes begin to cross again.

Dr. F.J. Schouten, who operated a drug store as well as a medical practice, widely advertised his celebrated "pheumatic liver and ague pills." A few years later,

Beginning in 1898 streetcar tracks ran along the center of busy 8th Street. (courtesy Myron Van Ark)

Train wrecks such as the ca. 1900 example above sometimes brought business for the
Citizen's Transport Company which rented out the rig below to carry grieving family members
during funeral processions. (courtesy Myron Van Ark)

Students of grades one through eight posed before their one-room
schoolhouse in Jamestown Township ca. 1890.

F.J. Goodby, proprietor of the Sanitarium Treatment Room at 42 E. 8th Street, offered his electric light bath, various sprays and douches, massage, electricity, vibration and many other forms of treatment as cures for everything from rheumatism to gout. Goodby also made a specialty of treating bunions and corns.

Fortunately, there were some reputable physicians available to Holland sufferers. None was more respected than Dr. Henry Kremers. Born in nearby Zeeland in 1850, Kremers graduated from the University of Michigan Medical School in 1876. In an age when house calls were the norm, Kremers made long rounds in his familiar horse and buggy and was "considered as a friend in nearly all the homes" he ministered to. The house he built for his family of five sons in 1889 would become the city's first hospital 28 years later.

The doctor had a busy year in 1889 when he also served as Holland's mayor. One of the few Democrats ever to be elected in the Holland vicinity, Kremers delighted in loudly calling to his dogs and horses, all named after prominent Republicans. Kremers' mayoral term ushered in a period of dramatic growth for the city. In 1890, Holland's population numbered 3,945. During the succeeding four years it would increase by 62 percent, reaching 7,790 by the decade's end. The city had finally shaken off the effects of the disabling fire of 1871 and local industry began to prosper. In 1891 alone, Holland experienced a building boom that brought the construction of several new business blocks and more than 100 homes.

Many of the handsome new structures that dotted Holland's downtown had been constructed in part of Waverly sandstone. A vast deposit of the fine grained, bluish-gray sandstone, which takes its name from a prominent outcropping near Waverly, Ohio, had first been quarried locally one mile east of Holland in 1857. The rock was floated down the river in scows and used for the foundations of Hope College's Van Vleck Hall. In 1867, John Roost purchased the quarry and increased production. By the 1880s proprietors had begun shipping the stone blocks to other west Michigan communities. A variety of schools, factories, and public buildings in Allegan, Kalamazoo, Grand Rapids, and Muskegon were constructed entirely of the attractive stone. Allegan, in particular, proved a good market and the Waverly stone went into the construction of the imposing Romanesque courthouse built in 1889, the Allegan High School Building and for the abut-

Dr. Henry Kremers and his family enjoyed a camp out on their lawn during the summer of 1888.

(photo from Holland Historical Trust Collection of the Joint Archives of Holland)

ments of the historic Second Street Iron Bridge, the last of the three still extant. The Waverly Stone Company was incorporated in 1889. An enlarged work force and a steam-derrick at the quarry nearly doubled output in one year alone.

The Holland City State Bank, an architectural gem in the fashionable Romanesque style, crowned with a clock tower, was built of Waverly stone in 1892. Two years before, the institution that occupied the structure had been incorporated as a state bank. Dirk Van Raalte, Civil War hero and son of the city's founder, became the bank's first president. The rival Holland State Bank received its charter in 1889. Leather mogul Isaac Cappon served as its president. Those lending institutions helped stimulate the continued business development that marked the decade.

Holland's excellent transportation facilities also spurred economic growth. By 1891 the Chicago & West Michigan Railroad offered direct rail connections with the Midwest's largest markets, as did the Detroit, Lansing & Northern Railroad. Thirty-two passenger trains and 18 freight trains left Holland daily. In addition, harbor improvements allowed the largest of the Great Lakes vessels then in use to dock along much of the northern waterfront of the city.

Long known for its printing presses, by 1891 the city boasted six locally published newspapers. The Dutch-language newspaper, *De Grondwet*,

In 1905, a cartoonist lampooned Arend Visscher, president of the People's State Bank, Ottawa Furniture Co. and Holland Sugar Co. In his spare time Visscher practiced law.

65

Periodic wrecks such as this ca. 1910 catastrophe interrupted service of the 50 trains that left Holland daily.

enjoyed the largest circulation. Other secular papers included *De Hollander,* the Republican-oriented *Holland City News,* and the newly established Democratic journal, the *Ottawa County Times. De Wachter* and *De Hope* were Dutch religious periodicals, and the students at Hope College published *The Anchor.* The first daily newspaper, the *Holland Daily Sentinel,* began its notable run that would span more than a century in 1895.

Beginning in the 1870s Grand Rapids had established a reputation as "furniture city" to the nation. Holland manufacturers also capitalized on the locally available lumber resources, transportation facilities,

and the presence of skilled Old Country craftsmen to create a thriving furniture industry. The Lake Side Furniture Company, founded in 1889, specialized in round oak and library tables, which it shipped to eastern markets. Holland's largest furniture manufacturer of the 1890s, the West Michigan Furniture Company on West 7th Street, also went into operation in 1889. It turned out quality bedroom furniture in fashionable oak, ash, and maple. In 1891, its woodworkers produced 20,000 bedroom suites and 10,000 bedsteads. By the decade's end the company billed itself as the "largest furniture factory in the world." Five hundred craftsmen working in four buildings comprising a total

Holland's largest furniture factory of the 1890s sprawled along West Seventh Street.

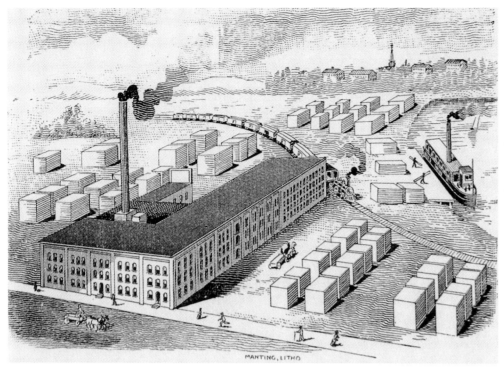

The Holland Furniture company received shipments of lumber via steamship.

of 100,000 square feet produced furniture valued at over $700,000 in 1898.

James Huntley, the brother of the city's electric pioneer, established the Ottawa Furniture Company in 1891. By 1899, 130 employees produced bird's-eye maple bedroom suites and oak sideboards at the factory on the corner of 5th Street and River Avenue. The Holland Furniture Company, founded by Herman Van Ark in 1894, turned out a similar line of furniture at its plant one block south on River Avenue. Four years later the Bay View Furniture Company, located on Lake Macatawa west of the city, began manufacturing a line of extension and library tables.

A caricaturist in 1905 pictured Holland Furniture Co. secretary Jacob. G. Van Putten balancing the firm's books.

(L)The Holland Furniture Company's 1911 catalog featured its line of "tiger oak" bedroom sets.

Holland's Alpena Restaurant ca. 1910 drew its name from the steamship that sank with all aboard, probably near the harbor entrance, in 1880. (courtesy Myron Van Ark)

Holland's able police force posed on the steps of the newly constructed City Hall ca. 1911. (courtesy Myron Van Ark)

The Graham & Morton Steamship Line *Holland* plowed through the waters of Lake Macatawa loaded with excursionists at the turn-of-the-century. (courtesy Myron Van Ark)

Eighth Street was a busy place on the Fourth of July ca.1905. (courtesy Myron Van Ark)

69

These turn-of-the-century bathers did not require much sun screen. (courtesy Myron Van Ark)

Surfmen of the U.S. Life Saving Station (later the Coast Guard)
at Macatawa prepare for a rescue drill ca. 1910.

The Drenthe Canning Co. employed more women than men in the 1890s chiefly because it could get away with paying them less.

Other factories that made use of the region's timber resources included the J. & A. Van Putten Company, manufacturer of wooden butter and lard tubs, candy pails, kitchen pails, etc. It had moved from Montague to Holland to take advantage of the city's superior transportation facilities. By 1891, 70 employees worked at its factory that covered two acres at the foot of Lake Street and Lake Macatawa. The C.L. King Company specialized in making hard-wood veneers, maple butter plates, splint market baskets, and fruit baskets. By 1891 some 12,000 freight cars loaded with those carefully stacked products left Holland each year. The rapid rise of Holland's furniture industry so

impressed the Buss Machine Company, which manufactured ingenious planing, gluing, and joining machines used in making furniture, that it relocated from Grand Rapids to Holland in 1895.

While Holland's booming industrial growth offered a source of livelihood for hundreds of factory workers, agriculture remained the backbone of the area's economy. By 1890 Ottawa County boasted farms totaling 203,228 acres. Wheat, corn, and oats were the major crops. But increasingly, the Dutch settlers utilized the age-old techniques they had used to reclaim their native country from the sea to transform the swamps that lay along the Black River and in northern Allegan

The Holland-St. Louis Sugar Co. factory, in the Romanesque style, was constructed on Harrison Avenue between 12th and 15th streets in 1898.

71

The H.J. Heinz workforce posed before the factory established in Holland in 1897.
(photo from Holland Historical Trust Collection of the joint Archives of Holland)

County into fertile muck fields, ideal for cultivation of potatoes, celery, and onions.

The climate-tempering influence of Lake Michigan also made the Holland environs ideal for fruit growing. By 1890 nearly 3,000 acres of apple trees and 400 acres of peach orchards had been established in Ottawa County. Each year, increasing quantities of fresh fruit and vegetables were shipped from Holland via Great Lakes vessels to ready markets in Chicago and Milwaukee.

The region's agricultural possibilities also spurred the creation of specialized processing plants in Holland. Following the passage of the Dingley Tariff of 1897, which protected domestically produced sugar from foreign competition, Michigan farmers began growing enormous quantities of sugar beets. In 1898, under the leadership of that old entrepreneurial workhorse, Isaac Cappon, the Holland Sugar Company constructed a huge plant able to process 350 tons of sugar beets daily. Soon, long lines of wagons loaded with the bulky vegetables became a common sight in Holland. At the plant, the sugar beets were sliced up and boiled in water and the syrup was extracted and processed into sugar crystals. In November 1899, plant manager C.M. McLean proudly produced the first batch of sugar.

The commercial preparation of pickles, a product destined to bring national fame to Holland, also began about the same time. In 1896 agents of Henry J. Heinz,

the "pickle king" from Pittsburgh, surveyed Holland as the site for a salting station where locally grown cucumbers could be preserved in huge vats of brine for eventual processing. A successful campaign to secure the new factory brought pledges by area growers for pickle acreage, a free site for the plant and other allurements. The following summer a salting house and a cider-pressing works opened. A vinegar generator was installed in 1898. Several buildings for the manufacture of tomato ketchup soon followed. By 1906 the Heinz operations in Holland encompassed eight "large modern structures" containing over 200,000 square feet. The erection of a three-story processing building in 1907 made the Holland factory Heinz's largest manufacturing facility outside the main plant in Pittsburgh. Soon, H.J. Heinz of Holland gained distinction as "the world's largest pickle plant," from which a steady stream of pickles, relishes, vinegar, and related products flowed to the nation's tables.

During this period of dynamic industrial growth, Holland paused briefly in August 1897 to celebrate the semi-centennial of its founding. The ranks of the original colonists had grown thinner with each passing year but descendants continued to revere their sacrifices. "We bless the year 1847, when once more the stream of emigration began to flow with renewed vigor from the land of the dykes and dunes into this land of enlarged freedom and rich in material resources," declared

Downtown Hamilton sported a pickle field at the turn-of-the-century.
(courtesy Allegan County Historical Society)

Holland's Semi-Centennial queen and her court climbed aboard a wagon for the gala parade in August 1897.
(photo from Holland Historical Trust Collection of the Joint Archives of Holland)

Hope College Professor Gerrit J. Kollen at the opening address of the festivities. U.S. Army Captain Cornelius Gardner waxed poetic over the founder's achievements: "Tis fifty full years since departing in sadness, from the land of their birth to face hardships untold, their journey here ended their hearts filled with gladness, our fathers knelt down as the pilgrims of old . . ."

Downtown Holland buzzed with excitement that August. The city's skilled carpenters had nailed together a gigantic wooden arch that spanned the street between River and Central. Topped by a full-sized statue of a white horse, the American and Dutch flags and the word "Welcome" in great letters, the magnificent monument also featured the likenesses of Van Raalte and other founding fathers. Hundreds of electric light bulbs illuminated the arc at night. Holland citizens and those from surrounding Dutch settlements thronged the city to marvel at the gaily festooned business blocks and colorful parades including a long line of floats highlighted by one loaded down with the Centennial Queen, a buxom Dutch lass named Mary Vander Haar (later Steketee) and a bevy of runner ups.

The occasion also afforded an opportunity for some of the area's finest public speakers to dazzle the huge crowds with their elocution. Old Simon Pokagon, hereditary chief of a band of southwestern Michigan Potawatomi, journeyed from his home in Allegan County's Lee Township to deliver one of his last public speeches. An author known as "the most highly educated Indian of his time," Pokagon urged the Hollanders not to forget the Native Americans who had once occupied the forests they had transformed into rich farmlands.

Progressive Governor Hazen Pingree, nicknamed Potato Pingree when as mayor of Detroit he provided tracts of city land for the poor to cultivate into gardens, told the audience that "as the race from which you have sprung has scooped their native land out of the ocean, so you have wrestled a garden out of the wilderness, and fertile plains out of swamps and sand hills." In his address of welcome Congressman William Alden Smith, who would represent the district that included Holland for two terms before serving as U.S. senator from 1907-1919, stated "the same kind of Providence that directed you here for your own good, gave you to Michigan for the good of the state."

Local son Gerrit J. Diekema, who over a political career that spanned five decades would win the title of Holland's premier orator, delivered a stirring address on "The Dutch Immigration and Colonization of 1847." Consider his elocutionary prose – one sentence a full paragraph long: "We have come here to pay homage to the men of 1847; to record our appreciation of their courage, our veneration for their piety, our sympathy in their suffering, our admiration for their virtues, and our attachment to those eternal principles of religion and civil liberty for which they left the graves of their ancestors and severed the tender ties of home and native land to dwell under other skies, to swear allegiance to another flag, to work out their destinies in a

Minister to the Netherlands Gerrit J. Diekema did not seem particularly pleased when Big Chief White Horse Eagle and wife paid him a visit in the 1920s. (photo from Holland Historical Trust Collection of the Joint Archives of Holland)

new world's western wilds."

A pamphlet entitled "Semi-Centennial Reminiscences" that preserved transcripts of Diekema's and other key speeches delivered at the celebration also carried many pages of local advertisements. One such advertisement urged in boldface type "Smoke Star Green Cigars." Herman Van Tongeren had established a cigar factory on East 10th Street in 1894 that within five years turned out 800,000 "Star Green" brand cigars annually. In an era when "real men" smoked cigars, Holland also boasted a number of other firms that manufactured the large "brown rolls."

In 1895 Albert Vegter had gone into production of "Country Girl," "Little Cuban," and "Lily Belle" five cent cigars. W.R. Reid and O.R. Johnson formed the ORJ Cigar Company in 1898 that within three years had rolled 500,000 "Just What You Want," "Knights of the Grip," and "Best" cigars. Under the motto "If you want a good smoke go and get a Snag," the Snag Cigar Company employed several expert cigar makers to roll "Snag," "Hoboe," "Old Rounder," and "Star of Liberty" brands. Other turn-of-the-century cigar makers included Leonard DeLoof, Frank De Later and George and

(Above) This Holland cigar "manufactor" utilized six roustabouts plus a wooden Indian to promote his stogies in the 1890s. (photo from Holland Historical Trust of the Joint Archives of Holland)

(Below) These workers at the Holland Shoe Factory took home about $1.30 for an entire 10 hour day in 1908.

These cigar box labels capture the glory days when Holland cigar makers hand-rolled hundreds of thousands of stogies each year.

In an era when Holland Township residents could work part of their taxes off by performing road maintenance these men are seen excavating gravel near the country club off Paw Paw Drive. On the far right is Johannes Naber. (photo courtesy Myron Van Ark)

Charles Brownell.

When *Holland City News* editor Nicholas J. Whelan took a ten-day vacation to Cuba in 1908, he sent back for publication in the newspaper a running account of his adventures. He recorded a humorous incident about the famed Cuban cigars, in particular, a brand named "Magoon," after the U.S. Provisional Governor of the island Charles Edward Magoon. Whelan wrote:

"The Provisional Governor passed the box when we called upon him, and we all standing 'side by each,' took one. Later in the day I handed mine to the porter at the hotel when he handed me a blotter. Still later in the day I found these cigars cost 62 cents per, and although I do not smoke, I envied the porter. I am sure he did not appreciate it, for they like stogies better than good goods, and I would have preferred seeing a man like Leonard De Loof or Herman Van Tongeren, our Holland manufacturers, attached to the business end of it for I think they would understand that it was a cigar whose sweetness should not be wasted on the desert air. After that when I was offered a cigar I ask how much it cost."

To fully comprehend Whelan's concern over that 62 cent cigar, its value needs to be placed in perspective of what Holland workers earned at that time. The 486 laborers at the West Michigan Furniture Company's two plants, the city's largest employer, took home a average of $1.68 for their 10-hour work day. Sixty-hour work weeks were standard at that time and the concept of extra pay for overtime had yet to be conceived by the unions. Workers at the Holland Furniture Company and the Ottawa Furniture Company earned an average of 12 1/2 cents per hour. Employees of Cappon and Bertsch earned 16.3 cents per hour if they made harness leather and 17.5 cents an hour if they worked at the sole leather plant. The 164 workers at the C.L. King Basket factory took home 93 cents for their ten hour day, and the Michigan Toy and Novelty Company paid its employees only 8.8 cents per hour. In other words, those workers would have to labor slightly more then seven hours to enjoy the luxury of one of those Magoon cigars.

Nevertheless it was an age of smoke. Men smoked cigars. Factory smokestacks belched soot into the sky proclaiming to all the world that business was brisk. Steamships and

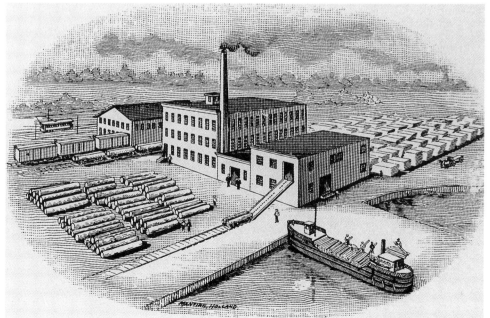

The Bay View Furniture Company plant stood for many years on West 15th Street.

railroad locomotives puffed long trails of wood or coal smoke as they hurried to and from the bustling city. But change also was in the air. By the 1890s new electric arc streetlamps had began to replace Holland's traditional kerosene lamps. The romantic old lamplighter would soon be a thing of the past. Electricity also powered the modern new streetcar line that opened on June 27, 1898. Then on October 14, 1901, the interurban that linked Holland with Grand Rapids ran its first regular passenger car.

Trolley cars, the two regular railroad lines, and, beginning in 1893, the Holland and Chicago Transportation Company's steamships *City of Holland* and *Soo City* carried increasing numbers of vacationers lured by Holland's recreational opportunities. With one way tickets from Chicago to Holland priced as low as one dollar in 1899, even the working class could enjoy a weekend cruise on Lake Michigan. Later, the Benton Harbor-based Graham & Morton Transportation Company operated its fleet of passenger and freight vessels that included the *Puritan, City of Grand Rapids, City of Saugatuck, City of Holland, City of Benton Harbor,* and *City of St. Joseph.*

As early as the 1870s the picturesque sand dunes at the mouth of the Black River and the miles of dazzling sugar sand beaches stretching along Lake Michigan attracted vacationers. Holland newspapers carried accounts of camping and fishing parties from Chicago and elsewhere. In 1879, for example, a contingent of Odd Fellows traveled from Grand Rapids by rail to spend a day cavorting in the Lake Michigan surf, picnicking, and rambling over the wooded sand hills. That same year the Holland *City News* reported: "Two different parties from Allegan have been camped out near the harbor of Black Lake for the past two weeks, and are infatuated with the fishing facilities which Black Lake affords — on one day catching over 100 black bass. It seems surprising to the gentlemen

The Graham & Morton Line steamer *Holland* was built in Wyandotte in 1881. Originally named *City of Milwaukee*, it was renamed *Holland* in 1905 and kept that name until 1919.

Looking as prim as the name of the vessel she was aboard, the turn-of-the-century Holland tourist at the center clutched a "Brownie" box camera.
(courtesy Myron Van Ark)

from abroad who love that sport that somebody doesn't improve the opportunity to build and fix up a regular pleasure resort, to make this spot one of the most romantic and attractive watering places in the United States."

It did not take long for some of that newspaper's

In 1885, a party of Alleganites, including Martin Ryan, Fred Hall, Will Vosburgh and Charley Smith, camped near the future site of the Hotel Ottawa. (courtesy Allegan County Historical Society)

A crowd of Macatawa resorters waits to board the City of Holland in this ca. 1910 photo. (courtesy Myron Van Ark)

The majestic Hotel Ottawa opened in 1886. It burned to the ground in 1923. (courtesy Myron Van Ark)

readers to take the hint. The exploitation of Holland Harbor's recreational possibilities began in earnest in August 1881, when a group of Holland citizens formed an association that purchased land on the south side of the mouth of the Black River. Macatawa Park was soon platted, lots sold, cottages erected, and by the end of the year, three hotels welcomed guests. Another large hotel, wrapped on two sides by spacious verandas, opened in 1884. Macatawa's most luxurious hostelry, the Hotel Macatawa, was constructed in 1895 for Mrs. M.A. Ryder, who also operated the Hotel Holland located downtown.

In 1885, the West Michigan Park Association, made up predominantly of Grand Rapids residents, was organized. The association platted another resort development on the north side of the harbor mouth. When the Hotel Ottawa, a fashionable two-story structure with a large observation deck, opened in 1886, the resort adopted the name Ottawa Beach. By the century's end, a smaller resort had also been established at Jenison Park on the south shore of Lake Macatawa, as promoters with an ear for the Indian names that the back-to-nature craze then found irresistible soon dubbed Black Lake. Begun in the 1880s as Scott's Grove, in 1888, W.A. Williams renamed it Shady Side. Three years later Luman Jenison purchased the resort, renamed it after himself, enlarged and remodeled the hotel there and platted out 300 lots that he offered for as low as $25. each. Waukazoo, on the north side of the lake at the site of the ill-fated paper city of Superior, became a resort in 1901 when local attorney J.C. Post and a Judge

Everett from Chicago purchased the 600–acre tract from Hope College. Each summer increasing throngs of cottagers and recreationists made their way to Holland's resorts via steamship, train, and interurban.

Many Hollanders, particularly the merchants who profited heavily from the tourist trade, welcomed the resorters. Summer vacationers from less conservative regions also offered a healthy cosmopolitan leavening to Holland's culture. But those "big city liberals" sometimes ran afoul of the area's strict religious expectations. In 1883, for example, the pastors of Holland's four main churches petitioned the Macatawa Park Association to respect the "sanctity of the Sabbath" by not operating the passenger vessel that transported park visitors to Holland on Sunday. When the captain

These turn-of-the-century resorters donned their Sunday best to frolic on Macatawa's sugar sand. (courtesy Myron Van Ark)

80

The success of fishing excursions such as this two-hour catch ca. 1910 of *De Grondwet* manager J.B. Mulder (right) and companion spurred tourists and townspeople alike to crowd the interurban bridge at Macatawa shown below ca. 1906.

FISHING IN BLACK LAKE- HOLLAND, MICH. 128-9

Henry Schaap delivered milk to Holland customers in 1911.

Dorothy returned to the plot of that work, but little Toto stayed in Kansas with Auntie Em. Baum, incidently, had coined the word "Oz" when he spied the alphabetical label on the bottom drawer of a file cabinet, "O-Z." And contrary to local tradition, Dorothy was not modeled after a Macatawa urchin - Baum had placed the character Dorothy in a short story published before he ever visited the resort.

In 1907, Baum turned briefly from Munchkins and cowardly lions to pen the first novel set in the Holland area, *Tamawaca Folks*, published under the pseudonym John Estes Cooke. The slim volume documented in thinly veiled characterizations the true story of how a coterie of cottagers wrested back control of the Macatawa Association from two unscrupulous locals who had usurped the public domain there and the lucrative concessions, creating a monopoly in grocery sales, launching service, ferry rides, etc. Baum described one of the scoundrels as a "fine old religious duffer, who loves to pray for your spiritual welfare while he feels for your pockets." Baum served as one of the directors of the Macatawa Association which succeeded in regaining the property owner's rights to the resort.

of the steamer *Macatawa* refused to eliminate this primary means of reaching the city and the railroad terminal, the ministers preached in sour unison to their congregations on the subject of "Sabbath Observation."

In 1899, a 43-year-old children's author from Chicago chanced to visit Macatawa. He found the resort so charming that three years later, when he had accomplished what few authors ever do—become financially successful—he purchased a cottage there. The man was Lyman Frank Baum and the funds used to purchase the cottage flowed from royalties of his best selling juvenile volumes, *Father Goose: His Book* and *The Wonderful Wizard of Oz*.

Baum named his cottage "The Sign of the Goose" in honor of his first successful book. A large sign bearing a white goose, modeled after W.W. Denslow's illustrations in the book, hung from the cottage porch. Baum also had crafted oak furniture decorated with geese for the cottage. At his Macatawa cottage Baum worked on some of his sequels to the *Wizard of Oz* including, *The Marvelous Land of Oz*, published in 1904. In that volume, a new character, Professor H.M. Woggle-Bug replaced Dorothy Gale from Kansas as the main character. Baum had gotten the inspiration for that character when as he walked the beach at Macatawa, a little girl held up a curious insect and asked what it was. "A Woggle-Bug," he told her.

Baum signed the foreword to his second Oz sequel, *Ozma of Oz*, "Macatawa, 1907."

Marinus Van Ark, on the far left, awaits customers at the Haveman Grocery Store on the southeast corner of 24th Street and Colby. (courtesy Myron Van Ark)

Managed by the Rathbone Brothers who also ran the Morton House in Grand Rapids,
the Hotel Ottawa charged guests $10.00 - $14.00 per week in 1897.

The rival Macatawa Hotel can be seen across Black Lake from the porch of the Hotel Ottawa in 1897.

This 1912 view shows the city's original automobile garage operated by Fred W. Jackson at 25 West 7th Street.

Each summer for a decade, Baum, his wife and their four boys spent the entire season at Macatawa. In 1909, possibly in reaction to a burglary of his boathouse, Baum sold his Macatawa cottage and moved to Palm Springs, California. The "Sign of the Goose" burned to the ground during the summer of 1927.

Another of Holland's literary lights, Arnold Mulder, a grandson of one of the original Dutch colonists to settle in the area, graduated from Hope College in 1907. After graduate studies at the University of Michigan and University of Chicago, in 1901, he became editor of the *Holland Daily Sentinel*. In 1913, Mulder published *The Dominie of Harlem*, the first of his four novels set in Holland and the outlying rural Dutch settlements. The first Michigan novelist to make use of a Dutch background, Mulder emphasized the ultra-conservative lifestyle of his fellow Hollanders. He viewed the strict Calvinist theology that permeated most aspects of the Hollanders' lives as repressive, limiting their freedom, intellectualism, and aesthetics. Although Mulder's *Dominie, Bram of the Five Corners* (1915), *The Outbound Road* (1919), and

In 1913, the camera captured a rare view looking down Angels' Flight, a trolley that carried many Macatawa resorters the 225 feet up the dune to a lookout platform. (courtesy Myron Van Ark)

Holland & Chicago Line.

THE only direct line between Chicago and the famous Michigan Summer Resorts Macatawa Park and Ottawa Beach, and the shortest, cheapest and best route between **Chicago, Holland, Grand Rapids, Lansing, Detroit, Saginaw** and all intermediate points. Close train connections made at Holland for above points.

Steamers "Soo City" and "City of Holland."

SUMMER SCHEDULE JUNE 23d TO SEPT. 3d, INCLUSIVE.

Leave Holland, Daily	8:00 P. M.
" Holland, Friday and Saturday (Special)	6:30 A. M.
" Holland, Sunday (Special)	2:00 P. M.
" Chicago, Daily (Except Friday, Saturday and Sunday)	8:00 P. M.
" Chicago, Friday and Saturday at	9:00 A. M. and 4:00 P. M.
" Chicago, Sunday at	9:00 A. M. and 11:30 P. M.
After September 3d steamers will leave Chicago daily	7:00 P. M.

Above special rates for transportation only.

Fare between Chicago, Macatawa Park, Ottawa Beach, Jenison Park and Holland, single $2.25; round trip $3.50 berth included. Grand Rapids, single $3.15; round trip $5.00. Allegan, single $3.00; round trip $5.00.

SPECIAL RATES CHICAGO TO HOLLAND AND RESORTS.

Friday and Saturday, leaving Chicago 4:00 P. M.—One way $1.75; round trip, $2.50.

Friday, Saturday and Sunday morning, leaving Chicago at 9:00—One way $1.00.

Friday and Saturday morning, leaving Holland at 6:30—One way $1.00.

Above schedule subject to change without notice.

Through tickets can be purchased at all stations on the C. & W. M. Ry., D. G. R. & W. Ry. and G. R. & I. Ry.

W. H. BEACH, President,
Holland, Mich.

CHARLES B. HOPPER, G. F. & P. A.,
Chicago, Ill.

CHICAGO OFFICE: No. I STATE STREET.

In 1899 the Holland & Chicago Line steamers *Soo City* and *City of Holland* made fast trips back and forth from the "Windy City."

These Grand Rapids Press newsboys posed during the summer of 1915 on the Fris Book Store vehicle. Note the ad for Arnold Mulder's new book. (courtesy Fris Office Outfitters)

The Sand Doctor (1921) were not particularly well liked by elements of the Holland community, they are now considered minor classics in the "local color" genre of fiction. He eventually left Holland to accept a professorship at Kalamazoo College. His nonfictional *Americans From Holland,* published in 1947, celebrated the Dutch heritage and earned Mulder a decoration from the Netherlands government.

An interesting chapter in Mulder's *The Sand Doctor,* portrays the wreck of a ship attempting to enter Holland Harbor during a fierce storm, an event that actually occured several times in the early 20th century. In October 1902, the *Hattie B. Pereue,* a steamer out of St. Joseph loaded with salt, attempted to take refuge in Holland Harbor during a gale in which "the sea was running mountain high, the waves dashing completely over the piers." Just as she was about to enter the piers a great wave struck the vessel, flinging her broadside into a trough and she struck a sandbar. When another huge wave washed the vessel free, the captain quickly rammed her bow into the north pier and all 13 crew members scrambled to safety.

On November 24, 1905, the Graham and Morton Steamship Line passenger ship the *Argo* ran aground near the entrance to the piers under similar circumstances. The surfmen of the Holland Lifesaving Station rushed into action, firing a line to the ship and setting up the breeches buoy apparatus. One by one the

23 passengers aboard were pulled along the line. Some took a dunking in the ice cold waves but all survived the ordeal. The *Argo* remained stranded in the ice until the last week of January 1906, when a crowd of onlookers watched a tug pull her loose.

The buxom Holland High girls basketball team stood before the school located between Graves and 10th Street in 1913. (courtesy Myron Van Ark)

You Can't Beat the Dutch

"DUST - ODOR - LESS"
FOR CLEANLINESS
You don't remove
the cover until the
can is full.

IT'S
ALL IN
THE LID

Sold under abso-
lute guarantee
to please or
money refund-
ed.

This ca. 1910 product was one of many made in Holland that capitalized on the city's Dutch heritage.
(courtesy Myron Van Ark)

By 1910 long freight trains carried pickle products by the barrel from the H.J. Heinz plant.

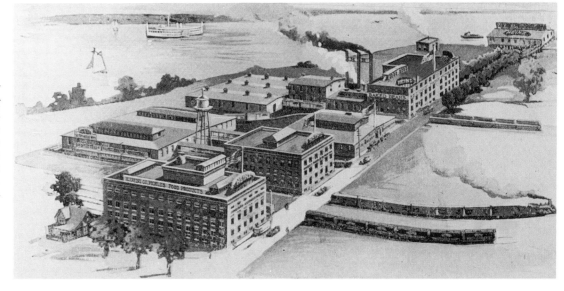

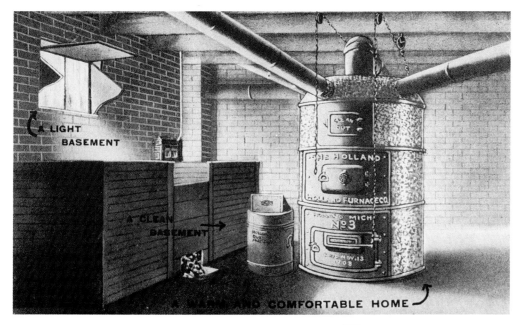

The famous Holland Furnace Company's product heated hundreds of thousands of homes across the nation.
(courtesy Myron Van Ark)

(Right) The Pere Marquette Railroad promoted Holland as a tourist resort in this 1909 pamphlet.

(Left) This 1908 Holland Furniture Company catalog emphasized the area's ethnic traditions.

L. Frank Baum wrote this sequel to the *Wonderful Wizard of Oz* at his Macatawa cottage during the summer of 1907.

In the decade prior to World War I, Holland area tourists took home souvenir ceramic treasures such as this hand-painted plate depicting the harbor entrance when "Big Red" was yellow.

88

The first person to be rescued from the Argo slides along the breeches buoy apparatus on November 24, 1905.
(photo from Holland Historical Trust Collection of the Joint Archives of Holland)

Another of the region's authors and probably the most famous, Paul De Kruif, chose the field of popular science as his theme. Born in Zeeland, Michigan, in 1890, De Kruif earned his doctorate from the University of Michigan in 1916. His first book, *Our Medicine Men* (1922), an expose of medical frauds and hoaxes, cost him his position as a pathologist at the Rockefeller Institute. But medicine's loss proved the gain of thousands of readers'. De Kruif's *Microbe Hunters*, published in 1926, became a best-seller. *Hunger Fighters* (1928), *Seven Iron Men* (1929), about the Upper Peninsula's mining heritage, and *Men Against Death* (1932) were written in part at his mother's beachfront cottage, "Blue Water." In the summer of 1932 De Kruif and wife Rhea built a log cabin amid the tree covered dunes on the shore of Lake Michigan. His autobiography, *Sweeping Wind* (1962), portrays the exuberant life of a master story teller.

The era that saw the rise of a notable literary tradition also witnessed the birth of a number of local industries that brought the city national prestige. Part of Holland's success in attracting new manufacturers came through the development of an industrial bonus program

Paul De Kruif was the Holland area's most successful literary native son. (photo from Holland Historical Trust Collection of the Joint Archives of Holland)

by a group of local promoters. Holland's unique bonus plan did not offer money directly to prospective business but instead provided land and sometimes factories which reverted back to the Bonus Committtee if the company failed. If the manufacturer proved successsful the property was eventually deeded to it. The Bush and Lane Piano Company, for example, was established in Holland in 1905. It would become one of the city's largest employers. Using specialized machinery invented by company president Walter Lane, by 1912 some 200 employees fashioned high-quality upright, baby grand, and player pianos at the 135,000 square-foot factory.

The following year saw the establishment of an industry destined to put Holland in the national spotlight. John P. Kolla, an expert foundryman who had immigrated to Ohio from the Alsace Lorraine region of France at the age of 19 in 1879, teamed up with his son-in-law August H. Landwehr, a crack young salesman, to form the Holland Furnace Company. They had chosen Holland as the site of their operation because of the bonus plan, the abundant supply of sand available for foundry moldings and the recently

89

Holland has long "loved a parade." The top view of a drum and bugle band dates from the 1880s. The bottom view of 8th Street ca. 1905 shows a nautical float. (courtesy Myron Van Ark)

The Bush and Lane Piano Factory produced thousands of pianos beginning in 1905.

improved harbor entrance and channel which permitted large ships to transport scrap iron for smelting into furnace parts. Production of central heating furnaces began in a small one-story frame building in 1906. By 1912 six expansions had increased the factory to 68,000 square-feet.

The Holland Furnace Company's quality products sold well initially. But the independent dealers who marketed the furnaces did not follow recommended installation procedures and that hurt business. So following the example of the successful Kalamazoo Stove Company, which marketed its ranges and stoves directly to the consumer under the motto "Kalamazoo Direct To You," the Holland Furnace Company established a system of factory branches that eventually numbered 500 in 44 states. Adopting the slogan "Holland furnaces make warm friends," the company soon became "the world's largest installers of home heating and air conditioning systems."

Attracted by the presence of the major furniture manufacturers in the city, in 1905, the Kinsella Glass Company began producing mirrors. Its quality beveled mirrors, engraved with ornate patterns, proved popular in the furniture industry. Soon Bernard Donnelly and a partner took over the operation they renamed the Donnelly–Kelley Glass Company. By 1912 nearly

Holland Furniture Co. employees were a patriotic lot during the World War I era.
(courtesy Allegan County Historical Society)

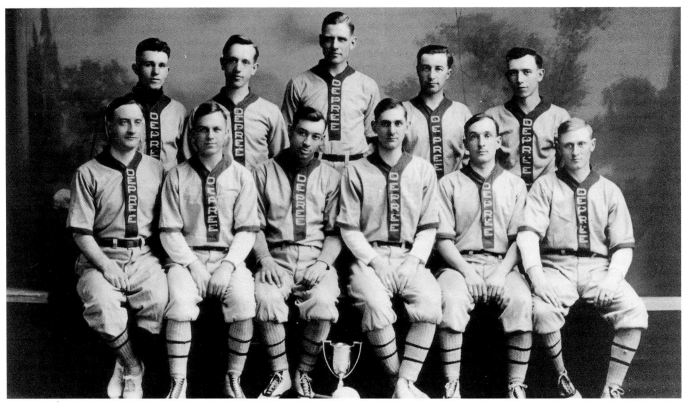

When not manufacturing formaldehyde fumigators and embalming fluid, De Pree Chemical Co. employees enjoyed playing softball. (courtesy Myron Van Ark)

These Holland women formed a Wooden Shoe Drill Team to entertain the old Civil War veterans who held a convention in the city in 1910. (courtesy Myron Van Ark)

Some of these proud 1917 Holland High champions may well have enlisted in the Army when America entered World War I that April. (courtesy Myron Van Ark)

50 craftsmen worked at the factory, "one of the most up-to-date mirror plants in the country, the most modern machinery being used and a grade of mirrors being manufactured that is second to none."

Other firms established during the early 20th century brought a healthy industrial diversity to the city. Local druggist Con De Pree launched the De Pree Chemical Company to manufacture formaldehyde fumigators in 1906. He began production in two small rooms over a downtown store. Business boomed as 80 percent of the health boards in the country adopted the fumigators. In 1909, the company moved to a new brick factory which was expanded to 30,000 square feet within five years. De Pree later branched into other chemical specialties including embalming fluid. Beginning in 1906, the Holland Shoe Company opened a factory in Holland to utilize leather produced at the huge Cappon and Bertsch Tannery. By 1914 nearly 400 employees produced over 3,000 pairs of shoes daily.

The staccato roar of hammers rapping away at shoe lasts in Holland resembled the sound of the machine guns that raked European battlefields that year. As the conflict escalated into a world war, President Woodrow Wilson's campaign slogan "He kept us out of war" helped win him reelection in 1916. Nevertheless, Wilson found it impossible to maintain neutrality, and on April 6, 1917, the United States entered the war. Holland displayed the same exuberant patriotism it had during the Civil War and Spanish American War as hundreds of young men rushed to join the colors. Two Holland men, Private Willard G. Leenhouts and Corporal Henry Wolters, made the supreme sacrifice. The Holland VFW post was named in honor of Wolters, who was fatally wounded at the Battle of Chateau-Thierry in July 1918. In 1920, the local American Legion post took Leenhouts' name.

Probably the earliest of the city's young men to serve in World War I, Cornelius Van Putten, enlisted in the

Kiltie McCoy was a Holland boy with an Irish name fighting in France as a Scotch soldier.

British Army in 1914. Born in Holland in 1887, the grandson of the founder of the First State Bank and a member of the family that achieved prominence in various wood manufacturing enterprises, Van Putten grew bored with the humdrum life in Holland where, he wrote, "the principal excitement is going fishing and making furniture." He took to the road as a traveling salesman, knocking about much of the country. October of 1914 found him in London, where a young woman hung a white feather on his shoulder, a sign that he was a slacker who should be in military uniform. Shamed, Van Putten enlisted in a Scottish regiment, changing his name to Patrick Terrance McCoy. Garbed in the traditional kilts he soon took the nickname Kiltie.

Van Putten fought in European battlefields for three adventure filled years, until he was severly wounded in the arm in 1917. Returning to Michigan he wrote a fascinating account of his military career called *Kiltie McCoy: An American Boy with an Irish Name Fighting in France As A Scotch Soldier*. Based on the horrors he had seen Van Putten concluded: "the only good German is one that is fertilizing the ground."

Throughout the war, books like Kiltie McCoy and the work of propagandists whipped anti–German sentiment to a frenzy. Liberty Loan drives went over the top, sauerkraut was dubbed "Liberty cabbage," and residents changed the name of the Ottawa County village of Berlin to Marne in honor of the battle that proved the turning point of the war. Slackers received harsh treatment in the Dutch communities. In Zeeland, for example, a "vigilance committee" tarred and feathered the poor old horse of a cookie peddler who they felt had not bought enough war bonds. The editor of the *Holland Sentinel* noted that "the punishment had been inflicted on the wrong animal."

Meanwhile the Ottawa County Red Cross helped harness some of the Home Front energy to better uses

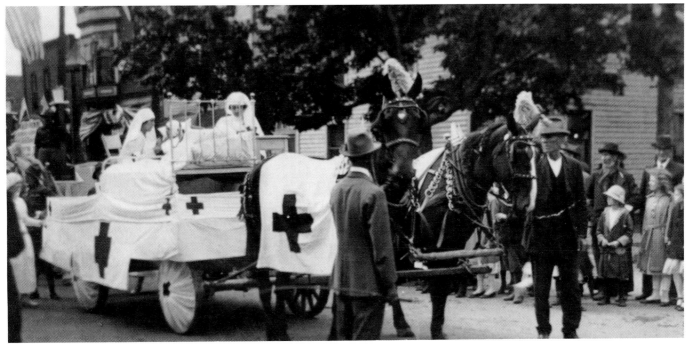

In 1918 the Ottawa County Red Cross promoted its work with a parade float showing "angels of mercy" at the bedside of a patient. (courtesy Ottawa County Red Cross)

by conducting a special drive to collect fruit pits and nut shells. After being thoroughly dried and delivered to collection centers, 555 pounds of the pits and shells were shipped for use in the manufacture of carbon for gas masks.

When Holland received news of the signing of the armistice that ended the war on November 11, 1918, the entire city went wild. Factory whistles and church bells blared out the tidings. A huge crowd paraded through the city with hanging effigies of the Kaiser. Nearly every store in the city soaped windows with "closed, gone to the Kaiser's funerals." Fireworks and a huge bonfire made from grease barrels lit up the early morning sky. One 80-year-old woman beat two kettle lids together as cymbals for five hours.

As the excitement died down and the doughboys returned to the farm or to jobs in Holland's diverse industries, the city gradually returned to normal.

The gala parade to celebrate the end of World War I featured a giant flag carried by local Boy Scouts. (courtesy Myron Van Ark)

A hoard of glass plate negatives that survived the ravages of time captures everyday life down on the farm. These six photos (ca. 1914) depict the George and Kate Kaper family on their 46 acre farm about one mile southeast of Hamilton (courtesy the Zeeland Historical Society)

The "corn was as high as an elephant's eye" in 1914.

Not all was hard work on the farm. The camera caught numerous parties and celebrations. Here the family prepares for a birthday party.

This party featured ice cream, hand cranked by family members.

The Kapers enjoy a watermelon party.

The men folk had their own version of a good time before Prohibition took away that pleasure.

Tulips Bloom & Downtown Blossoms

53. Big Day at Holland Fair, Holland, Mich.

Huge crowds gathered at the fairgrounds near Pilgrim Home Cemetery ca. 1919.
(courtesy Myron Van Ark)

A wave of excitement rippled through the many Dutch farm families of southern Ottawa and northern Allegan counties as September, 1919, approached. Teamsters allotted extra grain to their prize draft horses and working cattle. Children carefully brushed their Shetland ponies and Shropshire sheep and eyed flocks carefully for the best silver spangled Hamburg roosters or white Wyandotte hens. Gardeners selected their biggest and best mangle wurtzels and kale, their finest marblehead squashes and conehead cabbages. Housewives made repeated trips to the cellar to double check gallon crocks of June butter, shelves of pickled crabapples, canned whortleberries and grape catsup. And on bake day they fired up the big wood burning ranges that dominated their kitchens to bake fragrant nut cakes, molasses cookies and golden loaves of Graham bread.

It was fair time! And many a rural resident aspired to carry off first prize ribbons in the hundreds of categories as well as the 50 cents or so in premium money. They called it the "Victory Fair" that year. The boys in khaki had been fighting in France the season before but now they were back. And the organizers of the South Ottawa and West Allegan Agricultural Society's Fair intended their sacrifices not be forgotten. That Victory Fair held at the fairgrounds on the south side of East 16th Street opposite the Pilgrim Home Cemetery featured a display of "war relics," jagged chunks of shrapnel, German helmets and daggers and other souvenirs the doughboys had brought back from "no-man's land." And as if they hadn't seen enough action overseas, the veterans staged a "great sham battle" for fair goers.

The Holland Furnace Company had generously donated the funds for the hundreds of premiums awarded at that year's fair. Of all the Holland manufacturers that company could well afford to. Sales of its big furnaces approached $4 million in 1919. Much of that success came through massive advertising cam-

The Brownwall Co. promoted its stationary gasoline engines in the 1919 Holland Fair catalog.

paigns that blanketed selected zones of the mid west. By 1924 sales surpassed $10 million. The previous year, as the company had increased its force of traveling salesmen who periodically reported to the home office and other important clients traveled to Holland, furnace company manager August H. Landwehr had decided the city needed a suitable place for them to stay.

Landwehr had kicked off the campaign to bring a luxury hotel to Holland in 1923 with an open letter in the newspaper that announced "every man who has the interests of Holland at heart will want to help this proposal along." Given the public reluctance to fund civic improvements, however, it was not exactly the most propitious time to ask for financial backing. Voters, for example, had defeated a bonding proposal to build a badly needed new hospital in 1921 and again in 1922. The primary concern voiced by citizens seemed to be that non-residents might use the facility at the same rate as taxpayers. Finally, in 1925 the city bypassed the electorate by using surplus funds from the municipal power plant, and began construction of a new hospital.

The Holland Furnace Company, which had become the city's major employer, promised financial backing for the new hotel project. The company offered to assume $200,000 of construction costs in six percent realty bonds and raise the remainder by offering $100 shares of common stock. The Chamber of Commerce and other civic groups lent their support, and the necessary stock subscriptions were sold within weeks.

Local contractor Frank Dyke won the construction contract and he utilized local labor entirely to build the structure completed at a cost of $500,000 in April 1925. It was called the "finest hostelry on the entire west coast of Michigan," "a dream built of stone, steel and concrete," and "a monument to Holland and an incentive for its citizens to do even greater things." The Warm Friend Hotel stood on the

The new Holland Hospital was constructed in 1925 with Board of Public Works funding. (courtesy Myron Van Ark).

Jo Kools, shown here while in training in a New York City hospital, was one of eight nurses who staffed the Holland Hospital in the 1920s. (photo from Holland Historical Trust Collection of the Joint Archives of Holland)

By the late 1930s the marquee of the Warm Friend Hotel advertised the Warm Friend Tavern. (courtesy Myron Van Ark)

Eighth Street site formerly occupied by the City Hotel, built in 1872, and remodeled into the Hotel Holland in 1891. Designed to resemble a large scale version of a classic Frisian home, the six-story hotel boasted 144 plush rooms. The best materials went into its brick and sandstone exterior and its elaborate interior decor featuring oak ceilings and wainscoting. Practically every piece of furniture within had been created at local factories, including the walnut beds and dressers from the Holland and West Michigan Furniture Company, desks from the Bay View Furniture Company, chairs from the C.P. Limbert Furniture Company, and dining tables and chairs from the Ottawa Furniture Company. Unique leaded glass hanging lamps in the form of windmills accentuated the Dutch motif (these lamps now decorate the Chamber of Commerce offices). By the late 1920s the hotel's bellhops and waitresses wore Dutch costumes. "Trust to the Dutch," the hotel's

This Hope College graduating class (ca.1923) assembled before Graves Hall.

101

Constructed in 1910, the Knickerbocker Theatre offered Hollanders of the 1920s the opportunity to view Charley Chaplin, Mary Pickford and other stars of the silent movie era. A 1922 city ordinance that prohibited, among other things, any picture of "bloodshed, lust or crime" would have outlawed just about any modern-day movie.

(Below)
The Holland Concert Band performed for local audiences during the "Jazz Age."
(courtesy Don van Reken)

In 1926 Hope college students staged an historical pageant in honor of the school's 60th anniversary. These co-eds portraying water seemed to have fallen under the sway of Isadora Duncan.
(photo from Hope College collection of the Joint Archives of Holland)

advertising boasted, "to have the best."

In 1927, Holland's first radio station, WHBM, began broadcasting from the Warm Friend Hotel. Originally many of the live musical numbers were performed by the office staff of the Holland Furnace Company.

The Holland Furnace Company made extensive use of the hotel and, after Prohibition, its private "Tavern Club" to accommodate visiting branch managers, important customers, and other dignitaries. But other "traveling men," as salesmen were then known, as well as the increasing number of tourists drawn to Holland, also enjoyed the opulent hotel.

The burgeoning resort communities at Macatawa Park, Ottawa Beach, Jenison Park, Virginia Park, Waukazoo Park and Alpena Beach attracted thousands of vacationers during the 1920s. Another major drawing card of the era, the Getz Farm, originated in 1910 when wealthy Chicago entrepreneur George F. Getz purchased a tract of land north of Holland on Lake Michigan. Within three years he had transformed the sterile sandy soil into a fertile farm that soon became the showplace of the region. In 1913, Getz erected a

special pavilion at the Ottawa County fairgrounds to display his prize flowers, fowl, and a menagerie of exotic animals.

Following a trip to the Holy Land that same year, Getz imported donkeys and two camels named Hammid and Said. George Mansour, a Palestinian trainer also journeyed with the animals to Getz Farm. His flamboyant garb, including a turban, baggy trousers and Aladdin-like slippers with upturned toes and ever-present Turkish cigarette, proved almost as popular as the camels. Getz soon opened his estate to the public, and by the early 1930s as many as 75,000 tourists a day strolled through the manicured gardens, the greenhouses filled with rare plants, and the private zoo containing monkeys, bears, elephants, leopards, lions, hippopotamuses, rhinoceroses, and a 33-foot-long python. Some 800,000 visitors arrived at his Lakewood Farm in 1926 alone. Getz charged no admission fee until 1931. That year he charged adults 25 cents to demonstrate Lakewood's fund-raising potential to state officials. The estate had been offered for sale, but unfortunately Michigan officials declined because of state bud-

Nancy the elephant and Tiny Mite the miniature horse stand before the entrance to the Getz Farm, Lakewood.
(courtesy Myron Van Ark)

getary constraints brought on by the Depression.

In 1933 Getz transferred most of his animals to Chicago's Brookfield Zoo. Getz died in 1938 and his farm was eventually platted and sold to resorters. One little known heritage from the Lakewood Zoo, however, survives to provide pleasure for thousands. By the turn of the century, deer had been hunted to extinction in southern Michigan. A group of Allegan area sportsmen headed by Guy Teed purchased a small herd of white-tailed deer from Getz and set them free in the

Allegan State Forest. From there they spread throughout the region. Descendants of Getz's deer herd continue to provide thrills for naturalists and game for the annual army of hunters.

Holland lost a major attraction on November 6, 1923, when the historic Ottawa Beach Hotel burned to the ground. That grand structure had originated in 1886 as the Hotel Ottawa. In 1895 it was moved and completely remodeled. The loss of that landmark, however, proved beneficial in the long run when the State Park

Periodic conflagrations such as this 1925 blaze destroyed numerous structures at Macatawa Park.
(courtesy Myron Van Ark)

MACATAWA FIRE
APRIL 18 1925

The Holland State Park officially opened in 1928. (courtesy Myron Van Ark)

Board purchased 32 acres at Ottawa Beach a few years later. A new concrete road was completed to Ottawa Beach in 1927, and the following year the Holland State Park opened. An oval drive afforded a picturesque view of the lake and parking for beach goers. WPA funding during the 1930s allowed an expansion of the oval and other improvements, and by 1937 over 1,300,000 recreationists visited the park annually (although as late as 1931 beach etiquette prohibited men from appearing in public clad only in swim trunks). The quality of the water at local beaches also improved beginning in 1927 when the city's first sewage treatment plant went into operation. Previously the city's sewer mains emptied directly into the river, resulting in extensive fish kills and beach closings each year.

Another tourist attraction came to Holland in 1924 when the Chicago, Duluth and Georgian Bay Transit Company relocated its winter docking facilities from Saugatuck to Holland. On September 9, 1924 the 321-foot *S.S. South American* caught fire while docked at the foot of 16th Street. The crew escaped, although the cook bailed out of a porthole to do so and the captain burned his hands as he scrambled along a chain to the dock. The entire superstructure of the vessel burned, but the flooded hull was salvaged and rebuilt in time for the next season to carry passengers from Chicago to Duluth. Until the 1960s the Georgian fleet, *South American, North American* and *Alabama,* were a

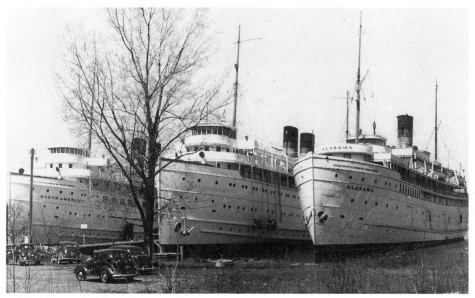

The Georgian Bay Transit Company ships, (left to right) North American, South American and Alabama docked for the winter at the foot of 16th Street until the 1960s.

Appointments & Service Equal to Crack Atlantic Ships

DINING SALON

PARLOR ROOM

STATE ROOM

SPACIOUS DECKS

The Great Oil-Burning White Liners
"NORTH AMERICAN"
and
"SOUTH AMERICAN"

offer you Seven pleasure-filled days—New Sights— New Experiences—New Friends

THESE sister ships are specially equipped for cruising service—Spacious decks; Commodious Lounge Rooms; Large comfortable berths or parlor rooms; Excellent Meals, daintily served.

You can enjoy quiet or gaiety on shipboard, as you prefer. The canopied palm garden on observation deck is ideal for relaxation. The vigor-laden breezes will put new life into you. Pleasures on board for old and young. Come—even if you come alone. A social hostess will introduce you. Enjoy to the utmost the dancing, entertainments, deck games and social life. Make this the vacation of vacations—the one you'll always remember.

In 1930, a week's cruise from Chicago to Buffalo and back on the *North American* or *South American* including meals and berth cost $79.50.

106

River Avenue looked like this in the "Model T" era. (courtesy of Myron Van Ark)

familiar winter sight docked in Lake Macatawa.

The Roaring Twenties also witnessed the birth of the festival that would be destined to outdraw all other area attractions — Tulip Time. During a speech delivered in 1927, Lida Rogers, a biology teacher at Holland High School, suggested the planting of flowers as a community beautification project. The idea caught on and the city's Dutch residents soon settled on the tulip as the appropriate flower. The following year, the city imported bulbs from the Netherlands and planted them along the street curbs and in parks. When they bloomed the following year, visitors' response was so encouraging that the program was augmented.

In 1930, news releases first advertised the "Tulip Time in Holland" festival and 50,000 visitors showed up. The following year, 175,000 tourists arrived. Beginning in 1930 Hollanders also began celebrating other ethnic traditions. Clad in colorful Dutch peasant costumes, Hollanders kicked off the event with the traditional street scrubbing. Klompen dancers, wearing wooden shoes, clacked through the city in elaborately choreographed dances. A marching band contest drew contestants from many area schools. Additional attractions were added throughout the Depression, including a miniature Dutch village. By 1938 annual attendance had reached 500,000. The festival was temporarily suspended during World War II, but in 1946 some 1.5 million bulbs again lined city streets and bloomed brightly in extensive public gardens.

The Holland Furnace Company gave Tulip Time further national exposure when it brought famous screen personalities to Holland during the late 1930s and ear-

ly 1940s. Pat O'Brien, Dorothy Lamour, George Raft, Bob Cummings and King Kong's heartthrob, Fay Wray, rode in Tulip Time parades, posed with local politicians and in general brought the golden age of Hollywood to Holland. Later a nationally broadcast radio show featuring Arthur Godfrey and the Holland Furnace Company's team of eight miniature ponies brought additional fame to Tulip Time.

The company itself, however, experienced its ups and downs during the Depression. In the early 1930s the Holland Furnace Company pioneered with the "first, simple, practical air conditioning system" for domestic use, the Holland Vaporaire Systems. In May 1931, office personnel moved into a modern new structure with many innovations, including a private telephone exchange. This building became the nerve center of local manufacturing operations and of the hundreds of sales and service branches across the continent.

But the company fell on hard times in the depths of the Depression. In 1933-1934, sales of only $3.5 million resulted in a loss of $100,000. P. Theodore Cheff, a dynamic young executive who had married cofounder Kolla's daughter, took over the reins of leadership to bring the company out of its slump. He introduced new business policies and revamped the entire organization. By the end of 1935, sales for the previous nine-month period soared to $8 million with nearly $1 million in profits.

The Great Depression that gripped the nation throughout the decade of the 1930s left invisible scars on all who lived through it. Despite a cost of living that remained remarkably low in Holland – 35 cent

Holland, Mich

**Decades before Tulip Time had been conceived Holland citizens promoted their Dutch
heritage with attractions such as this monster booth, probably at the Holland Fair ca. 1920.**
(courtesy Myron Van Ark)

Tulip Time Through the Years

Tulip Time 1931 brought 175,000
visitors to Holland.
(courtesy State of Michigan Archives)

The makers of Old Dutch Cleanser sensed a promotional
opportunity at Tulip Time ca. 1932.
(courtesy State of Michigan Archives)

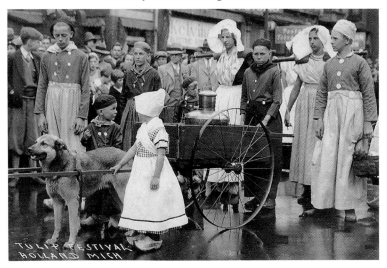

Even the city's dogs got into the
mood during the early years.
(courtesy Louis Hallacy, II)

Pipes were often
a part of the cos-
tuming ca.1933.
(courtesy Louis
Hallacy, II)

Women's costumes resembled nurse's uniforms during the 1930s. (courtesy Louis Hallacy, II)

Tulip Time was canceled from 1942-1945 because of World War II. But in April 1945 Holland held instead a flower show. The flower girl award went to Delores De Vries.

Cute Kids and pretty girls have long been an integral part of Tulip Time.

The year 1961 saw the tulip fields bloom with pretty Dutch girls. (courtesy State of Michigan Archives)

Michigan Governor George Romney (left) scrubbed Holland's streets ca. 1964.

Tulip Time Grand Marshall Mrs. George Bush with Holland Area Chamber of Commerce President Louis Hallacy, II, in 1987. (courtesy Louis Hallacy, II)

By 1952 costumes had become more historically accurate. (courtesy State of Michigan Archives)

Tulip Time began anew in 1946. Shown are Willard Wichers' wife Nell and daughters Janet and Elizabeth. (courtesy State of Michigan Archives)

Dignitaries have often traveled to Tulip Time. Scrubbing the street left to right in 1947 are Consul General of the Netherlands Jay Vande Mortel, Michigan Governor Kim Sigler and Holland Chamber of Commerce Secretary William H. Vande Water. (courtesy State of Michigan Archives)

Eighth Street dancers drew the traditional crowds in 1965. (courtesy State of Michigan Archives)

One of the most memorable Tulip Times was that of the nation's Bicentennial year. Left to right are; Madeline Hallacy and Mayor Louis Hallacy, II, presenting President Gerald Ford, daughter Susan and wife Betty with the traditional sets of klompen on May 15, 1976.
(courtesy Louis Hallacy, II)

These girls scrubbed vigorously in 1974.
(courtesy State of Michigan Archives)

112

This famous Holland landmark gas station was constructed in the 1920s.
(courtesy Boeve Oil Co.)

Holland Red Cross, recorded an incident typical of the hard times in her report for May 1931. When she arrived for work at the office located in City Hall she noticed an old battered Ford parked in front: "This was packed full of all kinds of junk also an expectant mother and 13 month-old baby and the father. They followed me into the office and said that they arrived the night before and had been given lodging and breakfast by the Legion. They had only four pennies left and no gas so could not buy milk for the baby or get out of town. When asked why they were so far away from home they said they had been looking for work and asked if we could not find them something." After conferring with a local attorney, the Red Cross worker gave the family a check for $2 so they could "move along out of town."

restaurant meals, 75 cent hotel lodgings and an overnight stay in the hospital merely $3 – many remember bread lines, going on the dole, bank failures, and Roosevelt's emergency jobs programs — the PWA, WPA, and CCC.

Katherine Van Duren, executive secretary of the

The glum 1930s were also the heyday of the likes of Machine-Gun Kelley, Baby Face Nelson, Ma Barker and Pretty Boy Floyd. Vicious hoodlums, many with Robin Hood-like reputations, sometimes won the affection of the common folk. Their colorful life-styles

During the Depression, Bert Kruiswyk's Jobbers Super Market at 139-141 River Ave. featured ridiculously low prices such as 6¢ loaves of bread and potatoes for a penny a pound.
(photo from Holland Historical Trust Collection of the Joint Archives of Holland)

relieved the monotony of the hard times, and the banks they robbed, then foreclosing on many a mortgage, were not that popular anyway.

Older residents still talk about the time Holland got a dose of this excitement. On September 29, 1932, a gang of bank robbers pulled a job on the First State Bank straight out of *Bonnie and Clyde.* Five or six "yeggs" armed with pistols and machine guns entered the bank shortly after it opened, ordered customers and bank employees to the floor in the middle of the building, and forced the cashier to open the vault. When the cashier moved too slow he earned a pistol thump on the head. A customer entering the bank, spun around and ran out into the street shouting that the bank was being robbed.

When Police Chief Peter A. Lievense ran to the scene one of the gang members shouted "There's a bull!" and shot him through the glass door. The bandits snatched up $12,000 in cash and ran to their getaway car, a Whippet sedan, while the wounded police chief and another officer opened fire. Shop owners and other citizens grabbed their guns and peppered the robbers' car as it raced through downtown streets and alleys. Bursts from one outlaw's machine gun spattered the sides of the Warm Friend Hotel, sending splinters of stone and glass flying. One pedestrian was shot. The bullet-riddled car sped away, heading east out of the city. As it raced through the rural Allegan County community of Burnips, farmers and other vigilantes fired a hail of bullets. Despite the 200-man dragnet that combed the woods in northern Allegan County, the yeggs had disappeared.

The great Holland bank robbery inspired coffee klatsch chatter for years to come, but for most Holland area residents the excitement was only a temporary lull in the business of making a living. Despite the

The great snowstorm of February 1936 that closed roads for more than a week required the hand shoveling of U.S. 31. (courtesy Myron Van Ark)

Depression, many area farmers managed to earn a good living through hard work and cooperation, characteristic of their Calvinist tradition. In Hamilton, a Dutch community originally called Rabbit River because of its location on that northern Allegan County stream, talk centered around eggs rather than yeggs. The Hamilton Farm Bureau, a cooperative organization founded in 1920 by 138 farmers was originally located in a corner of a local pickle factory. It gradually expanded and in 1932 under long-time general manager Andrew Lohman it erected a modern, three-story egg exchange. That facility joined the Co-op's grain elevator, warehouse, gasoline and oil storage units, garage, and mercantile outlets that had ensured success for its members, even during the darkest days of the Depression.

(Above) Holland fielded a semi-pro baseball team in the 1920s. (courtesy Myron Van Ark)

(Below) Silvia Vander Bie delivers an order at the A & W Rootbeer Stand across from the Buick dealer on E. 8th Street (photo from Holland Historical Trust Collection of the Joint Archives of Holland)

By banding together to buy feed and other supplies at bulk prices and by establishing quality standards for poultry and eggs, the Co-op's output commanded the

For many years beginning in 1939 the Chris-Craft factory turned out its quality boats.
(courtesy State of Michigan Archives)

highest market prices. The millions of eggs produced annually by local poultry keepers flowed to the egg exchange, located adjacent to the railroad, to be processed by automated grading, candling, washing, and packing machines. Since its founding, the co-op had not failed to yield a good dividend for its members. Sales rose from $101,000 in 1923 to $516,000 in 1930. By 1934 two freight cars of prize eggs per week were shipped to an eager market in New York City, packed under a cooperative brand.

Not all Holland area businesses weathered the Depression as well as the Hamilton Farm Bureau, but those that failed were usually succeeded by new enterprises that kept the local economy healthy. When the Thompson Manufacturing Company, which specialized in bent wood toilet tanks and other wooden novelties, went out of business, its factory was snapped up in 1933 by the Sligh Furniture Company. Sligh, founded in 1880, had grown to become one of the leading furniture manufacturers in Grand Rapids. But a depression in the furniture industry that began in 1926 brought mounting losses and in 1932 the Sligh Company closed its doors and began liquidating assets to pay off creditors. The following year, Charles R. Sligh, Jr., the 27-year-old son of the company founder, acquired some of the Sligh Furniture Company assets and, forming a partnership with Bill Lowry, began production in Holland. The Holland venture was an attempt to capitalize on its famous name on a smaller scale. By specializing in quality office desks, Sligh enjoyed a successful

rebirth in Holland. Similarly, when the big Bush and Lane piano factory lay vacant on 24th Street, the Baker Furniture Company relocated to Holland from Allegan during the Depression.

Other area entrepreneurs founded niche businesses that prospered despite the harsh economic times, Phillips Brooks, for example, became intrigued with the potential of a novel soft drink called "Bib Label Lithiated Lemon-Lime Soda." Originally marketed as a health drink because it contained a larger percentage of CO_2 "Life Gas," the product sold better when it changed its name to 7UP. Brooks acquired the southwestern Michigan franchise for 7UP in 1934. His initial efforts brought losses but he persevered and by 1937 his company was producing 60 cases of 7UP an hour.

By 1939, due largely to increased military spending following the outbreak of hostilities in Europe, the United States had begun to shake off the Depression. That same year proved important for Holland's economy as well. The Holland Shoe Company merged with the Racine Shoe Company, revamped the Holland factory, and ultimately doubled its work force. The newly organized Holland Precision Parts Company announced plans for a new factory to manufacture automobile and aircraft parts, slated to employ 1,000 workers. The Chris-Craft Corporation of Algonac, the world's largest producer of motorboats, also began construction of a 600-foot-long boat building plant in Holland. It had been attracted to the city largely because of the availability of skilled woodworkers. The city also

Holland Hitch employees made over one million pintle hooks during World War II. (courtesy Holland Hitch)

sales in a single week.

But on December 7, 1941, reports of the sneak attack on Pearl Harbor shattered the sanctity of the Sabbath for Hollanders and Americans everywhere. Few ever forgot where they were and what they were doing when they first heard the news. Most Holland factories soon turned to production of vital defense needs. The Holland Furnace Company cast over 25 million pounds of armor plating for tanks and manufactured miles of heavy anchor chain for the Navy during the war years. The Holland Hitch Company manufactured more than one million pintle hooks for military vehicles. The Donnelly-Kelley Glass Company converted from mirror production to fashion aerial gunsight reflectors and precision parts for tank periscopes. Hart & Cooley began making air intake covers for tanks and 60mm mortar shell casings. In 1942, half of its plant space was relinquished to a subsidiary, The Fafnir Bearing Company, which rolled out millions of ball bearings for military needs during the war. Even

launched construction of a new $1.5 million power plant financed in part by PWA funding. The James DeYoung power plant, named in honor of Holland's first superintendent of the Board of Public Works, opened in 1940.

The Holland Furnace Company also enjoyed continued growth. The September 4, 1941, issue of the company newsletter, the "Holland Firepot," trumpeted the new company record of over one million dollars in

The Fafnir Bearing Division of Hart & Cooley won a coveted "E Award" for its outstanding production record in 1944.

During the late 1930s this sign greeted visitors to Holland.
(courtesy Don van Reken).

An aerial view of the H.J. Heinz "tank farm" where millions of pickles were preserved in brine in huge cypress vats during "green season.

smaller firms got into the Homefront spirit. The Boeve Oil Company, for example, collected huge piles of old tires at its Lincoln Avenue site to be recycled for military use.

Thousands of Holland area men and women served on active duty in the far-flung battlefields of World War II. They fought the Japanese in Pacific naval engagements and in bloody South Sea Island battles. They fought the Nazis in Northern Africa and Europe and the Fascists in Italy. They flew B-24 Liberators, manufactured at the world's largest bomber plant at Willow Run, as well as fighter planes and cargo planes, and served around the world in aircraft ground crews. On the third anniversary of Pearl Harbor, the *Holland Sentinel* outlined the area's "roll of honor." Forty-six men from the Holland area had been killed, 10 were missing in action, 16 were listed as prisoners of war, and 66 had been wounded in action, some as many as three times. Lt. Col. Matt Urban, who later moved to Holland, received the Congressional Medal of Honor in 1986 for his combat heroism and leadership in France in 1944. That and other medals awarded for bravery made him "the

The Boeve Oil Co. collected mountains of scrap tires for the homefront war effort. (courtesy Boeve Oil Co.)

most decorated combat soldier in U.S. history." By the war's end, Holland servicemen had contributed to the defeat of the Axis powers to a degree equaled by few communities of a similar size.

In 1947, Holland celebrated its centennial with four days of activities in August, featuring an exhibition of art objects sent from the Dutch government, a dramatic production about the coming of the Dutch pioneers, barbershop singing, swimming contests in Lake Macatawa and consumption of a gigantic cake decorated with a replica of the first log cabin.

The Sligh family, local furniture manufacturers, brought national attention to Holland the same year as the centennial. The third annual National Water Ski Tournament, held on Lake Macatawa in 1941, had been won by Charles R. Sligh, Jr. The tournament was suspended during the war and then held again in Holland in 1946 and 1947. Sligh's son, Robert L. Sligh, won the national championship in 1947. During the late 1940s and 1950s Charles R. Sligh's daughter Patti Sligh Ver Sluis, also an expert water skier, taught at the water ski school the family operated on Lake Macatawa.

The industrial evolution that had kept Holland's economy vital for nearly a century continued in the

Patti Sligh and other Sligh family members demonstrated their skill at the water ski school they operated on Macatawa Lake in the 1940s & 1950s.

In 1951, Parke-Davis acquired this abandoned Armour Leather Co. plant and converted it for production of pharmaceuticals.

West 8th Street looked like this in the late 1940s. (courtesy Myron Van Ark)

Despite it being a pagan celebration, Hope College co-eds cavorted around the May Pole each spring for many years. This is the 1962 festival. (photo from Hope College collection of the Joint Archives of Holland)

post war era. By the late 1940s the last of the city's once dominant leather factories, the Armour Company Tannery on the north shore of the Macatawa River, had closed. The Chamber of Commerce promoted the availability of the site and in 1951 the Detroit-based pharmaceutical giant Parke-Davis purchased the 30-acre tract and remodeled the structures. Its first major product was the antibiotic chloromycetin, a wonder drug discovered during World War II and released for general use in 1949.

Millions of patients had been successfully treated with the drug. By June 1952 Parke-Davis held 38% of the antibiotic market in the U.S. Then a bombshell fell in the form of a Los Angeles newspaper story about a local physician's claim that a side effect of chloromycetin had killed his son. The AMA followed by issuing a warning to doctors, and the wire services splashed the story across headlines around the country. Panic set in, and by October Parke-Davis' share of the antibiotic market had dropped to five percent. Work at the Holland plant came to a stand still. Parke-Davis employees voluntarily shifted to a part-time schedule to rescue 382 laid-off workers.

Parke-Davis weathered the crises by cooperating wholeheartedly with an FDA investigation and by following its time honored slogan, a Latin phrase meaning "Truth in Medicine." Soon chloromycetin had been vindicated and production at the Holland plant was up and running again.

In 1955 the Holland Chamber of Commerce celebrated another industrial victory when it won competition with other cities to land a new General Electric plant on East 16th Street.

In the meantime Holland youths were again called upon to fight for their country on foreign soil when in June 1950 the Cold War heated up in Korea and President Harry Truman committed U.S. troops to combat. Twenty-two-year-old U.S. Army Corporal John Essebagger, Jr., was posthumously awarded the Congressional Medal of Honor for his valor and devotion to duty when he singlehandedly engaged an overwhelming force of communist soldiers near Popsudong, Korea, on April 25, 1951. After three years of bitter fighting a final truce agreement signed on July 27, 1953, brought an uneasy peace. Korea would remain divided at the 38th parallel.

The postwar period brought to Hope College a rush of veterans eager to capitalize on the GI Bill. Enrollment jumped from 400 in 1945 to 1,200 in 1947, including 533 veterans. Hope launched a hectic building program facilitated by Federal Housing Authority funds that saw many new dormitories constructed. Enrollment dropped again during the 1950s, but the impact of the postwar baby boom and Hope's national reputation enabled it to reach an all-time high in the 1960s. During the late 1940s Hope emerged as one of the country's leading producers of candidates for Ph.D. degrees in chemistry. In 1959 the *Chicago Tribune* rated Hope as one of the nation's 10 best liberal arts colleges.

Three years before, nature at its most destructive, in the form of a killer tornado, had indelibly etched the date April 3, 1956, on the minds of Holland area resi-

Chester Van Tongeren's Dutch Novelty Shop on River Ave. featured a wooden shoe that would fit Paul Van Bunyan, ca. 1945. (courtesy State of Michigan Archives)

dents. Tornados whipped through 12 states killing 49 people, and Michigan received the worst of it. Spawned over Lake Michigan, a huge twister swept toward Holland, but miraculously leapfrogged the city. Hudsonville to the east was not so fortunate. A sickening yellowish cast to the evening sky and an ominous black cloud front preceded the disaster. Families sitting down to their evening meal glanced up to see the furious funnel sweeping toward them. It struck the center of Hudsonville, smashing houses into kindling wood and tossing cars around like toys. Thirteen were left dead in Hudsonville, and five more were killed in Standale and Thompsonville. Tornado victims overflowed into the corridors of Holland Hospital.

Five years later, with memories of the killer tornado still fresh, Holland turned to exploiting the more beneficial aspects of air movements — in the form of a historic Dutch windmill. In 1961, Holland businessman Carter Brown conceived of transplanting an authentic windmill from the Netherlands as a memorial to the city's Dutch heritage. Aided by Mayor Nelson Bosman and Henry S. Maentz, Willard C. Wichers, the guiding light behind the formation of the Netherlands Museum in the late 1930s and early 1940s and director of the Midwest office of the Netherlands Information Service, led the search for a suitable windmill. As Wichers emphasized the importance of strengthening the cultural and historic ties between Holland and its American namesake, prolonged negotiations with Dutch officials finally resulted in permission to remove one of the ancient windmills, which are considered national treasures by the Dutch. The Holland City Council authorized the issuance of $450,000 in revenue bonds to fund the project.

Wichers located a suitable 200-year-old windmill known as "De Zwaan" near Vinkel, Noord Brabant, and he bought it on the spot for $2,800. As Dutch millwright Jan Medendorp supervised the careful dismantling of the huge structure, construction crews readied its new site on Windmill Island. Bulldozers created a 10-foot-high mound, upon which masons constructed a historically accurate brick tower to support the windmill. In October 1964, the Dutch vessel *Prins Willem Van Orange* conveyed some 70 tons of windmill parts to Muskegon. A convoy of specially decorated trucks paraded the windmill through the streets of its new home. Workmen labored through the bitter winter weather to complete the project in time for the next May's Tulip Festival. On April 10, 1965, Prince Bernhard of the Netherlands, Michigan Governor George Romney, and other dignitaries joined Wichers in dedicating the majestic 125-foot-tall "De Zwaan."

True to tradition, a pretty Hope College co-ed dressed in ethnic costume met the prince on the drawbridge to Windmill Island and requested he be the first to pay the one dollar admission fee. Each year thereafter thousands more were happy to purchase tickets to tour a genuine bit of old Holland.

Holland's windmill coup, however, coincided with some bad economic news. The mighty Holland Furnace Company tottered on the brink of failure, despite highly visible promotional campaigns such as boxing great

Rocky Marciano
WORLD'S HEAVYWEIGHT CHAMPION
AL WEILL, MANAGER
HOLLAND FURNACE COMPANY
TRAINING CAMP
HOLLAND, MICH

In 1953 and 1954, one of boxing's all time greats trained in Holland for the match he won over Jersey Joe Walcott. (courtesy Myron Van Ark)

Rocky Marciano's training camp in Holland provided by the company. Its troubles had begun in the mid-1950s. At that time the Federal Trade Commission leveled charges that some high pressure company salesmen had routinely recommended replacing furnaces that could have been easily repaired. These allegations shook consumer confidence in the once highly respected firm and sales fell sharply. Company president Cheff announced he was selling out to a West Coast industrialist named M.J. Stevens in 1962. But the deal fell through amid a flurry of contradictory statements by both sides after Stevens revealed plans to streamline the massive organization. Nevertheless, Cheff bailed out the following year. The company failed to modernize its product line and its bulky furnaces lost out to competitors who introduced smaller, more efficient models. Shortly after it was purchased by the New Jersey-based Athlone Company, the Holland Furnace plant closed forever.

Motivated in part, no doubt, by the decline of the city's largest employer, a group of local business leaders grew worried over the potential lack of available jobs for upcoming generations. Discussions held during a Chamber of Commerce board meeting on September 15, 1958, ultimately gave birth to the Holland Economic Development Corporation (HEDCOR). Over the next two years, Clarence Jalving and Mayor Bosman consulted the Michigan Department of Economic Development about the possibility of utilizing land on Holland's southside as an industrial park. After visits to other communities to study their industrial planning, chamber members proceeded to organize a nonprofit corporation to purchase land through stock offerings and promote Holland's industrial possibilities. While not officially a Chamber of Commerce entity, HEDCOR shared office space and an executive director with the chamber, and the two organizations worked hand in hand.

Despite its potential, HEDCOR encountered public controversy during its developmental years. Citizens and downtown merchants worried that an industrial park project would lead to the decline of the city's downtown. Industrial leaders wrote angry letters to the editor opposing the park. But HEDCOR representatives persevered. Fund drives yielded enough money for the acquisition of land, and in 1968 HEDCOR celebrated the dedication of the first manufacturing facility constructed on the southside park, the massive Lifesavers plant.

The Holland Area Chamber of Commerce Early Bird Breakfasts begun in 1965 have featured inspiring speakers such as Michigan Attorney General Frank Kelley.

The Prince Machine Co., founded by Ed Prince in 1965, looked like this ca. 1970. (courtesy Prince Corporation)

The 1960s also witnessed the birth of a variety of companies that would play important roles in the city's future ranging from Charles Conrad's Thermotron in 1968, LeRoy and Cheryl Dell's environmentally–oriented engineering firm in 1968 and Ed Prince's shoestring venture in die-cast machinery production in 1965 that seven years later would diversify into the first lighted vanity visors and begin its climb to greatness. The 1970s brought further industrial diversification to the city. Some firms such as J.B. Laboratories were spin-offs from prior companies. Many, including Trendway and Metal Flow, achieved success through the energy and hard work of the entrepreneurial families who guided them. Gail and Alan Hering brought Atmosphere Processing to Holland in 1975 in part because of the excellent source of electricity available through the Board of Public Works.

But amid those years that saw Holland secure employment for the coming generations came America's entanglement in another foreign war. Beginning in 1965 with the deployment of the 173rd Airborne Brigade to Viet Nam increasing numbers of Holland's young men would find themselves fighting for their lives in jungle battlefields.

Twenty-two year-old Sgt. Gordon Douglas Yntema gave his life for his country during hand to hand fighting with the Viet Cong in 1968. His bravery in the face of insurmountable odds won him posthumously the Congressional Medal of Honor. U.S. Army Sgt. Paul Ronald Lambers also won the Congressional Medal of Honor in 1968 for "conspicuous gallantry and intrepidity in action at the risk of his life above and beyond the call of duty." Lambers survived Viet Nam and returned to Holland only to tragically drown in Lake Michigan in 1970.

The Viet Nam era would be remember as a time that tested the very fabric of American society. And the Holland that had so successfully retained its traditional atmosphere also found itself a community in transition. New industries and the resultant population growth produced a building boom. Old traditions — closing downtown shops on Wednesday afternoons, the strict observance of the Sabbath, and local ordinances resembling "blue laws" — gradually succumbed to more mainstream practices. As Holland grew, it suffered some of the negative aspects of urban life – an increase in crime and traffic jams.

As late as the 1950s Holland still boasted of its ethnically homogeneous population—90 percent of Dutch heritage. But that too would change with an influx of Hispanics and, more recently, Southeast Asian refugees, who were able to come to Holland through the sponsorship of various churches. In the 1930s Mexican nationals and Mexican-Americans from Texas had begun to migrate into the area to harvest fruit and vegetable crops. In 1939, for example, a local professor proposed to the Chamber of Commerce that he start a program to teach Spanish to local merchants so that they could better serve the growing number of Hispanic migrant workers. The labor shortage that developed

Hispanic migrants working in the Holland area gathered each week during harvest season for fellowship at the Olive Township Hall in 1948. (photo from Holland Historical Trust Collection of the Joint Archives of Holland)

during World War II lured increasing numbers of Hispanics to the north and some found employment in Holland factories. By the 1950s many Hispanics had established residency in Holland and they promoted more migration into the area by friends and relatives.

The Hispanics arriving in the Holland area spoke a different language, belonged predominantly to the Catholic Church, and retained distinct cultural values. Their introduction into the conservative, largely homogeneous Dutch Calvinistic community was not without its abrasive encounters. Hispanics encountered discrimination in housing and employment opportunities. Yet by the 1960s and 1970s, the bridal pages of the *Holland Sentinel* revealed an interesting fact—considerable intermarriage between Dutch and Hispanics. Older generations might frown on such developments,

Celia Martenez (center) was named queen of the Mexican Fiesta held in Holland in May 1968.

126

A "Morale Girl" offers encouragement as a member of the Hope College class of 1984 strains hard during the traditional freshman - sophomore rope pull.
(photo from Hope College Collection of the Joint Archives of Holland)

but love was doing what legislation could not.

Holland was a community in flux in other ways. Fueled by the burgeoning and diverse industrial base that had arisen since HEDCOR's campaign in the 1960s and the quality of life of the region Holland's population had climbed to 69,407 in 1990, a 56 percent increase since 1960. Scores of suburban housing developments blanketed the surrounding townships. And in response to the automobile culture that had transformed American life, fast food restaurants, outlet stores, strip malls and other multipurpose megaliths, such as the Westshore Mall that opened in 1988, increasingly lined the U.S. 31 corridor and contiguous streets.

Holland's downtown core faced the same deterioration that had plagued most other Michigan cities. But the Chamber of Commerce, city officials, a Downtown Development Authority, Hope College and other interested backers and, in particular, Ed and Elsa Prince, fought back to preserve the best of what downtown Holland had long been to the community. Building on a common concern for the city they had demonstrated with their support for the Evergreen Commons senior citizens facility in 1985, the Princes saved the historic

Tower Clock building from the wrecking ball in 1988. That year the city completed its Streetscape project complete with a subterranean "snowmelt" system. Soon three mini-parks had been added to the downtown. Two were decorated by the Princes with bronze statuary crafted by Colorado sculptor George Lundeen. Another major attraction came with the city's Window on the Waterfront Walkway. The 1990s brought continued revitalization to the downtown with the restoration and adoptive reuse of the Amtrack Railroad Station, the conversion of the old Post Office into the Holland Museum and Hope College's restoration of the Knickerbocker Theatre. Architecturally pleasing new buildings also arose including the Curtis Center, the Freedom Village campus, the new Post Office and Hope College's Haworth Learning and Conference Center.

As Holland prepared for a gala celebration of its sesquicentennial it was clear that the city had weathered yet another threat to its continued vitality. But underpinning all the grandeur of new bricks and mortar, population growth and quality of life was Holland's commerce, its industrial, business, banking and educational strength. The stories behind those firms, young and old, most proud of their heritage follow:

The old Holland Post Office shown here ca. 1947 now houses the museum.

Eighth Street looking west in late fall at dusk. (photo by Vito Palmisano)

The Holland Harbor piers have beckoned boaters for decades. (photo by Vito Palmisano)

Sunset from the south shore at the harbor entrance. (photo by Vito Palmisano)

Holland State Park looking north on a Labor Day weekend (photo by Vito Palmisano)

An eye catching entry in the 1995 Children's Parade at Tulip Time. (photo by Vito Palmisano)

Constructed in 1892 of Waverly sandstone, the Tower Clock Building is one of downtown Holland's architectural treasures. (photo by Vito Palmisano)

Autumn's golden orbs accentuate the Farmers Market at the Civic Center. (photo by Vito Palmisano)

Placed by Ed and Elsa Prince in downtown pocket parks, sculptor George Lundeen's bronze statuary delights residents and visitors alike. (photo by Vito Palmisano)

Michigan Governor John Engler and wife Michelle with their triplet girls, appeared at the 1996 Tulip Festival. (photo by Vito Palmisano)

De Zwaan in Tulip Time. (photo by Vito Palmisano)

Maureen Massie "tiptoes through the tulips" in Centennial Park in 1996.

Pilgrim Home Cemetery, where sleep the pioneers of 1847. (photo by Vito Palmisano)

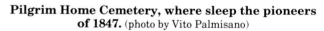

132

A.D. Bos Company

As a boy in the 1950s Thomas Bos often accompanied his father Alvin D. Bos as he delivered wholesale candy and tobacco to little corner grocery stores and gas stations throughout Allegan County. He remembered his father telling stories about the various businesses along the way - why some prospered and others failed. In high school when young Tom took over that Allegan route he was struck by the high degree of customer loyalty his father had earned through his fairness and accuracy. Those factors, his father's ethics and his ability to learn from the mistakes of others - to adapt to changing circumstances and to innovate - continue to spell success for the A.D. Bos Company .

The Bos saga began in 1919 when Alvin D. Bos' brother William married Janet Van Tongeren. Janet's father Herman ran a cigar and candy store at 12 East 8th Street where he also hand rolled Knickerbocker brand cigars. The following year William went to work for his father-in-law, wholeselling Knickerbocker cigars throughout the area. Soon he became an independent salesman, adding tobacco and candy to his stock.

At first the Bos Tobacco and Candy Company operated out of the basement of the Van Tongeren Cigar Company but later moved to the former Blom Saloon on River Avenue. Bos traveled the road selling out of a Dodge panel truck emblazoned with a Knickerbocker cigar advertisement. Gerald, another brother, joined the firm in 1923 and he opened up the Grand Haven and western Allegan County territory. During Prohibition the company also distributed near beer and soda pop manufactured by Blatts.

In 1928, the Bos Company moved to a house at 203 East 8th Street. The following year Alvin began working for the company, concentrating on sales in Grand Haven and Allegan. Following the repeal of Prohibition in 1933 the Bos Company began distribution of beer. During the Depression years the company enjoyed growth, purchasing new and larger trucks. Employment rose to 15 or 20, including many family members.

By 1939 the company had stopped handling beer and the following year Alvin bought the trucks and started operating as the Alvin D. Bos Company, predominately in Allegan County. The World War II years proved tough with sugar rationing and tobacco allocated to military needs. Bos judiciously parceled out what stock he could acquire and earned customer loyalty for many decades to come.

Bos bought his first cigarette vending machine in 1955 and then candy and coffee machines. In 1959, he installed his first full bank of machines dispensing candy, cigarettes, pastry, coffee, pop and chips in the basement of Hope College's Kollen Hall. Three years later Bos pioneered with the first successful unsubsidized venture in the country serving food from machines to high school students when he installed two banks of machines in the newly opened Holland High School. An attendant stocked the coin operated machines from the back with hotdogs, hamburgers, cold sandwiches and other foods. The Bos Company continued to maintain that food service for the following 16 years.

In 1962 Bos sold his wholesale and outside vending business to concentrate on the Holland area vending business. Four years later his son Thomas left his teaching position at West Ottawa High School to join the family business. The company expanded into a 3,000 square-foot building at 434 West 22nd Street and moved increasingly into the field of commercial vending accounts. Early customers included the Holland Color Co. and Home Furnace Co. In 1975 the company was incorpo-

Alvin D. Bos prepares to hit the road in 1936

rated as the Alvin D. Bos Vending Company.

The company moved to its present location at One West 5th Street, the former office and warehouse of the DePree Chemical Co., in 1981. Under Thomas' leadership the firm moved into the computer age. Current technology allows for almost hourly reconciliation of accounts by delivery persons.

During the 1980s and 1990s the company continued to expand through innovative response to changing tastes and circumstances. The surgeon general's report on the hazards of smoking brought a phasing out of cigarette machines. The company responded to the drop in coffee consumption by adding flavored coffees, espresso and cappuccino. The health conscious movement spurred Bos to label healthier products in its machines.

In 1996 the firm's 80 employees cater to 30,000 customers each day in factories in Allegan, Ottawa and Kent counties. Those consumers quaff an amazing one million cups of coffee each month!

Atmosphere Processing, Inc.

The Atmosphere Processing, Inc., headquarters at 100 North Fairbanks Avenue.

Gail Hering never forgot her first impression of the old building where her husband Alan would launch Atmosphere Processing in the fall of 1975. The structure had served as part of the original plant of the Home Furnace Company, which from small beginnings had become a major competitor to the industry giant, Holland Furnace Company. A fire had blazed through the structure about the time the furnace company was sold and moved in the mid 1960s. As Hering surveyed the ruins ten years later it was "like the firemen had put out the fire and history stood still." Soon the Herings were shoveling dump truck loads of refuse out of the old building and Atmosphere Processing was "picking up where the cinders left off."

Born in Port Huron, Alan Hering moved to the Detroit area and attended Eastern Michigan University before getting a job with the Ford Motor Company as an apprentice in the field of industrial pyrometry, the measurement of heat. There, he was fortunate enough to be trained by Thomas Padden, a legendary pioneer in the field who had been hired by Henry Ford himself. Padden proved a brilliant teacher who would not accept less than Hering's best efforts, and a firm friendship also developed between the two. In recognition of that, when Atmosphere Processing built new offices in 1981, they named the library conference room "The Padden Room."

During his 12 years at Ford, when he worked at industrial instrumentation in the general parts division for transmissions and chassis, Hering learned his craft well. By then he had stifled his entrepreneurial spirit long enough. Feeling strongly that the heat treat process could function better as a separate business with management focused strictly on its needs, he sensed the time was ripe to start his own independent operation.

After two years' intensive research he had narrowed down the possible locations for the new venture to the Detroit area, Georgia, or Holland. But at that time the U.S. was in the midst of a fuel crisis with long lines of automobiles at gas pumps and natural gas nearly unobtainable. Electricity was a viable option to natural gas, and Holland won out because of its excellent source of cheap electricity offered by the Board of Public Works. Although the plant later switched to natural gas, electricity continues to provide

a back up source.

Another factor that proved important for the company's success was Holland's location midway between Detroit and Chicago, amid one of the nation's fastest growing industrial areas. And once in Holland the Herings found a new home "with a wonderful quality of life."

The first year of business was "touch and go." Gail Hering, who had married her husband in 1961 and started her own career teaching theater and English in the Livonia Public Schools and at Madonna College, originally planned to pursue teaching in Holland. But, one day Alan called and said, "I need you here to help me. The truck's on the way." She soon found herself loading furnaces, conducting tests, and driving a semi and a fork lift. In 1979, she bid farewell to the thespian world and officially became CEO of Atmosphere Processing.

By then the operation which specialized in annealing and normalizing processes, offering as well air and water quench hardening, stress relieving, carbide removal and shot blast cleaning, had cleared the hurdles of the first year's start-up and became profitable, doubling in size every three years.

In 1985, when the company earned Ford's coveted Q-1 award, it was processing around five million pounds of iron castings and steel forgings each week. Growth continued strong through the late 1980s thanks to an ongoing boom in automobile production. But by the early 1990s the "Big Three" automobile manufacturers began putting pressures on suppliers to reduce prices. And even with a revenue of $11 million, precious little in the way of profits was left.

The Herings countered with a major change in strategy - shifting the company's customer base away from the automobile industry, down-sizing from 180 to 60 employees and making major capital investments in state-of-the-art technology. The company also entered into new markets such as straight-length steel bars as long as 45 feet and expanded its capacity to handle more pounds per hour. A major breakthrough came with the "Dura-Blue" process, a rust resistant coating procedure developed by Hering.

As a result of its response to the threats of a changing marketplace Atmosphere Processing revitalized its operations to continue as a force in the heat treating industry and in Holland's economy.

Baker Book House

Arlene Popma remembers well the luncheon she enjoyed in 1987 at Granny's Kitchen Restaurant on 28th Street in Grand Rapids. It proved a milestone in her personal development and in the annals of the Holland Baker Book House.

For the previous 15 years she had been working at the Fruit Basket Flowerland, but that job had begun to cloy — she felt the need of a new challenge. Popma's husband Gary, general manager over retail of Baker Book House, had mentioned his wife's dilemma in passing to Pete Baker, vice president of the retail sales division and son of the company founder, Herman Baker. Baker invited her to lunch and then he popped the question - would she become manager of the new Holland Baker Book House store the company was planning to open at the Cedar Village Mall on Chicago Drive? It would be a big career change but Popma took one night to mull it over, discussed it with husband Gary and the next day said yes to a new vocation that she soon learned to excel in and to love.

The firm that Popma cast her future with originated in 1939. Fourteen-year-old Herman Baker had immigrated to Grand Rapids from the Netherlands with his family in 1925. Soon he began working part time in the famous religious bookstore operated by his uncle, Louis Kregel. There, Baker learned to love the biblical classics and by studying them he developed a knowledge of theology that would rival many pastors.

When he was 28, Baker opened his own religious bookstore at 1019 Wealthy Street in Grand Rapids. The rent was $18.00 a month and his entire stock consisted of the 500 used volumes he had collected over the years. Baker's business grew slowly but steadily at first. Three years later he was able to purchase the Wealthy Street structure.

In 1940, Baker had ventured into book publishing with a commentary on the book of Revelation, More Than Conquerors, by Dr. William Hendriksen. Fifty-six years later the volume remains in print and continues to sell well at Baker Book House Stores.

In 1948, Baker made the decision to launch an expanded publishing effort. The store celebrated its tenth anniversary with the reprinting of the multi-volume 19th century classic, Barnes' Notes on the Old and New Testaments. Next came the massive New Schaff-Herzog Encyclopedia of Religious Knowledge. Due in part to the strong demand for reference books, commentaries and textbooks occasioned by the rapid growth of seminaries and Bible colleges after World War II, the Baker publishing business flourished. By 1959 the Baker catalog included 147 active titles.

Baker constructed a new 25,000 square-foot facility in Ada in 1966 to keep pace with the vigorous growth of the publishing division. Over the next two decades that structure was expanded twice. When the acquisition of the W.A. Wilde publishing company of Natick, Massachusetts in 1968, the following year's Baker catalog listed 747 active titles. The 1970s witnessed Baker's venture into the mass-market field and the 1980s brought an increasing emphasis on new titles rather than reprints of classics. By 1989 the Baker Catalog contained approximately 1,300 active titles, some of which approached one million copies in print.

The Grand Rapids Wealthy Street location remained Baker's sole retail outlet until 1968 when a bookstore was opened at 501 Chicago Drive in Holland. Popma became manager of that store on April 30, 1987, and a few months later of the new 3,000 square-foot Baker Book House at Cedar Village Mall which replaced it. Under Popma's philosophy that "it is important to constantly have goals, to expand, to grow, you should never be satisfied" and with the teamwork of her fellow employees the store grew to encompass 5,000 square feet after four years. In October, 1995, a new expansion increased it to 7,000 square feet. There, an amazing inventory of 11,000 religious titles as well as related videos, software, CD's, cassette tapes, music books and gift items dazzle browsers.

In 1977, founder Herman Baker articulated his business philosophy: "We love to sell a good book. There is no better business to be in. In books we have the richest treasures on earth, the output of the best minds of the ages." The firm's current president Richard Baker and in the Holland Baker Book House, Arlene Popma and her staff that has grown from five to 17 employees, continue to honor and practice that vision.

The Baker Book House at 716 Chicago Drive.

Beverage America

"If at first you don't succeed, try, try again," might well have been a favorite motto of Seven-Up Bottling Company of Western Michigan founder Phillips Brooks. It was during the beginning of the Great Depression while Brooks was working in Cincinnati that a new beverage product "Bib Label Lithiated Lemon-Lime Soda" caught his attention. When he moved to Holland to work for his brother Ernest's insurance agency he continued his interest in that soft drink which, fortunately, shortened its name to 7UP. In 1934 Brooks received a franchise to bottle and sell 7UP in 19 counties in southwestern Michigan. He, his wife Ruth and children Jim and Janet labeled bottles in the basement of their home. The family car, a 1929 Buick sedan, was Brooks' first delivery vehicle.

Demand for 7UP, inspired Brooks to expand production. He sold his home to purchase more bottles and cases. But at the end of two years of hard work the bottom line read zero profit. Discouraged, he sold his business for $400.

But Brooks refused to let his entrepreneurial dream die. A year later he bought back the business for the same price and borrowed enough money for a down payment on a building at 99 River Avenue and some second-hand equipment. In March, 1937, the 7UP Bottling Company of Western Michigan began producing 60 cases of 7UP an hour.

Business boomed! By 1942 a fleet of 30 delivery trucks handled an annual output that had soared to ten million bottles. Sugar rationing posed a threat during the war but Brooks served on the home front as chairman of the Ottawa County Rationing Board and his company survived.

James F. Brooks returned from service in the Air Corps to join his father's business. The company was incorporated in 1953 with James Brooks as president. The plant on River Avenue had to be expanded twice to meet growing demand for 7UP. New products were added in 1959 including Like, a diet version, and Howdy, "the friendly drink," line of flavors.

In 1967, the company consolidated operations with the Seven-Up Bottling Company of Northern Michigan based in Cadillac. The following year the Grand Rapids Bottling Company joined the corporation, bringing new product lines of Hires Root Beer, Dr Pepper and Sun-Glo. The year 1969 brought the acquisition of the Vernors Bottling Co. of Southwestern Michigan in Battle Creek whose product line included Orange Crush and Vernors. To reflect this expanded product line the company changed its name to Brooks Products.

On August 16, 1969, Brooks Products, Inc., celebrated the gala opening of its new state-of-the-art bottling plant at 777 Brooks Avenue, capping nearly four years of construction at the HEDCOR Industrial Park site. The 50,000 square-foot facility was capable of filling 960 bottles and cans per minute.

James W. F. Brooks, who had worked for the company during high school, joined the firm full time following graduation from Michigan State in 1971. Ten years later this third generation of Brooks had worked his way up to become president and CEO of Squirt & Company.

Brooks Products, Inc. had become Squirt & Company in 1977 following the acquisition of the Squirt franchise. Squirt traces its origins to 1937. Over the next ten years the company grew through innovations such as the first diet soft drink sweetened entirely by NutraSweet and vitamin fortified Diet Squirt. Industry restructuring spurred sale of the Squirt division in 1986.

During the late 1980s the company acquired Flint 7UP and Detroit 7UP and changed its name to Brooks Beverages, Inc. The year 1988 brought the acquisition of Beverage Management, Inc., an Ohio based giant that started up in the 1920s. The newly named Brooks Beverage Management, Inc. continued to grow through the introduction of "New Age" beverages like Snapple, Evian and Royal Mistic as well as the development of the Pro*Pak hot pack operations started in 1992.

In 1995, Brooks Beverage Management, Inc. merged with Mid-Continent Bottlers, Inc. of West Des Moines, Iowa, and Seven-Up Bottling Company of St. Louis (MO) Inc. and formed a new holding company called Beverage America, Inc. The merger created the largest 7UP/RC bottler in the United States that delivers its diverse range of beverage products to 13 states, producing at six sites, with 50 distribution centers and over 3,000 associates.

A busy scene at the 7-UP Bottling Company of West Michigan ca. 1938.

BLD Products

The BLD Products Ltd. headquarters at 534 East 48th Street. (photo by Karen L. Dirkse)

Dave Dirkse, president of BLD Products, still chuckles when he recalls the original purchase order his young company received in the fall of 1974. It was an order for 200 of the automatic choke pull offs that were its first product. But he and partner Larry Neighbor, the entire work force of the operation, had only 196 of them in stock. No problem - he typed, "consider this order completed" on the form, packed the parts, happily shipped them to the Philadelphia purchaser and BLD was off and running.

Dirkse had grown up in Holland where his father and uncles sold automobiles. As a teenager he had always been around cars, working on them and he liked cars. He knew even then that someday he would be involved in some aspect of the automobile business and he would own and run that enterprise. After graduation from Holland High School he spent a tour of duty with the U.S. Air Force, graduated from Ferris College in 1968 and took a job in sales with the Bendix Corporation. But he never relinquished that dream to operate his own business.

His chance came in July 1974, when he and Neighbor took control of the day to day operation of BLD Products, a company incorporated in Flint, Michigan, the year before by Ben Benjamin, Leon LaVene and Duane Walper - the firm's name comes from the initials of their first names.

Originally the company operated out of a little 800 square-foot building on Dye Road in Flint. Dirkse and Neighbor did all the work themselves - drove a truck to pick up stock, unloaded it, filled orders and packed and shipped them. Soon the hard work and energy they put into the business began to pay off. Major clients were added and the company began manufacturing its own products. In January 1976, BLD relocated to a 12,000 square-foot facility to accommodate its rapid growth.

As the company continued to boom, the decision was made to move away from Flint. Various cities were considered but thanks in part to the very receptive attitude displayed by HEDCOR, the firm purchased five acres in the Southside Industrial Park. In February, 1980, BLD moved into its new 26,000 square-foot facility.

New products such as brake hardware brought additional growth. In 1982 BLD acquired Spinett, Inc. of Claremont, Minnesota, and moved that company's diesel engine water pump operations to Holland.

Tragically Neighbor drowned in a boating accident in June, 1983. The flag pole and memorial pedestal that graces the front of the BLD building honors him as "partner - executive - friend."

By 1985, the plant had grown to 50,000 square feet as the company developed temperature sensor and idle air control product lines. Precision Compressors of Bad Axe, Michigan, a manufacturer of air conditioning compressors, was acquired in 1985 and moved to a new 20,000 building adjacent the main factory in Holland the following year.

MascoTech, Inc., of Taylor, Michigan, acquired BLD in 1986. BLD continues to operate under its own management as a wholly owned subsidiary.

The following decade saw hectic growth for BLD. In 1986, BLD acquired Superior Push Rod of Port Clinton, Ohio, and moved its operations to Holland the following year. A line of heavy duty truck parts were purchased from Sloan Valve Company of Franklin Park, Illinois, which were also moved to Holland. A reorganization by MascoTech resulted in BLD acquiring the aftermarket portion of McGuane Industries, major product lines including transmission modulators, choke thermostats, in 1992. Production equipment moved to Holland from Corunna, Michigan.

To supplement the heavy duty truck parts purchased from Sloan Valve Company, the brass fuel cap business of Lincoln Brass Works, Inc. of Detroit was purchased in 1993. Two years later the company acquired Novo Products Inc., a manufacturer of PCV valves. Production continues at its Ocala, Florida, plant with administration provided from Holland. Production of a line of dash pots, throttle kickers and vacuum motors was moved to Holland in 1995 from Saturn Electronics and Engineering.

Currently BLD Products employs more than 200 people, most of them at its beautifully landscaped facility in Holland. Those employees, Dirkse readily admits, have been the major factor in his company's success - "absolutely nothing could have been done without those people."

Boeve Oil Company

Human nature being little different in the late 1920s than today, a large crowd of Holland residents had flocked to the scene of the fire at the Boeve farm on 48th Street south of the city near the present site of the Lifesavers plant. But this was no ordinary conflagration. While filling the 15,000 gallon Pure Oil gasoline tanks from a railroad tanker, the tank had overflowed and a spark from the pump engine set it afire. The blaze burned for about half an hour while the curious gathered when suddenly the cast iron top of the tank blew up and a jet of flames shot 300 feet into the air. Hysterical women ran screaming with children in their arms. Russell A. Boeve, co-owner of the bulk oil facility, never forgot fireman Andrew Klomparens yelling as he ran "legs don't fail me now." Boeve's wife ran so fast she lost a shoe. Fortunately the fiery liquid was consumed in the air and no one was hurt. The damage to the facility was covered by insurance

Founder Russell A. Boeve hand carried five-gallon buckets of fuel oil to customer's tanks in the 1930s.

and that near catastrophe proved but a memorable pyrotechnic interlude in the Boeve Oil Company annals.

Russell Albert Boeve had been born on the family farm in 1902, one of 14 siblings. Childhood memories included the 1 3/4 mile walk to the country schoolhouse, inspecting periodic train wrecks on the nearby Pere Marquette tracks and plenty of hard chores on the farm. After he left high school he worked until he was 21-years-old on the farm of cousin Nick Dykhuis for $60 a month, the highest wage paid among any of the area hired hands.

In 1926, Boeve entered the oil business, forming a partnership with Dykhuis, Art Boeve and John Boeve. They constructed a bulk storage plant on a side track across the road from the Boeve homestead. There, petroleum products from Texas and Oklahoma were delivered by rail. A Model T Ford truck with a 400 gallon tank and a supply of five gallon buckets completed their stock of equipment. It was no easy matter to merchandise gasoline to area farmers in those days. The product had to be lugged in buckets to rural gas tanks and threshing rigs.

Shortly after that the partners, then known as the Main Oil Company, purchased a little two pump gas station and garage on Lincoln Avenue, about one block south of 32nd Street. Russell and Art Boeve took turns driving the delivery truck and manning the station.

In 1928 Russell Boeve paused briefly from his hard work to marry Antoinette Schrotenboer. She survives as proud matriarch of the Boeve family. After the big fire destroyed their storage plant, the Boeves sought a new location closer to Holland. They purchased the site on Lincoln Avenue which still remains their main office. Beginning in 1929 the Great Depression brought hard times for everyone. At the station the Boeves bartered chickens, potatoes, beef and other commodities for gasoline. They survived those bleak days and even prospered.

Beginning in 1931 the Boeves branched into Kalamazoo. After selling the business to the Pure Oil Company in 1935, they bought it back a few years later. By the early 1940s the company operated 20 stations in Holland and another 20 in Kalamazoo. The World War II years brought gasoline rationing stamps and scrap drives. The Boeves did their bit on the home front by gathering great piles of used tires for the war effort. Following the war, the Boeves built a state-of-the-art $20,000 gas station on the northeast corner of 8th Street and Columbia Avenue where they operated under the motto "We Serve Cars from Bumper to Bumper."

Russell's son Paul Boeve, who had started working part time in the gas station while in high school in the late 1940s entered the fuel oil delivery business after graduation. He witnessed the company phase out the majority of its gas stations to concentrate on supplying industrial and commercial petroleum users. In 1950, the Boeves discontinued Pure Oil products and began supplying Mobil Oil products, their current brand.

Over the succeeding decades the Boeve Oil Company expanded to include: Geerlings Oil in Zeeland, part ownership of the Ottawa Oil Co. and the industrial oil business of Superior Oil Co. of Muskegon. In 1975 the Boeves purchased the Cook Oil Co. of Allegan. Paul Boeve, Jr. started with the company then, in the office of the Allegan facility. In the 1980s, the Boeves branched into oil recycling, developing procedures for cleaning hydraulic oils and returning them to use, thereby benefiting the environment. In 1995 the Boeves also added the Wedge Oil Co. of Allegan to their holdings. Currently the Boeve Oil Co. numbers 27 employees, seven delivery trucks and state-of-the-art facilities equipped with computers and other technological marvels.

The Bradford Company

The Bradford family's association with the Holland area began during the first decade of the 20th century - the golden age of the resort industry. Then scores of Chicagoans, including L. Frank Baum, originator of *The Wizard of Oz*, sought refuge from the hectic pace of big city life by spending their summers at Macatawa Park. William J. Bradford's family eagerly looked forward to climbing aboard one of the big steamers that carried them from Chicago to the cottage they rented at Macatawa.

Bradford had established with a younger partner a company that produced fancy cardboard partitions used to separate and cushion candy in boxes. Tragically, Bradford died in 1923. Using the life insurance settlement, his wife and son bought out the partner's interest. William J. Bradford, Jr., then brought his brother-in-law into the business, and later a younger brother, Charles L. Bradford.

In 1924, Mrs. Bradford, Sr., purchased her own cottage at Macatawa. The earliest recollections of Judson T. Bradford, born in 1928 and who would later head the firm, were of delightful times spent amid the sand and surf at his grandmother's cottage.

manufacturing - such as, zinc die-cast chrome-plated parts that needed to be protected from scuffing. These partitions were made out of cardboard, which offered a light weight and less expensive alternative to traditional corrugated boxboard dividers.

The business in Holland grew under its first manager, Bradford's son, William J. Bradford III. But when he resigned, his brother Jud who had begun a career in St. Paul, Minnesota, obeyed his father's summons and joined him in Holland in 1956. For 20 years he worked at the 16th Street plant, becoming president of the firm in 1973.

Two years later, wishing to expand beyond that location's capacity, he purchased a 30 acre tract on the then rural northside and in July 1976, the company moved into its newly constructed factory.

Around 1984 a major turning point in the company development came with the automobile industry's decision to replace expendable paper board packaging with returnable, reusable material handling systems. The company decided to battle what was clearly a threat to its future by "rolling up its sleeves and jumping into the fray full force." It

**The Bradford Company moved to its plant at 13500 Quincy Street in 1976.
Over the succeeding two decades it was enlarged several times.**

W.J. Bradford Paper Company managed to survive the Great Depression of the 1930s. Among its customers was the Hollander Co. which produced chocolate covered cherry candies at a factory on the corner of 16th Street and Van Raalte in Holland. Jud Bradford never forgot the wide-eyed wonder with which as a boy he viewed the huge vats of chocolate in that factory.

World War II brought demands of conversion to production of packaging for the war effort. Following the war came another spurt of growth. In the early 1940s William J. Bradford, Jr., and his wife had purchased their own cottage at Macatawa through Henry Maentz, president of the Holland City Bank. When Bradford sought to expand the business by establishing a second plant in Holland in 1951, Maentz sold him the same building that had previously housed the Hollander Candy Co.

In 1951 when Bradford Paper Co. started at its new location, it had but few customers. It began specializing in constructing box partitions to cushion parts used in automobile

became the pioneer packaging company to do so in the United States. The outcome was the development of its "Just In Time" system of customized reusable shipping containers. The company, which shortened its name to Bradford Company, also established an aggressive continuous improvement program. In 1995 alone the company achieved an amazing 1,100 documented improvements in product designs, manufacturing methods and operating procedures.

In March 1996, Jud Bradford became chairman of the board of the company, turning over the reins of management to his sons Thomas R. and Judson A.

Bradford credits his employees with the company's continuing success. In 1971, the Bradford Co. began rewarding employees by sharing costs savings through bonuses. Beginning in 1987 the company established an employee stock ownership plan. As Jud Bradford has often said "every person here is absolutely necessary and we can not continue to be successful without you."

City of Holland

Holland City Hall, constructed in 1911, is being restored to its original splendor for the 1997 Sesquicentennial Celebration.

Mayor Albert McGeehan warms to his subject when he speaks about Holland's heritage. An author and scholar of the area's past and a 30 year veteran of the high school classroom where he taught generations of Holland students their American roots, the mayor knows well the lessons history offers. And from his perspective: "The greatest challenge the city faces is how well it will assimilate the diverse ethnic population being drawn to Holland to partake in the fruits of its success." Fortunately, Holland can look to its century and a half record of overcoming adversity and solving problems through joint efforts as a guide to surmounting the challenges of the future.

When the Rev. Albertus Van Raalte led a ragtag band of followers to the wintery wilderness that was Holland in 1847 the most pressing challenge was survival. Ignorant of frontier skills such as log cabin building, hunting and living off the land, the settlers suffered that winter through lack of shelter and food. The following summer brought hordes of biting insects including malarial mosquitoes. Others perished from a smallpox epidemic that raced through the colony. So many colonists died the first year that one of the original community projects was the building of an orphanage. Luckily the orphans were adopted and the structure served instead as the first schoolhouse. Through perseverance and hard work Holland survived those first "bitter times." By 1849 thousands of other immigrants had arrived in Ottawa County and 236 houses dotted the city's sandy streets.

The city had been officially platted by Allegan County Surveyor E.B. Bassett in 1847. From the start River Street and 8th Street became the main arteries and their intersection the heart of downtown. Holland Township was also organized that year, but because the immigrants had not been in the state long enough to become naturalized citizens they could not vote until 1850. Instead, under Van Raalte's leadership they held town meetings where they discussed issues and developed ways and means to work together to solve their common problems apart from the regular political channels.

Among the most pressing needs once they had shelter over their heads was to establish a source for the local economy. Early efforts included grist and sawmills and the sale of tanbark and wood ashes. They were hampered in those efforts by the lack of a decent harbor. The sand bar at the mouth of the river prevented commercial vessels from entering. After petitioning the state and federal government for assistance failed the Hollanders turned to their own resourcefulness. In 1858 citizens in Holland, Zeeland, Overisel and Fillmore townships voted to tax themselves to fund harbor improvements and they built it themselves. By the fall of 1859 Holland Harbor was able to accommodate large great lakes ships which ushered in a era of steady economic growth.

Following the Civil War, in which Holland volunteers distinguished themselves through their bravery, the city had grown so that it required a government organization beyond that supplied by the township. In 1867 Holland incorporated as a city. Isaac Cappon, a local leather entrepreneur, served as the first mayor.

Amid another economic boost brought by the recent arrival of two railroad lines, the city suffered the worst setback in its history in 1871. On the same day as the Chicago Fire a fierce fire fanned by gale force winds left most of the city in ashes. Two days later at a citizen's committee that met in City Hall to coordinate relief activities Van Raalte announced "with our Dutch tenacity and with our American experience, Holland will be rebuilt." Residents set to work with zeal and the city made a dramatic comeback. In September of the following year Holland staged a gala celebration marking its 25th anniversary attended by a crowd of 5,000.

In 1876, months before Van Raalte's death, citizens created Centennial Park that continues as a shade-covered oasis and focus of civic pride. The year 1884 witnessed completion of a fashionable Italianate brick city hall, fire station and city library that still stands on 8th Street. The 1880s brought the beginnings of a tourist industry that would make the city and outlying resorts a mecca for generations of Chicago residents in particular. During the 1890s the city aggressively wooed new factories and by the first decade of the 20th century Holland boasted a diverse manufacturing base that included the production of cigars, pickles, mirrors, furniture, furnaces and shoes.

The decade of the 1890s also saw the city launch a unique experiment that would evolve into the Board of Public Works. Set up as a separate organization with its own fiscal accountability, the board first implemented a municipal electrical plant in 1894 then a water system in 1895 followed by the beginnings of a sanitary sewer system in 1899. Over the decades the board would modernize and expand its capacity with the first sewage treatment plant in 1925, the state-of-the-art James De Young generating station in 1940 and a plant to treat water pumped from Lake Michigan in 1957. Over the years profits generated through the sale of utilities were returned to citizens by helping to fund the hospital, fire department apparatus, school needs and park improvements, by assisting the city's general fund thereby lowering the tax burden and many other community projects.

Under Mayor Jacob B. Van Putten the city adopted a new charter in 1907 that changed its government to the alderman form with two aldermen elected from each of the five city wards. Four years later the new city hall with its marble stairway paneled with fine wood and the public library on the second floor opened on River Street.

In response to a suggestion made by Lida Rogers, a biology teacher, the city planted tulip bulbs imported from the Netherlands along streets and in parks in 1928. By 1930 some 50,000 tourists were being attracted to the Tulip Festival. Throughout the 1930s the festival grew to incorporate costumed dancers, street scrubbing and marching bands. By 1938 annual attendance reached a half million. The festival was suspended during World War II. Beginning in 1946 it again lured hundreds of thousands of visitors each May. It continues to form an important segment of the local economy and of fund raising opportunities for community groups. Despite the Depression that took its toll on local industry in the late 1930s, the city in concert with the Chamber of Commerce succeeded in diversifying its industrial roll by convincing Chris Craft and a shoe company to relocate to Holland.

In 1950, the city adopted a new charter which gave it a city manager form of government. Four years later the Civic Center opened at the former site of an abandoned leather factory. In 1960 the public library moved from city hall to a new building on River Street named in honor of Ray Herrick, a former Holland native whose generosity made the structure possible. Following the extension of utilities to portions of adjacent townships, the late 1950s witnessed the annexation of neighborhoods that increased the city's area to 14 square miles. By 1960 the city's population had jumped from 15,858 to 24,916 over the decade.

In 1962 the Holland Economic Development Corporation was formed as a an affiliate of the Chamber of Commerce. HEDCOR created industrial parks south and north of the city. The success of HEDCOR and the city government in attracting new industries and retaining manufacturing operations started by local entrepreneurs which developed into global competitors transformed Holland from an ethnic enclave to one of the state's fastest growing and most prosperous communities.

But the rapid growth of shopping malls, commercial strip developments and suburban residential developments fueled by the automobile culture threatened the continued vitality of Holland's historic downtown core. In response, the city created a Downtown Development Authority (DDA) in 1978. Six years later the city received designation as a "Main Street" community and it began receiving technical support from the National Main Street Center and the Michigan Department of Commerce. In 1988 the city accomplished a $3 million Streetscape Project which refurbished and beautified the downtown and included an innovative subterranean snowmelt system. Other projects which revitalized the downtown included the restoration and adaptive reuse of the historic post office building as a museum, the transportation depot, City Hall, the Town Park and Window on the Waterfront plan. The private sector participated with projects ranging from construction of architecturally appropriate new structures, the restoration of historic properties such as the Knickerbocker Theater and the development of the Freedom Village campus. In 1995 the Strategic Planning Committee was formed with representatives from various downtown organizations to create "a comprehensive vision for downtown." Its report, "Broadening the Vision," which outlined a strategic framework for future downtown development was adopted by the City Council in late 1995.

The Windmill Island Project, an initiative begun in 1995 to invigorate that part of the city, includes a world trade center. Another element of Holland's emerging global focus came with the designation of Queretaro, Mexico, as a sister city in 1996 in recognition of the increasingly important role taken by the area's Hispanic citizens.

Holland received national recognition for its civic accomplishments in June 1996 when it was chosen as one of ten All-America Cities by the National Civic League because of its innovative ways of solving community problems.

The All America City Presentation Team returned from Texas, June 16, 1996, with the Holland All America City Award in hand.

Davenport College

It began in 1990 with a wave of the hand and a simple question, "Well, how about here?" Don Maine, president of Davenport College, and Prince Corporation CEO John Spoelhof had been driving around Holland while discussing the need for a local business college campus. The Prince Corporation placed a high value on practical training and business education applicable to the job and while Davenport had been offering a smattering of such courses in various Holland area facilities since 1974 many prospective students still faced the obstacle of long evening drives after work to the Grand Rapids campus. That's when Spoelhof pointed to a vacant 10-acre field adjacent the Prince Tech Center on Waverly Road and suggested an innovative partnership between business and education.

The Davenport College Campus at 643 South Waverly Road.

The two institutions worked quickly to cement that relationship. Ground breaking for the campus took place in January 1992. By September the Byron Center-based Dykhouse Construction Inc., had completed an architecturally dazzling two-story, 32,000 square-foot structure containing 15 classrooms, an 8,000 volume library, state-of-the-art computer labs, seminar facilities and an innovative learning center designed to help students acquire special skills via one on one tutors and computers. When classes opened on September 21, 1992, more than 600 students had enrolled. A staff of 24 and some 40 adjunct professors offered customized education and training tailored to the needs of local businesses as well as a nearly 60 practical day and evening classes.

The Holland facility was the 11th campus of the educational institution that traces its origins to 1866. German immigrant and Civil War veteran Conrad Swensburg founded the Grand Rapids Business College that year on the site now occupied by the Grand Rapids Public Library. The original 16 students studied bookkeeping, business law, penmanship and arithmetic in a single classroom, with tuition as little as $5.00 a semester.

Swensburg retired in 1891, turning the management of the college over to staff member Aaron Parrish. Unfortunately Parrish proved a poor administrator, the once dynamic college deteriorated and in 1910 he absconded with the institution's bank roll and was never seen again in Grand Rapids. That is when a young instructor named Michael E. Davenport came to the rescue. He and his brother purchased the college's assets for $500 and saved it from oblivion. Year by year the Davenports rebuilt the curriculum, attracting more students and recapturing its esteem.

By 1918, when the school was renamed Davenport Business Institute, enrollment had climbed from 10 to 150. Six years later it became the Davenport-McLachlan Business University. During the Depression, Davenport recognized the need for a four year college for area students without the means to leave Grand Rapids. In 1935, he established a separate institute, the Grand Rapids College of Applied Science, later renamed the University of Grand Rapids. In 1945 that campus was sold and it became Aquinas College.

The original business college was named Davenport Institute in 1948. Under Robert W. Sneden, who became president following Davenport's death in 1959, the college began offering associate's degrees and was granted North Central accreditation. When Sneden retired in 1977, enrollment at the renamed Davenport College had climbed from 250 to 1,900.

Maine succeeded Sneden as president and under his leadership the college launched a dramatic expansion campaign. A Lansing campus was opened in 1979 and two years later Parson's Business College of Kalamazoo, which also dates back to the 1860s, merged with Davenport. Other campuses followed in Battle Creek, South Bend and Merrillville, Indiana. With the acquisition of the Detroit College of Business and its campuses in Dearborn, Flint and Warren in 1985, Davenport became the largest independent college in Michigan.

When the Holland Campus opened in 1992, Davenport employed 1,500 at its 11 campuses with a total enrollment of 14,000 students. Under Dean Tom Carey's leadership enrollment at the Holland campus grew to more than 1,000 in three years. In 1995, Carey retired to be succeeded by Al Wetherell. Davenport continues to develop its special relationship with the Prince Corporation and other area businesses and to offer Holland area students, an opportunity to learn and advance.

Dell Engineering, Inc.

Amidst a gala celebration to mark the nation's bicentennial in 1976 came a growing consciousness by many Americans that all was not right with "mother earth." The decades of unbridled industrial activity had taken their toll in the form of water, soil and air pollution. In concert with the beginnings of the environmental movement, in 1976 Leroy and Cheryl Dell launched Western Michigan Environmental Services, Inc. (WMESI), a pioneering venture to offer environmental engineering and environmental analytical work.

Leroy Dell had grown up in the Montcalm County community of Stanton and Cheryl hailed from nearby Sidney, the heart of a region settled in the 19th Century by Danes. Their descendants nurtured hard working, ethical traits, not unlike those of the Dutch who pioneered Holland. That cultural similarity would be one of the factors that motivated the Dells to locate in Holland.

Dell had started working at the age of seven with his father, a Montcalm County engineer, helping him survey roads. Following graduation from high school he entered a state highway department training program. After earning engineering degrees from Ferris College and, in 1966, Michigan State University, Dell gravitated toward the field of water and waste water treatment.

For ten years beginning in 1968 he worked for an Ann Arbor-based engineering firm, spending most of his time near Holland while serving as the resident engineer for treatment plants in Grand Rapids, South Haven, Muskegon and elsewhere.

As WMESI received strong support from area businesses additional employees were hired to handle an expanded customer base, in 1978 Dell was faced with a major career choice. He could either leave Holland and advance up the corporate ladder or stay in the area he had learned to love. Fortunately he chose the latter. That year he founded Dell Engineering as a sole proprietorship to incorporate his engineering expertise with the analytical and sampling services provided by WMESI.

As the business expanded the two companies moved from their original 600 square-foot facility on East 10th Street to a 10,000 square-foot former furniture factory at 146 South River Avenue in 1980. Continued growth and the development of additional capabilities such as water and waste-water services, solid waste management, instrumentation repair, installation and calibration and treatability studies necessitated another move. In 1984 the two firms, then comprising a staff of 15 professionals, relocated to a 15,000 square-foot former roller skating rink on Lakewood Blvd.

During the 1980s Dell Engineering completed such notable projects as the massive Bil Mar Wastewater Treatment System, several solid waste recycling systems and a host of industrial treatment systems for air, water and waste. Several projects beneficial to the communities were completed, such as the conversion of a former junk yard in Ann Arbor to a non-profit office complex and home of the Michigan Artrain, the reclaimed waterfront project in Muskegon known as Heritage Landing and other adaptive reuses of once worthless land containing hazardous properties.

Increasing federal, state and local environmental regulations also brought continued growth throughout the 1980s. As more businesses sought their environmental consulting services the staff grew to 23 employees by 1986. That year the two firms were restructured with Dell Engineering becoming a corporation while full ownership of WMESI was transferred to Cheryl Dell.

With the advent of the 1990s came an increasing need to provide a comfortable and attractive work environment for employees in a building that could be adapted to the varying operations of the two firms. In April 1991, David VerBurg and Associates was commissioned to design a new building on a lot in the Northside Industrial Park. Exactly one year later the two firms moved into a beautifully landscaped 32,000 square foot facility, housing state-of-the-art laboratories and modern offices. That same year the Holland Area Chamber of Commerce honored Leroy Dell with its Small Businessperson of the Year Award.

By 1996 Dell Engineering, Inc. and WMESI had grown to a combined professional staff of 85 employees offering a comprehensive variety of civil and municipal engineering, structural and geotechnical engineering, facilities engineering, process design, contract operations and management of water and wastewater facilities, environmental consulting services, aquatic toxicology testing and analytical laboratory services.

The Dell Engineering Corporate Office at 3352 128th Avenue.

Donnelly Corporation

It's a long leap from ornate hand-etched mirrors to "intelligent glass," capable of performing sophisticated tasks, but for a company that has done business in every decade of the 20th Century while winning recognition as one of America's best companies to work for - it was all in a day's work.

Founded in 1905 as the Kinsella Glass Co., its original work force of 40 made mirrors for the thriving Holland area furniture industry. In an era when massive oak sideboards and curved glass china cabinets were the height of fashion the company crafted huge, bevelled glass mirrors sometimes decorated with detailed hand-ground designs.

When Bernard Donnelly took over management of the company in 1910 it became the Donnelly-Kelley Glass Co. The decade of the 1920s witnessed hard times for the local furniture factories. Donnelly responded to this changing market by diversifying into the automobile industry, producing oval rear windows for touring cars.

When Bernard Donnelly died in 1932 his widow Mary became president of the company. Their son John F. Donnelly, who had studied engineering at Notre Dame prior to entering a seminary to become a priest, returned to Holland to help his mother run the company. By the late 1930s he became treasurer and later would take over as president.

Donnelly survived the Depression because of its reputation for skilled glass grinding, cutting, polishing and silvering, and its emphasis on quality and customer service. That tradition of excellence would continue as a company hallmark and a source of strength during the succeeding decades.

World War II brought conversion to military needs and the company produced aerial gunsight reflectors and precision parts for tank periscopes. During the war Donnelly grew adept at producing high volume glass components at very precise tolerances and it learned new techniques such as vacuum coating glass for varying reflection ranges.

After the war, Donnelly sought other markets including windshields and side windows for locally made Chris-Craft boats. Over the next two decades the company established itself as a leading supplier of a variety of interior and exterior automobile mirror components by adapting its core technology of glass processing to more sophisticated mass production techniques such as diamond grinding wheels and the vacuum coating process.

In 1952 Donnelly became one of the first American companies to embrace the concept of participative management when it applied the principles developed by MIT Professor Joseph Scanlon. Over the decades the company modified and bettered the plan to encourage employees to achieve their highest potential and to provide a work environment best suited to commitment and productivity. Currently, employee teams discuss work design issues, solve problems together and make decisions regarding equity issues while enjoying competitive wages, benefits and a Scanlon profit sharing bonus plan.

In the early 1950s Donnelly laid the foundation for expansion into the European automobile market. In 1968 the company established a major foothold when it established Donnelly Mirrors, LtD., in Naas, Ireland. Ultimately Donnelly would expand its international market to 30 nations and 30% of its total sales.

In the 1970s the company achieved a major technological breakthrough when it developed plastic molding skills. This led to its invention of modular windows for the automotive market in 1974. Between 1965 and 1975 total company sales grew from $3 million to $18 million. Modular window sales alone rose to more than $100 million in 1992.

In 1984, Donnelly Mirrors, Inc., became Donnelly Corporation. During the 1980s the company continued to develop innovative mirror assemblies and window systems. Following development of another core technology, electronics, it began manufacturing electronic lighting systems, compasses and indicator displays. The company also began a significant new business venture - coated glass used for liquid crystal displays and other specialty coatings for the computer industry.

Donnelly has continued to grow throughout the 1990s, and now employs 5,000 people in nine countries around the world. Still a leader in the development of new technologies, Donnelly is at the forefront of exciting new innovations such as low-cost diffractive optics and "smart glass," which holds enormous potential for use in vehicles and buildings. Last year, Donnelly had more than $600 million in total sales to customers worldwide.

The Donnelly Corporation's new interior mirror plant in Holland.

Drawform

The story behind Drawform began more than 40 years ago in the Mississippi River town of Quincy, Illinois. It was then and there that a high school machine shop course opened young Ron Griffith's eyes to his life's work. Griffith continued his education at a tool and die trade school in St. Louis, and then he began an apprenticeship at Drawn Metal Products near Chicago. During his nine years there, he rose to the position of plant production manager.

In 1970 Griffith joined two associates from Drawn Metal Products who had followed their entrepreneurial dreams to Holland, where they established Trans-Matic Company. Six years later, Griffith founded Drawform Stamping. He knew for his dreams to become reality, he had to produce a quality product and find a niche for the company. Consequently, Drawform Stamping took on the tough jobs that its competitors could not or would not.

At that time, Drawform Stamping was hardly cutting edge technology. It operated from 2,500 square-feet of rent-

Stamping hallmark. By 1977, ten employees were in place, and the company increasingly focused on deep draw stamping. Two years later, its name officially changed to Drawform.

In 1980, with seven presses and 20 employees, Drawform moved into a new 10,000 square-foot facility in Zeeland's Industrial Park. In 1985, an expansion to 32,000 square-feet allowed for the introduction of larger high tonnage presses, high-tech support equipment, and computers – all of which enabled Drawform to handle more complicated and challenging projects. The work force grew to 85 employees.

As Drawform gained a national reputation for developing complex, tight tolerated parts, it grew rapidly. By 1993, it was utilizing five separate buildings: a fragmented situation which did not enhance its emphasis on teamwork and the cell manufacturing concept. So, planning began on a "greenfield" facility to create a plant that would streamline product flow without compromising quality. In the interim, Draw-

Drawform's new 200,000 square-foot facility at 500 North Fairview in Zeeland was completed in 1995. (photo by Vito Palmisano)

ed space with two eyelet presses, a grinder, lathe and air compressor. An extension cord from a neighboring business supplied power, a semi-trailer served as the warehouse, and a '65 Chevy truck made deliveries. But what the company lacked in equipment, it made up for in determination.

Griffith hit the road with a bag full of samples, traveling wherever he had to go for business. It steadily paid off, thanks to early successes such as a project involving a microphone connector part. Drawform Stamping devised a method to produce the piece as one stamping, eliminating several secondary operations and attendant costs for the client. From that and similar experiences, Griffith realized that "next to its employees, customers are what makes an operation work." Customer service soon became a Drawform

form's growth continued unabated, with 141 million deep drawn stamped parts shipped (90 percent to the automotive industry) in 1994.

In July 1995, Drawform's nearly 250 highly skilled employees moved into a 200,000 square-foot, state-of-the-art facility at 500 North Fairview in Zeeland. Aided by its new plant containing the biggest and finest machinery and computers, production increased to 131 different types of products for 47 companies around the world.

In 1996, the desire for success sparked in a high school machine shop class remains alive and well — with plans to double Drawform's manufacturing capacity by the year 2001.

145

Elhart Dealerships

Ken Elhart's eyes still light up when he recalls the first new car he sold - a 1950 Ford Crestline, a two-tone, brown colored, chrome-plated beauty. Back then some models of Fords sold for around $1,000 new and it was no curiosity for a Holland area automobile buyer to count out carefully hoarded green backs and drive off the lot in a fully paid-for new vehicle. Now nearly a half century later technological change has wrought an entirely new automobile market and the dealership Elhart founded sells an amazing 3,000 new and used cars annually.

Born in Holland, Elhart had moved at the age of three with his family back to his mother's homestead north of Lowell when his father lost his job as a traveling salesman to the effects of the Depression. He grew up amid the hard lonely work on the farm and graduated from Lowell High School. Following the war his father, Ted Elhart, decided the family would return to Holland.

Ken Elhart was the first to make the move, taking a job at Vrieling Motor Sales, the Ford agency at 159 River Avenue, in January 1948. His original responsibilities were to pick up and deliver parts for customers. The following year R.E. Barber purchased the agency. From 1950-1953 Elhart took time off from his automotive career to serve a stint in the U.S. Coast Guard during the Korean War. Returning to R.E. Barber Ford, Elhart worked his way up to become sales manager from 1955 to 1965.

By 1965 the time had come to strike out and establish his own dealership. There were some Ford dealerships available but none in the Holland area and that is where he wanted to stay and raise his family. Then in March of that year when the Mutual Pontiac and GMC truck dealership at 150 E. 8th Street became available Elhart opted to make a "big emotional jump" from Ford to Pontiac. The Elharts sold their home to use the equity to finance the purchase of the dealership and he, wife Barbara and sons Wayne and Jeff moved to a rental unit.

That risk paid off thanks in part to community support and the backing of local businessmen who wanted to see Elhart succeed. Elhart and his eight employees were soon selling scores of GMC trucks and the popular high performance wide track Pontiac GTOs. Four years later Elhart added the American Motors franchise to his dealerships and transport trucks began unloading AMC Hornets and later Gremlins at the 8th Street sales lot.

On January 1, 1970, Elhart moved to a new facility, formerly a crop field on Chicago Drive. The firm's 20 employees began showing customers shiny new Pontiac Catalinas and Bonnevilles. That fall Elhart hired a used car manager and began concentrating on the sale of used cars of all makes and that evolved into a major aspect of the business.

In 1971 Elhart became one of the first in the area to sell van conversion models with custom interiors. But 1971 also brought a long GMC strike that crippled production and left Elhart facing the huge debt load of his new building with cars unavailable. The dealership survived but that experience convinced Elhart of the need to diversify further. In 1975 he added the Jeep franchise to his business.

Three years later came a 7,000 square foot expansion to the body shop and service department, which then numbered 21 service stalls and 11 body shop stalls. The Elhart work force had climbed to 35 employees.

The decade of the 1980s saw the second generation of Elharts enter the business full time. As teenagers Wayne and Jeff had worked for their father, mowing the lawn and washing cars. Following their graduation from Holland High School in 1972 and 1976 respectively, college degrees and the experience of working elsewhere, they returned to Holland. In 1985, Jeff became manager of the newly acquired Elhart Dodge franchise and Wayne the manager of Elhart Pontiac GMC Jeep-Eagle.

In the spring of 1987 Elhart moved into another new facility adjacent the lot on Chicago Drive. Two years later a 10 year campaign to secure the Nissan franchise finally paid off and with the completion of a $350,000 expansion scores of Maximas and Sentras found eager buyers.

In 1990 Jeff and Wayne took over as presidents and general managers of Elhart Dodge Nissan and Elhart Pontiac GMC Jeep-Eagle. By 1996 total employment numbered 124. Ken Elhart continues to serve the firm he started in a consulting capacity, especially in long range planning. Proud of the employees, past and present, and the family's many accomplishments, he is fortunate enough to be able to say that "if he had his life to live over he would do the same thing."

Founder Ken Elhart with sons, Wayne (left), president and general manager of Elhart Pontiac GMC Jeep Eagle, Inc., and Jeff, president and general manager of Elhart Dodge Nissan, Inc.

First of America Bank - Michigan, N.A.

The year was 1878. The "colony" established by the Rev. Albertus Van Raalte in 1847 had grown into a vibrant young city, despite almost complete destruction by fire seven years before. Yet among the many factories and other commercial enterprises that made the city bustle with activity one major institution was lacking - a bank. But before the year had ended Jacob Van Putten remedied that by establishing a private bank at 30 West 8th Street which "at once secured a large number of accounts and became popular with the businessmen of the city."

In 1890, Van Putten incorporated his bank under state law with a capital of $37,000. Two years later the Holland City State Bank moved into its new building at the corner of Eighth Street and River Avenue. The handsome three story structure constructed of Waverly sandstone from a local quarry included a tower containing the city clock. The bank offered three months certificates of deposit that paid 3% interest. By the turn-of-the century, Dirk Van Raalte, Civil War hero and son of the city's founder, became the bank's president.

Holland's second bank began when the First State Bank was incorporated on December 26, 1889. Isaac Cappon, wealthy proprietor of a local leather factory, served as the bank's first president. Within two years the First State Banks's accounts included "the names of many of the leading manufacturers, mill owners, and merchants of Holland and vicinity, while in the savings department, which this bank makes a specialty, there are over 600 depositors." By 1912, Gerrit J. Diekema, a prominent politician known as "Holland's premier orator," served as the bank's president.

The Great Depression that began in 1929 brought the biggest threat to its survival that the American banking system would face. "Runs on the bank" coupled with lax regulations and less than adequate reserves caused the failures of hundreds of banks across the nation. On February 14, 1933, Michigan Governor William A. Comstock ordered every bank in the state closed for eight days - a bank holiday, he called it. Then President Franklin Roosevelt declared a four day national bank holiday effective March 6th. On March 9, 1933, Congress passed the Emergency Banking Relief Act which succeeded in checking the national panic.

The First of America Bank-Michigan, N. A. at One West 8th Street.

Throughout this dark era, when bank depositors wondered if they would ever see their life's savings again, the Holland City State Bank and the First State Bank remained relatively strong and stable. Even a daring robbery of the First State Bank in September 1932 that witnessed more than 100 bullets fired, a high speed escape by a gang and a loss of $73,164.10 did not diminish the community's faith.

In November 1936, Holland's original two banks merged and the newly named Holland State Bank opened on December 3rd at the former location of the First State Bank, One West Eighth Street. Henry S. Maentz, a prominent civic booster who had headed the First State Bank, assumed the presidency of the new institution.

The Holland State Bank changed its charter from a state to a national bank in 1946 and became the First National Bank of Holland. On March 26, 1973, the First National Financial Corporation (now First of America Bank Corporation) acquired the bank as an affiliate. The bank later developed a trust department and changed its name to First National Bank & Trust Company of Holland. Past presidents include: Donald J. Thomas (1973-77), Robert F. Bishop (1977-82), and Timothy R. Taylor (1982-91).

In 1983, First of America Bank became the common name for all affiliates of First of America Bank Corporation to reinforce its region wide posture and provide a sense of continuity and unity to all of its member banks.

During 1991, the bank went through several mergers to link up with a much larger regional bank known as First of America Bank - West Michigan. This enabled the bank to serve a much broader base of customers while still maintaining the community bank spirit and ideal. Philip J. Koning, born and raised in Holland, has served as Community Bank President since 1991. The final evolution of First of America came in late 1995 when all Michigan regional banks merged into one statewide bank under the name First of America Bank-Michigan, N.A, As part of a $23 billion holding company, the bank maintains five offices in the Holland community and one in nearby Zeeland. Ranked as one of the largest holding companies in the midwest, First of America is a full-service bank offering a wide variety of products and services to cater to the needs of its customers.

First Michigan Bank Corporation

First Michigan Bank Corporation founder Jacob Den Herder died in 1916. But if he could return today to west Michigan, where he emigrated from the Netherlands in 1847, he would scarcely believe his eyes. He and his fellow colonists had labored hard to convert a wilderness into thriving farmland. That once-rural acreage is now laced by modern roads and is sprouting residential and commercial developments in place of agricultural crops.

But even more incomprehensible would seem the growth of his bank. In 80 years his single office in downtown Zeeland has burgeoned into 14 community bank affiliates, with 87 FMB banking locations stretching from Niles, near the Indiana border, to Sault Ste. Marie, a stone's throw from Canada.

Den Herder started his private bank in 1878, operating out of a rented desk in the back of a Zeeland clothing store. By 1900, when he incorporated as Zeeland State Bank, deposits had grown to $200,000. Following Den Herder's death, Frank Boonstra became the bank president, but he was succeeded in 1924 by the founder's son, Christian Jacob Den Herder. He would be the second of four generations of the Den Herder family to head the bank. Under Christian's leadership the institution continued to grow and, unlike

by Holland. However, it did not prevent FMB from building its East Town branch on Eighth Street, literally a few feet outside the Holland city line. FMB also established several branches in Holland Township, helping to fuel the growth of Holland's "north side." After the restrictions were dropped, FMB located its personal banking offices at the Curtis Center in downtown Holland.

Another change in banking laws fueled FMB's statewide expansion. Robert J. Den Herder became the fourth member of his family to serve as bank president when he succeeded Vanden Bosch in 1967. In 1973, the First Michigan Bank Corporation was formed under new bank holding company laws, with the Zeeland bank as the lead affiliate of the corporation. FMB started a bank in the Grand Rapids area and acquired other community banks around Michigan, adding the "FMB" prefix to their names but retaining a large measure of local identity and authority.

Robert Den Herder was succeeded as CEO of the corporation by David Ondersma in 1984, and three years later the company reached $1 billion in total assets. By 1992, when FMB moved into its new corporate headquarters on Adams Street in Holland Township, its assets totaled $2 billion. FMB passed the $3 billion mark in 1995 as the company con-

The First Michigan Bank corporate headquarters at One Financial Plaza 10717 Adams Street.

many other Michigan banks, successfully weathered the harsh financial times of the Depression. Christian's son Edward followed in his father's footsteps in 1937, becoming at the age of 37 one of the state's youngest bank presidents.

Fire ravaged the bank building the following year, but all customer records, rushed to the vault by employees, survived the flames. The building was restored and is still in use today. Edward Den Herder died in 1952 and was succeeded by Adrian Vanden Bosch, who was at the helm for several bank milestones. In recognition of the new trust department, the bank changed its name to First Michigan Bank and Trust Company in 1958. The first branch offices were opened in Allendale and Hamilton.

At the time, state banking laws prevented banks from establishing branches in any community where another bank was already chartered. While that prevented other banks from coming into Zeeland, it blocked First Michigan Bank from establishing offices within the city limits of near-

tinued to expand and pioneer new services. FMB opened the Holland area's first in-store branch in the new Family Fare supermarket on South Washington Avenue. It was the first Holland bank to establish a presence on the Internet, and in 1996 offered customers the opportunity to bank from home via personal computer.

While technological improvements brought additional convenience to customers, FMB has never abandoned its community banking philosophy, which combines the best attributes of a small community bank, including local decision making and personal service, with the multiple products and operating efficiencies of a large bank. FMB's success, including 14 consecutive years of record earnings and dividends, has been built on knowing the customer and meeting the customer's needs. It's the way Jacob Den Herder did business in 1878, and it's the way First Michigan Bank Corporation does business today.

Freedom Village Holland

The immaculately groomed campus known as Freedom Village sprawls across a 13-acre plat along the Macatawa River northeast of Holland's downtown core. Less than a decade before, the site had been disfigured by dilapidated housing and a crumbling factory building. Now four wings of concrete, brick and steel, seven stories tall, radiate from a central atrium and swimming pool complex. It is fitting that those five interconnected wings are named for the majestic Great Lakes the first letters of which spell the word "homes." And homes are what Freedom Village is about - homes where 500 senior citizens live in spacious apartments featuring spectacular views of the Macatawa River and Windmill Island, interact with one another in activity centers, a library, cafe' and dining rooms while enjoying the peace of mind that comes from "a life-care commitment."

Freedom Village is a friendly place and it came about as the result of a long time friendship between Bill Vanderbilt and Bob Roskamp. Following graduation from the University of Michigan in 1962, Vanderbilt taught high school in a Chicago suburb at New Trier High School. Roskamp taught at a nearby school. They met through attending the same church, and a friendship developed.

Vanderbilt left Illinois in 1967 to launch a teaching career at Hope College where he became chairman of the Physical Education and Athletic department. Roskamp also left the classroom to follow his star in the field of geriatric care. Expanding on his ideas of what was best for senior citizens he began a new concept of retirement community, a "life-care" facility which guaranteed that residents would continue to be provided health care as long as they lived, regardless of deteriorating physical

The atrium of Freedom Village's Lake Michigan Wing.

or financial conditions. Roskamp eventually became the CEO of Freedom Group, manager for eight life-care campuses in Florida, California, Arizona and Michigan in partnership with local investors.

The friendship of Vanderbilt and Roskamp continued over the years despite geographic separation. In 1986 their families enjoyed a North Carolina vacation together. There Vanderbilt became imbued with his friend's sense of mission. Returning to Holland, Vanderbilt contacted the Riverview Development Committee led by Gordon Van Wylen and John Tysse and Ron Boeve of Timber Brook Realty who had been acquiring property on a speculative basis along the

Macatawa River. When putting together a partnership, Roskamp had urged Vanderbilt to identify people who had been doing the most for seniors in the community. Edgar and Elsa Prince, with their involvement in building Evergreen Commons, were logical choices.

Vanderbilt remembered vividly what happened when he presented the proposal to Prince in the fall of 1987, Prince asked a couple of questions and then hitting the table with his fist, exclaimed "Let's do it!" The following week Vanderbilt, Prince and others flew to Florida to view Roskamp's life-care facilities in depth. He found a vital community of active senior citizens without the loneliness so common to retirement homes. Even more enthused with the concept, Vanderbilt assembled a partnership team of himself, Roskamp, Tysse, Boeve, Prince and Van Wylen, a retired Hope College president.

The partners unveiled to the community their plans for Freedom Village in December 1987. Following a favorable feasibility study, a model unit was constructed in November, 1988. A hard fought campaign to secure permission from the Michigan Department of Commerce to market the facility ended with approval in March 1989.

Prospective residents willing to place a $1,000 deposit began flocking from Muskegon, Traverse City, Chicago and 23 states, as well as the Holland environs. They chose from eight different apartment types ranging from a studio to a deluxe two bedroom, three bath, with den. On May 10, 1990, ground was broken for the project. Midway through the sales the partners decided to increase the number of units from 268 to 349 by constructing a fourth wing.

On August 19, 1991, the first residents moved into the dazzling complex that includes an indoor pool and spa, auditorium, library, gymnasium, bank, beauty salon/barber shop, gift shop, game rooms, craft room, wood working shop, five elegant dining rooms and a sidewalk cafe'. In May 1993, the Freedom Village campus concept was completed with the construction of the Inn in the traditional Williamsburg style. This unique 64-bed health care facility offers varying levels of personalized nursing care to both Freedom Village residents and the entire Holland community

By 1996 Freedom Village stood completely occupied with a waiting list of more than 125 prospective residents.

Fris Office Outfitters

"Dealer in General School Supplies, Stationery, Newspapers, Holiday & Fancy Goods, Bibles, Etc.," Lambertus Fris proudly proclaimed in his advertisement in the *Holland City Directory* of 1901. Fris had launched his business on January 1, of the previous year when he purchased the structure at 30 West 8th Street that had been constructed for Jacob Van Putten as his private bank in 1878. In 1885 the building housed a bookstore selling notions, candy and newspapers. The Fris Hallmark Shop continues to occupy that same original location.

Tragedy struck the Fris family in 1907 with the death of Lambertus. To help the family meet expenses his ten-year-old son Jacob helped his older brother and sister staff the store. By 1910, "L, Fris News Depot," had made a specialty of selling postcard views of the area. A big banner hanging over the store's door advertised "5 Postal Cards for 5¢." Jacob also earned money selling newspapers on the interurban cars and the excursion boats that carried tourists from the 8th Street docks to Macatawa Park. By the time Jacob graduated from Holland High School at the age of 17 he had added the care of his ailing mother to his heavy load.

The family suffered additional misfortunes. Jacob's older brother died the year he graduated. When his sister married, responsibility for running the store was left in his young hands. He managed to keep the business in the black until his mother's death in 1920. Fris was required to purchase the business from his mother's estate, but he met a stony reception from local bankers when he tried to secure a loan. Fortunately A.H. Landwehr, an expert salesman who had co-founded the Holland Furnace Company in 1905, had enough confidence in Fris' ability to loan him the money. Later Landwehr again came to his rescue. When Fris was forced to purchase the building or move, he advanced him another loan.

Over the succeeding decades, Jacob married Sara and began a family while they "literally worked day and night" to make the business known as Fris Book Store a success. By 1938 the store's motto "Everything for the Office" revealed that office supplies, furniture, typewriters, etc. had been added to the inventory.

Following World War II Jacob and Sara's son Dale, assumed much of the management of the store. By then, the wholesale distribution of magazines, newspapers and paperbacks had became a major part of the business. In the late 1940s, that division of the business known as Fris News Company was relocated to a new building at 109 River Avenue. Chris DeVries bought the news company in 1956 and moved it to the corner of 9th and Columbia Avenue.

That same year the Fris Book Store was renamed Fris Office Outfitters and Stationers. Soon the office supply and equipment part of the business moved to 109 River Avenue. It became Fris Office Outfitters and the downtown location was called Fris Stationers. As Fris Stationers centered its inventory around Hallmark products the store's name became Fris Hallmark Shop.

The fourth generation of Fris family joined the enterprise in 1974. That year Dale and Mary's son J became a partner in Fris Stationers and in 1988 he became vice president of Fris Office Outfitters. His brother John started with Fris Office Outfitters also in 1974. In 1986 he was elected president of the corporation.

Following the opening of another Fris Hallmark Store at Cedar Village Plaza in 1987, the three Fris stores were merged under the Fris Office Outfitters corporate name.

Currently, Dale Fris continues to serve as chairman of the board of the corporation which operates three stores employing 45 staff members, many of them long time employees. Operating under the motto "If its available anywhere, we'll find it!" Fris employees take pride in working for a firm that enjoys a sense of well earned heritage through its roots in the community and numerous long time customers.

Lambertus Fris with Grand Rapids *Press* newsboys in front of the original store, ca. 1900

GMB Architects–Engineers

Gordon Buitendorp formed a concept of an ideal company early in his career - "to create a professional work environment that recognizes the individual and permits an extreme amount of individual freedom." Fancy titles and strict areas of responsibilities and duties seemed to only restrict and hamper the creative freedom so important in his profession. As a result, over the nearly 30 years since he founded his own firm, GMB has earned a reputation of personal "team" attention to quality, innovation, and integrity.

Buitendorp grew-up in Muskegon. Following graduation from Muskegon High School, he studied at the University of Michigan where he received his Bachelor of Architecture degree in 1963. Then came five years of experience working for firms in Grand Rapids, Grand Haven and Muskegon. In 1967 he passed his registration exam. One year later, on November 1, 1968, he launched Gordon M. Buitendorp, Inc. Pete Elzinga of Elzinga & Volkers assisted by giving him a start and a corner in his basement on Sixth Street. By the early 1980s, Buitendorp was on his own. Since that time, many renovations have occurred from that basement space as growth has evolved the company into the present GMB Architects-Engineers.

Buitendorp's first major job came in 1968, designing a new factory for the ExCello Corporation on 48th Street. He accomplished other projects for ExCello and in the early 1970s designed a plant for Brooks Products and a new terminal for Holland Motor Express on 40th Street.

He carefully added to his staff until his team numbered eight architects. In 1976, Jim Vanderveen joined Buitendorp as a mechanical engineer, which led to the development of an engineering support within the firm. An electrical engineering team came next and most recently Buitendorp has complemented his staff with an interior designer and a landscape designer.

During the late 1970s GMB Architects–Engineers participated in diverse projects, including the Manistique Hospital, Negaunee High School, the Luce County Courthouse in Newberry and a nursing home in Munising.

By the 1980s Buitendorp had assembled a team which included diverse talents, still emphasizing teamwork, talent, and opportunity. As this growth occurred, so too, the projects expanded in a pleasing diversity and variety. Buitendorp decided to limit his firm to 50 people, so that he can continue to maintain the "family team" - so important in giving each project the "personal touch." And, as the firm grew, state-of-the-art technology was incorporated - the company now is completely computerized.

To assist in support and diversity, GMB acquired in the mid-1980s the Angus-Young architectural firm in Janesville, Wisconsin, which now numbers 20 employees.

GMB has accomplished outstanding projects in Holland, such as the new Sligh Furniture Manufacturing facility; the historic restoration of the railroad depot via adaptive reuse, and the return of Van Vleck Hall at Hope College to its former glory. Currently GMB is refurbishing Holland's historic City Hall.

While most of GMB's work has been in Michigan, major-out-of-state projects include the design of a state-of-the-art processing plant in Iowa, for Eagle-Ottawa Leather, an ink pigment plant for Flint Inc. Corp. in Elizabethtown, Kentucky, and various ventures for Bayer Inc. (formerly Miles Labs) in Indiana.

The 1990s witnessed GMB secure a continued array of educational projects, including elementary schools in Hudsonville and Zeeland; middle schools in Hudsonville and Forest Hills; and high school projects in Grand Haven, Allendale, Zeeland, Grandville and Big Rapids.

The spring of 1994 brought the affiliation of GMB with the Muskegon-based Hooker/De Jong firm, which has enabled growth there from three to 12 employees.

And, Buitendorp continues to practice the philosophy he developed some 30 years before - to allow and encourage team associates the freedom of innovative ideas and resourceful problem solving, maintaining a productive and enjoyable place to work.

GMB Architects-Engineers made downtown a better place when the firm revamped the Holland Transportation Depot at the corner of Lincoln Avenue and 7th Street.

Grand Rapids-Holland Insurance Agency

Dale E. Van Lente remembers June 4, 1981 well. He and fellow employees had just moved to their new office at 19 West 8th Street and were preparing for a gala open house when disaster struck in the form of one of the worst hailstorms of the century. His agency was soon deluged with over 1,000 claims for damaged automobiles and roofs. Worse even than the $1 million in damages was the paperwork nightmare of claim reports. But Holland Insurance Agency had survived many other crises over the years and it would weather the great storm of 1981 as well.

Holland Insurance Agency traces its origins to a little side venture Kommer Schaddelee added to his real estate business in 1873. Holland residents had learned hard lessons about not carrying insurance two years before when the great forest fire of 1871 swept through the city destroying all but a handful of buildings. The $900,000 loss was covered by only $35,000 worth of insurance.

Grand Rapids Holland Insurance Agency has helped keep downtown vital as shown here in a 1918 parade on River Avenue. (photo courtesy Myron Van Ark)

By the turn-of-the-century, attorney Arend Visscher had purchased the agency from his uncle. In 1921, Visscher's son Raymond and Ernest C. Brooks, one of the few Democrats to serve as Holland mayor and state senator, bought the firm. Visscher died in 1929 but Brooks continued to operate the Visscher-Brooks Agency out of the Visscher-Brooks Building at 8 E. 8th Street.

In 1956, Van Lente and C. Neal Wiersema, bought the agency, then with an office at 6 E. 8th Street. Van Lente, whose great grandfather had immigrated to Holland in 1848, was born in the city in 1924. In 1956 the entire volume of business was $100,000 a year, less than half of it commercial. When he retired 33 years later the business had increased many fold with 90% of it commercial. Following Wiersema's death in 1960, Van Lente chose John A. Heyboer as a partner in 1964 and the agency became Van Lente & Heyboer, Inc.

In 1971, Van Lente & Heyboer, the A.W. Hertel Agency and the Van Dort Insurance Agency merged to form the Holland Insurance Agency, Inc. The Hertel Agency had begun in 1917 when John Arendshorst bought the John Pessink Agency. Thirty years later, Arnold Hertel of Grand Rapids acquired the Arendshorst Agency then located at 429 E. 8th Street. Over the decades the A.W. Hertel Agency grew to embrace the Van Putten Agency, the Vande Vusse Agency and the Drew Agency. The firm's managing associates included James Hertel, Hil Buurma and David Lake.

Robert Yonker joined Holland Insurance Agency in 1973, becoming a stockholder two years later. That year also witnessed the acquisition of the Nykamp Agency following Richard Nykamp's untimely death. In 1980, Jack Heyboer, became associated with the agency. He too became a stockholder in 1982.

Holland Insurance Agency merged with Grand Rapids Insurance Agency in 1982. Two years later the corporate name became Grand Rapids Holland Insurance Agency, Inc. The Holland branch was bigger but the Grand Rapids area offered the greatest growth potential. By 1996 both branches would be about equal in size.

The Grand Rapids Insurance Agency had been formed about 1899 by C.W. Watkins. In 1906 his nephew, C.G. Watkins, joined the firm. Over the decades the agency included various partners, including Ferry Heath who served as assistant secretary of the U.S. treasury in 1928. The agency incorporated in 1964 with Ray L. Van Kuiken as president.

Following the merger, Grand Rapids–Holland Insurance Agency continued to expand. The 1980s saw new stockholders enter the firm including, David Krombeen and Richard Eming. Also in the 1980s the Art Hansma Agency in Grand Rapids and the Lewis Vande Bunte Agency in Holland joined the firm.

James Heyboer became a stockholder in 1991. The following year Don Schriber became a stockholder following the merger of the Don Schriber Agency, founded by his father in Grand Rapids in 1947. Other stockholders appointed in the 1990s include Wayne Walkotten, Mary Brandsen, Ed Hassenrik and Dan Rink. In 1994 the agency purchased the Merchants Mutual Agency and added Craig Reinke as a stockholder.

The agency now boasts four locations: Holland, Grand Rapids, Kentwood and Kalamazoo, with over sixty employees. Each office strives to maintain a vital role in their communities. The agency's mission statement echoes this; "Grand Rapids–Holland Insurance Agency, Inc. works faithfully to serve the risk management needs of its customers, the professional needs of its employees, and the civic needs of its community."

In 1992 the Holland office of the agency relocated to its present headquarters at 29 West 8th Street. As Dale Van Lente recalls, his agency was most proud of its commitment to remain downtown and help keep the historic core of Holland alive.

Hansen Machine Company, Inc.

Family members remember Carol Christian Hansen as a happy man who enjoyed life - someone whose personality and integrity placed him in constant demand. Employees recall a generous and loyal boss who inspired loyalty from them. Many in the congregation of the First United Methodist Church remember him as a stalwart member. But perhaps most of all his legacy continues in the name of the company he founded which carved out an important record in the annals of Holland area industry.

His father, Christian Martin Hansen, had emigrated from Norway in 1863, settling in Holland where he got a job as a tanner for the Cappon & Bertsch Leather Co. on West 8th Street. At his home on West 16th Street, his seventh son, Carol, was born in 1905. Because Scandinavian tradition decreed that seventh sons become doctors, young Hansen got the life long nickname "Doc."

By the time he was a teenager, Hansen had begun displaying the traits of an entrepreneur. He peddled horseradish door to door, hawked Grit newspapers and sold ice cream cones. With the onset of the Great Depression in 1929, Hansen "rode the rails" out west where he worked on farms and he had a brief stint as a state policeman. The year 1934 found him back in Holland, operating Doc's Barbecue Stand which he later sold to Russ' Restaurant. The following year he took time out from his busy work life to marry Ruth Reimink who had grown up on the family farm near Hamilton.

Soon Hansen took a job with the Keeler Brass Co. of Grand Rapids where he developed into a skilled tool and die maker. In 1943 Hansen vented his pent up entrepreneurial dreams and opened up his own little machine shop in a double garage building near Grandville. There he subcontracted military projects for Keeler Brass.

Following the end of World War II, Hansen sold his Grandville shop. But when the buyer went broke he got it back. In 1948 Hansen relocated his business to the basement of the Van Tongeren Dutch Novelty Shop on Third Street. The entire work force numbering three employees manufactured devices for the DePree Chemical Co., trim dies for Keeler Brass, machinery for Holland Wire and fancy brass knobs for the Baker Furniture Co.

Brothers Verne and Don Kane who joined the com-

Founder Carol "Doc" Hansen ca. 1940

pany about then, ultimately becoming president and vice president of Hansen, remembered some tough times. When business was slow Hansen had employees painting at his home rather than lay them off. After two years later Hansen moved again, to a former warehouse for used cars at the corner of Douglas Avenue and Jefferson.

During the 1950s the business began to grow as the company served an impressive list of Holland manufacturers. The Hansen Machinery Co. built machines that laminated plywood for Herman Miller's revolutionary Ames designed chairs, manufactured and maintained parts for H.J. Heinz' pickles can lines, parts for clocks and clock hands for Howard Miller, original tooling for trusses for the Flash Bridge Co., boat shafts for Chris Craft, aluminum ribbing for Roamer Boats and gas tanks for the Mac-Bay Boat Co. The company even built a machine that made pizzas. Hansen himself, continued to try his hand at inventions, some of which were good ideas but too far ahead of their time, including a prototype pogo stick and a garden tool set with handles dipped in rubber.

In the early sixties, Lou Lucarelli and Bill Van Harn joined the company. Lucarelli became the corporate secretary and Van Harn would ultimately work his way up to become vice president of engineering. During the mid 1960s the company began growing rapidly with electronic work in the appliance industry, projects for Oldsmobile and, in 1966, the advent of plastic molding. Beginning in 1968 the company launched a building program that expanded production space every four years. In 1973 Hansen Machine bought an old fruit exchange building in Douglas and opened a branch in that Allegan County community. Other additions came in 1977, 1981, 1985 when the Holland factory was completely remodeled and all stamping operations moved to Douglas.

Hansen retired in 1984, remaining chairman of the board until his death in 1988. The following year Hansen Machine moved to its new facility at 13040 Greenly Street, one of the first structures in HEDCOR's Northside Industrial Park. Employment numbered 120 there and at the Douglas plant. In November 1994 Hansen Machine was sold.

Heinz U.S.A. Holland Factory

It was the talk of the town that December in 1896. Not even the recent presidential campaign in which Ottawa County had overwhelmingly voted for William McKinley in opposition to William Jennings Bryan nor the pioneering horseless carriage experiments of Henry Ford and Charles King in Detroit streets earlier that year had sparked such a commotion. No, the topic that dominated Holland's coffee klatch chatter that December was neither automotive prototypes nor politics – it was pickles.

Specifically, the opportunity to land a new industry for the city – a projected pickle factory, to be built by the Pittsburgh-based H.J. Heinz Co., had the city abuzz. A Heinz representative had been favorably impressed with Holland because of its splendid rail and water shipping facilities. But there were a couple of catches – local farmers needed to pledge production of 300 acres of cucumbers and a suitable site with a railroad connection needed to be provided for the plant free of charge.

Holland's mayor and later U.S. congressman and minister to the Netherlands, Gerrit Diekema, spearheaded the campaign to secure the pickle plant prize for the city. A town meeting held at the local Grand Army of the Republic Hall on December 23 brought speedy results. By January 9 approximately 200 area growers had pledged a total of 500 acres, ranging from one half to 10 acre plats. Later in the winter, those growers also agreed to pledge $2.50 per acre to pay the $800 cost of a two-acre site on 15th Street adjacent to Lake Macatawa, conveniently available from Diekema's father, Wiepke.

Ground breaking for the plant came on April 19, 1897. On June 1 the 16,000 square-foot facility designated as H.J.

Heinz Salting House Number 16 stood complete in plenty of time for the upcoming "green season."

Henry J. Heinz, the proprietor of Holland's new industry, had launched his food empire in 1869 with the bottling of horseradish in a small, two-story house in Sharpsburg, a Pittsburgh, Pa., suburb. Careful concern with quality and advertising aplomb, including such famous gimmicks as miniature pickle watch fobs handed out by the millions at the Columbian Exposition and later World's Fairs, had by the mid 1890s rendered his company one of America's largest and most profitable businesses with more than 200 food products. His huge Pittsburgh plant, nine branch factories and 38 salting stations had made Heinz a "pickle king" and a millionaire in an era when that meant something.

With the start of the 1897 green season, long lines of horse-drawn wagons queued up before the plant. Cucumbers in crates and burlap bags were carefully sorted at the loading dock. Farmers ebullient over the high rate of 30 cents per bushel the company promised soon learned that strict company standards meant that they might cart back home half a load of nubs, crooks and too large pickles. In the early days tomatoes also were processed into ketchup at the Holland facility.

At the salting house, huge cypress vats of cucumbers were preserved in brine for processing during the winter months. Originally, little if any actual bottling of pickles occurred at Holland. The pickles were shipped in 46 gallon barrels back to Pittsburgh for their final careful packaging for delivery to the nation's grocery stores.

The Holland plant enjoyed success right from the start, and soon it began expanding exponentially. In the summer

Local growers waited in long lines in 1908 at the original H. J. Heinz Holland plant.

of 1898 the company erected a structure for converting millions of pounds of apples into cider vinegar and a five-story building for pickle processing. By the following year, Plant Superintendent A.E. Atwood managed five buildings comprising 82,500 square feet and capable of processing 550 acres of pickles, 250 acres of tomatoes and a half million bushels of apples each year.

On November 12, 1901, the Michigan factory inspector paid a visit to the Heinz plant in Holland. He found 46 male and 31 female employees who worked six 10 hour days each week at an average rate of 10 cents per hour. While that wage seems amazingly low by modern standards, it compared favorably with other Holland industries: workers at the Holland *Sentinel* earned only about eight cents per hour. And, in 1904, the state factory inspector would observe that the Holland factory "is a model for utility and neatness."

By 1906, the factory consisted of eight "large, modern structures" with a floor area exceeding 200,000 square-feet on 10 acres of land. That year a new vinegar building, devoted largely to the distillation of malt vinegar, "the finest building of its kind in the city," was completed. Following construction of a new, three-story processing building in 1907, the Holland factory became Heinz' largest manufacturing center outside Pittsburgh.

Over the succeeding decade the production of ketchup was moved to Grand Rapids and other locations and the Holland plant concentrated on pickles and vinegar. By 1913, the work force had grown to 131 employees. Four years later, with the entry of the United States into World War I, Heinz, who had pioneered in the "social welfare, health and happiness" of his workers, offered life insurance to his work force. He was probably the first Holland employer to do so.

The year 1929, which ushered in a decade-long Depression, saw Heinz employ 160 full-time employees and 225 seasonal workers. Throughout the Depression, Heinz helped stabilize the local economy through steady employment and purchase of pickles. During the 1930s the entire pickle bottling operation was moved from Pittsburgh to Holland. But the Depression era also produced a setback in the form of a blight known as mosaic virus which attacked Michigan cucumber plants. However, the Heinz research laboratory at Bowling Green, Ohio, developed a virus-resistant variety. Ultimately, Heinz distributed its own special hybrid seeds to its cucumber growers.

With America's entrance into World War II in 1941, many Heinz employees served their country in far-flung battle fronts. On December 6, 1942, 21-year-old Sergeant George Bruursema became the first Heinz employee to die in battle. Throughout the war Heinz participated in home front activities such as the big war bond rally held in February 1943. During 1944 and 1945 the manpower shortage was somewhat relieved through the use of up to 44 German prisoners of war who were bussed from the POW camp near the Allegan Dam to the Heinz factory.

Following the war, as the GIs returned to their jobs at Heinz, in 1949 the company completed a modern new salt house containing scores of big cypress vats. In 1950, two advanced technology acetator vinegar fermenters were installed in Holland. Those first such units in the United States continue to generate wine and malt vinegar 46 years later.

Continued factory growth marked the decades of the 1950s–1980s. With the development of the fresh pack pickle process during the mid 50s, Heinz launched the largest expansion in its history to install the requisite heat pasteurization equipment. Completed in 1959, that expansion rendered Heinz' Holland plant the world's largest pickle factory as well as the city's biggest taxpayer, water user and shipper.

By 1970 some 30 new buildings had been added to the site and more than 550 people found year round employment at the Holland plant. Another 300 workers, many of them area students working their way through college, swelled the payroll during each summer's green season. In 1983, a million dollar expansion added new cucumber handling equipment and an additional 300 salting tanks.

But the company also experienced problems during this period of phenomenal growth. When the U.S. Congress failed to renew the "Bracero Program" which allowed Mexican migratory workers to harvest crops in the United States in the early 1960s, a dearth of American pickers adversely affected the agricultural business. Heinz scientists responded by developing new dwarf varieties of cucumbers whose concentrated fruit set on the vine allowed machine harvesting. Heinz pioneered in developing such harvesting technology.

Rougher handling of cucumbers from machine harvesting as well as other automated handling techniques exacerbated a problem known as bloater damage. Bloaters are cucumbers with hollow centers which result from the sudden release of carbon dioxide gas. This gas is formed during cucumber fermentation as well as cellular respiration of the cucumbers. Studies proved that increased handling from machine harvesting, conveying and trucking increased respiration of the cucumbers leading to higher levels of gas. In the mid 1970s Heinz once again solved a major industry problem by inventing a procedure that bubbled nitrogen gas though the fermenting brine solution thus causing a gradual release of carbon dioxide from the pickles.

In 1996, as the Holland Heinz plant prepares for its centennial, the factory, includes 17 buildings totaling 500,000 square-feet. Two hundred and sixty-seven full-time employees, including Barbara Stegenga who has worked in the plant for 50 years, and up to 300 seasonal workers who annually produce nearly $100 million worth of pickles, peppers, relishes, vinegar and baby food fruit juices. For 100 years the Holland employees have upheld the founder's commitment to do a "common thing uncommonly good."

An aerial view of the massive Heinz factory and tank farm.

Haworth, Inc.

"From a tiny acorn the mighty oak grows." Few American corporations better exemplify that old adage than Holland's Haworth, Inc. From a humble beginning in a little workshop operated solely by the founder the company has burgeoned into a major force in the worldwide office furniture industry with more than 9,000 members who produce annual sales in excess of 1.15 billion.

The Haworth story began in the days following the end of World War II. Gerrard W. Haworth was employed as an industrial arts teacher in the Holland Public Schools. He liked his work and he enjoyed using tools, so as a second job he installed a wood working shop in his garage. Using that equipment he began moonlighting to help meet the demands of sending five children to college. That became so much fun he decided to leave the classroom and launch his own business.

When he sought start-up capital from a local bank, the banker turned him down as a bad risk because he had no experience in operating a business. But his parents had faith in their son's potential and loaned him their life's savings to pursue his dream. Haworth bought some used machinery and went into business in a small rented facility in 1948. Under the name Modern Products he began manufacturing custom designed wooden check-out counters, merchandise displays and other retail store furnishings. Determined to make his enterprise a success, right from the start he emphasized quality and customer service.

A major breakthrough came in 1950 when he introduced bank and floor-to-ceiling partitions which he distributed through a separate marketing group. Within four years the company had evolved its "Soundex" and "E-Series" of modern office partitions from prototypes designed for Walter Ruether's UAW headquarters in Detroit. The year 1955 saw the introduction of planters and room dividers. The company had grown to 47 employees.

The renamed Modern Products Company was incorporated in 1957 and two years later Modern Partitions was founded as a marketing arm. In 1961 the company's 80 employees moved into a new facility constructed on 32nd Street. The following year witnessed diversification into the academic market with the introduction of study carrels. In 1965 dormitory furniture was added. A year later the company's 101 employees generated $3 million in annual sales.

The decade of the 1970s witnessed the beginnings of dramatic growth for the company. The company pioneered with Modern Office Modules in 1971, the industry's first acoustical panel and universal panel hinge. These innovations would greatly increase the flexibility and responsiveness of modular office environments. By 1975 when Modern Products and Modern Partitions became Haworth, Inc., employment had reached 212. The following year G.W. Haworth became chairman of the board and his son, Richard G. Haworth, succeeded him as president and CEO. The younger

Haworth Corporate headquarters in Holland.

Haworth had joined the company following a stint in the military, bringing new dimensions and innovations that spurred growth. In 1976 he shifted the direction of the company to office furniture systems exclusively, as Haworth introduced two revolutionary panel features. Monocoque panel construction, similar to that used in airplane wings, resulted in a much stronger panel without stress points. And Haworth's invention of the revolutionary pre-wired modular office furniture panel, first enabled users to access power where needed without clumsy extension cords or expensive rewiring. In 1979, when Haworth formed four major sales divisions to replace independent sales subsidiaries, its employment had climbed to 713.

The decade of the 1980s brought an even greater rate of growth and development of new products. In 1981 a former corn field in HEDCOR's Southside Industrial Park sprouted Haworth's architecturally dazzling new corporate headquarters and manufacturing center. Ground was also broken for a quarter million square-foot national distribution center adjacent it. Haworth entered the office seating market that year with the establishment of a chair manufacturing facility in Allegan. By 1995 the Allegan plant would produce more than two million chairs.

Haworth introduced another office innovation in 1982, the first adjustable keyboard pad, which won the Gold Award from the International Association of Business Designers. Employment reached 1,250 that year and sales exceeded $100 million. Two years later, when the company produced its one millionth ERA-1® panel another 700 employees had been added and annual sales topped $200 million.

In 1986, Haworth introduced the Power Base®, the industry's first eight-wire power system with three dedicated circuits. Another revolutionary product designed in response to the growing use of computers in the work place, the Power Base® allowed users to dedicate electric circuits to specific uses and reduce destructive electrical interference. By year's end 2,500 employees worked in facilities that surpassed one and a half-million square-feet.

The year 1986 also saw Haworth aggressively enter the

international market with the signing of a licensing agreement with Okamura Corporation to manufacture and market products in Japan. Two years later Haworth purchased Comforto, with seating and office furniture plants in Germany, Switzerland, and North Carolina. It began construction of a wood manufacturing facility in Holland and opened a new sales office in the United Kingdom.

In 1988 Jerry Johanneson was elevated to the position of chief operating officer, and in 1994 to president, serving with Founding Chairman G.W. Haworth and Chairman and CEO Richard G. Haworth in an Executive Office which led the corporation to even greater levels. The decade ended with the completion of a new wood manufacturing facility in Holland. Employment stood at 3,700 and sales reached $500 million.

The 1990s brought continued efforts to expand Haworth product lines. In 1990, the acquisition of the RACE® systems furniture, brought high design and flexibility to office environments. Domestic facilities growth continued at a steady pace. That same year the corporation acquired the Mueller Furniture Corp. of Grand Rapids and Lunstead of Kent, Washington. It also completed its new Holland Panels Plant powder coating addition. The Myrtle Desk Co. of High Point, N.C., joined Haworth in 1991. Two years later Haworth acquired the Hendersonville, TN., based Globe Business Furniture, a major supplier to the small business and home office market. In 1995 the Ludington Components plant opened, followed by the Big Rapids Components plant the next year.

The international market was expanded during the 1990s as well. Kinetics of Rexdale, Ontario, was acquired in 1990. An interest in companies in Portugal and France followed the next year. The year 1992 brought acquisition of an interest in an Italian firm and the beginnings of joint ventures which created new Asian sales and service capabilities. In 1995, Haworth entered the Malaysian market with a joint venture to market and manufacture products in Kuala Lumpur and COM of Italy was acquired. By 1995, fully 25% of Haworth sales were outside the U.S.A.

Annual sales which surpassed $1 billion in 1994 brought the corporation growing international attention. *Forbes* magazine ranked Haworth 160th in its listing of the 400 largest U.S. private companies in 1995. Three years before, Haworth had become the first U.S. office furniture manufacturer to be certified with the coveted ISO 9001 quality standards rating. Soon all of Haworth's domestic and foreign businesses were also certified with that stringent set of international quality standards.

An honor of a different sort came in 1993 when Haworth was named one of "The 100 Best Companies to Work for in America." That reflected a commitment to the company's human resources that had characterized Haworth's entire evolution. Recognizing its employees as "diverse, talented and resourceful members of a worldwide team," the corporation provided a participative work environment that rewarded hard work and intelligence, a philosophy that could only continue to benefit its more than 9,000 members and millions of satisfied customers worldwide.

Haworth's Corporate Executive office is the company's top management team and is composed of (from left to right) G. W. Haworth, founding chairman; Jerry Johanneson, president and COO; and Dick Haworth, chairman and CEO.

Hart & Cooley, Inc.

Howard Stanley Hart, co-founder of Hart & Cooley Inc., was an amazing turn-of-the-century entrepreneur, an inventor, industrialist, builder and a man "with his fingers in many pies." Born in New Britain, Connecticut, in 1867, at the age of 16 Hart went to work for the Stanley Metal Works located in his hometown. Over the succeeding nine years he would rise to the rank of general manager in charge of manufacturing.

Like many another ambitious youth he wanted his own company. In 1892, he resigned his position at the metal works and in partnership with Norman P. Cooley, established the Hart & Cooley Manufacturing Company in Chicago, the first cold-rolled steel plant west of Pittsburgh. Over the next seven years Hart patented several of his inventions, including a steel heating register, that was superior to the traditional heavy cast-iron affairs.

In 1899 Hart and Cooley sold their Chicago plant and returned to New Britain. There, in 1901, they organized the Hart & Cooley Co. with a capital of $50,000. Their Booth Street factory became the first in the country to manufacture warm air registers from stamped steel, a product that gained almost instant success.

Not content with his booming register business, Hart felt the need for quality, American-made ball bearings. Following an investigative trip to Germany, then the world center of that industry, in 1910 he invested profits from the register business to begin manufacturing bearings, and soon set up a separate company called Fafnir Bearings. In 1912 Hart teamed up with another partner to form the Hart & Hutchinson Company to manufacture steel lockers.

The "Roaring 20s" brought the company into the Michigan market place. In 1924 it formed the Federal Manufacturing Company in Holland to supply the famous Holland Furnace Company with registers. In 1928 Hart & Cooley moved its Connecticut operations to Holland and merged with Federal under the name Hart & Cooley Co., Inc. Warm air products made in Holland soon supplied customers nationwide. The city, situated near the geographical center of the market, proved an excellent location. By the early 1930s, despite the Depression, Hart & Cooley had established itself as the world's largest producer of warm air registers.

Hart remained active in the business he had established until 1935. During his remarkable career he set a record for having the most register patents issued in his name. He died at the age of 76 in 1944.

By the time of his death the Holland plant had grown to 238,750 square-feet of floor space, with "unmatched facilities for register research and manufacture." Following America's entry into World War II in 1941 as Michigan became the "arsenal of democracy," register production took a backseat to military needs. During the war Hart & Cooley employees, who now numbered scores of "Rosie the riveters" worked around the clock to produce 60mm mortar shell casings. Approximately half of the plant space was relinquished to the Fafnir Bearing Company which moved its operations to Holland in 1942. Until it closed in August 1945, millions of ball bearings rolled off the Holland production line.

During the 1950s, when forced air heating became widespread, Hart & Cooley expanded its residential and commercial line of registers, grilles and diffusers with many new products. The Metlvent gas vents for gas-fired appliances were introduced in 1959. By 1962, when it won "Achievement of the year" honors during Michigan Week, Metlvent accounted for 16% of total sales. The Metlvent all-fuel chimney system followed that same year.

In 1963 Hart & Cooley completed construction of its award winning new office designed by architects Kammeraad & Stroup and furnished by the Steelcase Company.

Hart & Cooley became a part of the manufacturing division of Great American Management, Inc. (GAMI) known as Eagle Industries in April, 1986. Hart & Cooley continued to expand. Reliable Products of Geneva, Alabama, joined the corporation in 1988, Norflex, a flexible duct manufacturer with plants in Memphis and Jackson, Tennessee followed in 1989. In May 1995, Hart & Cooley acquired the assets of Flexible Air Movers, Inc., of Fresno, California, and in December of that year Cody West, Inc. in nearby Sanger, California, joined the corporation.

Hart & Cooley, Inc., at 500 East 8th Street.

Herman Miller

In 1988 Herman Miller's new CEO, Dick Ruch, met with every employee-owner of the company and articulated a fundamental truth: "Change is forever, and change is our only hope for managing what we must become." Change truly had been the essence of the company's history - its adaption and response to changing tastes and needs in the marketplace and its primary role in bringing beneficial change to the American office place.

The company traces its origins to 1905 when Herman Miller and a group of Zeeland businessmen founded the Star Furniture Co. to manufacture inexpensive bedroom furniture. Four years later Dirk Jan DePree, joined the firm as an office worker. In 1914, DePree married Miller's daughter Nellie

By 1923 the Star Furniture Company was in financial straits. DePree and his father-in-law bought a majority of the stock and renamed the company Herman Miller. The new company began placing an emphasis on quality rather than price while continuing to produce the traditional ornate bedroom suites popular during the period. But intense competition in the furniture industry coupled with the advent of the Great Depression brought Herman Miller dangerously close to bankruptcy.

DePree made a bold move in 1930, adding to its line furniture designed by Gilbert Rhode in response to America's changing lifestyles - more mobility and less living space in the home. That gamble helped the company weather the Depression. By 1945 it had completely phased out its traditional line of furniture to concentrate on modern.

That same year George Nelson, a young architect and writer who would win an international reputation, joined the company. Over the succeeding decades he emphasized quality, helped expand the company's design orientation via increased involvement in graphics, merchandising and advertising and broadened Herman Miller's reputation for innovation by engaging world class designers to create furniture pieces that became classics.

One such designer was Charles Eames, who nurtured a long relationship with the company, and was named the most influential designer of the century by the World Design Congress in 1985. Prior to his death in 1988 Eames designed revolutionary Herman Miller products including the molded plywood chair, the lounge chair and ottoman, tandem sling seating and the aluminum group.

The company entered the office furniture market in 1942 with the Executive Office Group, a component system designed by Rhode. In 1964, under the leadership of Depree's son Hugh, who served as CEO from 1962-1980, Herman Miller focused its energies to solve the needs of the office environment.

The company introduced the Action Office® system in 1968. Designed by Robert Propst, this radically different design known as the "open plan" featured work spaces defined and separated by modular panels. Those easily movable panels and other components enabled companies to adjust quickly and efficiently to changing needs. The often copied system would revolutionize the way people work. Named the best product of the decade by the 1985 World Design Congress, Herman Miller open plan office furniture has provided work spaces for over a million people.

Following Bill Stumpf's invention of an office chair based on ergonomics, the study of people's relationship to their environments and tasks, Herman Miller introduced the Ergon® chair in 1976. Design advancements brought the Equa® chair in 1985 and Aeron® chair in 1994.

Max DePree succeeded his brother as CEO in 1980, serving until 1987. Under his leadership the company expanded its pioneer participative management began in 1950 when it adopted the Scanlon Plan. In 1983, every full time employee with at least one year of service became a shareholder - bringing truth to what the company tells customers "When you place your order with us, everyone serving you is an owner."

In addition to sharing with employees the fruits of its success, sales of $1.28 billion in 1996, Herman Miller also practiced a responsibility to the environment through more than two decades of waste recycling. In 1993 Fortune magazine named its environmental record as one of the nation's top ten.

Dick Ruch served as CEO from 1987 to 1991, followed by Kerm Campbell and Mike Volkema in 1995. The company maintains its world headquarters and a manufacturing and distribution plant in Zeeland with additional Michigan facilities in Holland, Grandville, and Spring Lake. Mike Volkema is the company's current CEO.

The Herman Miller, Inc., World Headquarters.

Holland Area Chamber of Commerce

Louis Hallacy, II, who has guided the Holland Area Chamber of Commerce since 1981, likes to think of the organization as "the front door of the community" - the point of contact where visitors and prospective businessmen and citizens get their initial impressions of Holland's attributes. And behind that door lies a vibrant organization that has earned national recognition for its efforts to consistently promote the region and thereby ensure its economic vitality.

The precursor to the present Chamber began as the Holland Board of Trade on March 6, 1908. Jacob G. Van Putten, manager of the Holland Furniture Company, served as the first president of the group that numbered 25 members. Among the Board's earliest projects was to work with the City Council to secure the new City Hall that was constructed on River Avenue in 1911. One year later the board inaugurated a long tradition of publishing quality books and pamphlets promoting Holland's attractions and its heritage when it produced *Holland: The Gateway to Western Michigan for Chicago and the Great West.* Filled with rare views of the city and its industries, the volume remains a prime historical source for the period. The concluding page epitomizes a philosophy that continues as a theme to the present: "Holland wants you, and it invites you as a manufacturer, merchant or citizen to locate in Holland. Liberal inducements will be offered to responsible concerns."

In 1924, the Holland Chamber of Commerce was organized. Evert P. Stephan, then mayor of the city and manager of the Holland Furniture Co., became the organization's first president. Originally the Chamber maintained its office in the City Hall. Shortly after its organization the Chamber actively participated in a campaign to secure $150,000 in local support to assist in the Holland Furnace Company's efforts to build a new hotel for the city. The Chamber accomplished that task with aplomb, and the following year the landmark Warm Friend Hotel opened.

The Great Depression began in 1929 and three years later the Chamber reduced its annual membership dues from $25.00 to $15.00. The harsh days of the Depression also brought the need for a more sophisticated operation and on November 27, 1935, the Holland Area Chamber of Commerce was certified as a non-profit corporation. William M. Connelly managed the organization at that time. In 1938 the Chamber moved into its new office located on the ground floor of the historic Holland State Bank Building whose clock tower continues to dignify the corner of 8th Street and River Avenue.

The following year, Charles R. Sligh, Jr., who had relocated his furniture factory from Grand Rapids to Holland in 1933 with the Chamber's assistance, served as president of the organization. He long remembered that year's economic coup when the Chamber persuaded the Algonac-based Chris Craft Corporation to establish a boat manufacturing plant in Holland. As Chamber president, Sligh also conducted negotiations that resulted in the city's acquisition of an unsightly old leather factory site that ultimately became the location of the Civic Auditorium.

Similarly, in 1948, under Carl C. Andreasen's leadership, the Chamber purchased a plot of land on the shores of Lake Macatawa in Holland Township that was converted into a beautiful park and boat launching site. Henry S. Maentz, Sr., a long time First National Bank president who served as Chamber president in 1950, counted as his major achievements the Parke-Davis Company's conversion of an abandoned leather factory to a pharmaceutical plant, the expansion of the Baker Furniture Co. and the construction of a new H.E. Morse Co. factory on Douglas Ave. for the manufacture of novel ball point pens.

One of the highlights of 1952 was the speech Congressman and later President Gerald R. Ford made at the Chamber's second noontime "Cracker Barrel" session. Two years later came ground breaking ceremonies for a new General Electric Co. factory that had been secured for Holland via the Chamber's efforts.

The Chamber relocated its office to the newly constructed Civic Center in 1954 but shortly thereafter it moved to the

The Holland Chamber of Commerce float for the 1949 Tulip Time parade passes its office in the Waverly Building on West 8th Street.

The Holland Area Chamber of Commerce office at 272 East 8th Street.

ground floor of the Warm Friend Hotel. In 1956, the Chamber launched a major advertising campaign to promote its work and the area's many tourist attraction. That same year it sponsored a golf exhibition in conjunction with its annual membership meeting, during which Julius Boros broke the American Legion course record with a 62! That tradition continues to the present with the annual golf outing which draws 500 participants.

The Chamber's persistent goal to ensure the economic vitality of the area resulted in the seeds being sown for an industrial development corporation at the Chamber board meeting on September 15, 1958. Four years later the Holland Economic Development Corporation (HEDCOR) became a reality. From the beginning the Chamber shared office space with this separate entity and managed its affairs. A successful fund drive resulted in the acquisition of 100 acres of land on the city's southside in Allegan County. The Southside Industrial Park's first major tenant opened its massive Lifesavers plant in 1967. That brought national recognition, and the park grew by leaps and bounds. By 1996 it comprised 615 acres occupied by 52 factories. The success of the Southside Industrial Park and the growing scarcity of nearby land spurred HEDCOR to open a Northside Industrial Park in Holland Township in 1987. By 1996 that had grown to 535 acres and 20 plants. The companies in HEDCOR's two industrial parks employ more than 16,500 people.

The Chamber launched another Holland tradition at 7:30 a.m. on January 5, 1965, with its first Early Bird Breakfast held in the Tulip Room of the Warm Friend Hotel. During its first season average attendance of the event held the first Tuesday of every month, ten months of the year, was 53 persons. Over the decades inspiring speakers including Michigan Attorney General Frank Kelley, Detroit Tiger great Al Kaline and others would push the average attendance well over 200 at the gala coffee klatsch forum held at Hope College's Maas Center since 1987.

The Chamber continued innovations that bettered the community such as the Silent Observer program it launched in 1976. But by the dawn of the 1980s it suffered a period of stagnation. That would change in a big way with the appointment of Louis Hallacy, II, as president in 1981. Hallacy had grown up in Grand Rapids, moving to Holland with his new bride Madeline, in 1956, where they operated Hallacy Tire and Supply Company. Seven years later he started with R.E. Barber Ford of Holland as a car salesman, work-

ing his way up over the next 18 years to become secretary of the organization. In the meantime Hallacy had become actively involved in community affairs, serving on the Ottawa County Road Commission Board, the Tulip Time Board, and as a city council member. Beginning in 1973 he was elected mayor for three terms.

When Hallacy accepted the presidency of the Chamber in January 1981, membership stood at 375. The Chamber Board charged its new president with the "responsibility to promote membership growth, add new programs and put the organization on a sound financial footing." Over the succeeding "dynamic decade" he would accomplish those goals and much more. By 1990, the Chamber numbered 1,000 member firms.

Some of the highlights of the 1980s include: the formation of a Small Business Development Center with programs ranging from counseling and seminar series to Small Business Week activities; the establishment of the Holland Area Convention and Visitors Bureau to better promote Holland as a tourist destination; the creation of the Allegan Ottawa Development Corporation, and a foreign trade zone for West Michigan. The Chamber participated with local government in establishing an Airport Task Force, Traffic Task Force and by conducting Industrial Retention Surveys. It expanded its program to benefit members by establishing the Chamber Foundation, the Holland Chamber Political Action Committee, Health Insurance Programs and the HollanDollar Gift Certificates plan in 1988. Its Leadership Holland program began training community volunteers for future leadership roles. To keep pace with its burgeoning membership and array of new programs, in 1987, the Chamber moved from its cramped and antiquated office in the Warm Friend Hotel to a completely remodeled structure at 272 E. 8th Street equipped with state-of-the-art computers and electronic communication facilities.

A rapid rate of progress continued into the 1990s. Membership surpassed 1,400 in 1996 when the Chamber inaugurated a web site on the internet. Three years before, the Chamber had won national recognition when it was named the number one Chamber of Commerce in America. As the Chamber faces the changes and problems of the future brought about by its unparalleled success in revitalizing the area's economy it will continue to mirror the quality of life that makes Holland so attractive a place to live, raise a family, work and retire.

Holland Board of Public Works

As a consumer-owned utility, the Holland Board of Public Works (HBPW) provides testimony to the power of a community's citizenry. As late as the 1880s, the city was without electricity and consequently electric street lights. Drinking water came from hand pumped shallow wells or directly out of the Black River and city scavengers were hired to empty backyard privies by hand. A citizen's campaign for a municipal water system culminated in the passage of a bond proposal in April, 1883. Two years later with 4.5 miles of water mains completed, the new water works system was turned over to a Board of Water Commissioners. In 1893, that unit was abolished in favor of a Board of Public Works. Alfred Huntley, a local machine shop operator, served as the first superintendent of the Water Department.

Huntley also became involved in the introduction of electrical power to Holland when he and W. A. Holley constructed a small electric plant for use in their machine shop. Citizens urged them to build a larger plant and furnish electricity to downtown stores. In July, 1890, the Common Council granted Huntley and Holley's Wolverine Electric Light Co. permission to erect power poles along city streets.

Street lighting proved a bone of contention when some citizens wanted gas lights and others wanted electric lights serviced by the Wolverine Co. A referendum vote in 1892 decided the issue in favor of establishment of a city owned power plant. A legal suit against the city by the Wolverine Co., the need for a revised city charter and another referendum vote intervened until finally in March 1894, what became known as the "Fifth Street Station" began operation. The plant was built at a cost of $12,000. Shortly after, the Board of Public Works was charged with the control and management of the water works, electric light plant, sewer system, and other such public improvements.

During its first year of operation, the demand for electricity increased so rapidly that capacity was doubled. In 1897 the electrical system was altered from the original direct current (DC) to alternating current (AC) and two years later all day lighting service first became available.

In 1899 the Board of Public Works responded to the need for a sanitary sewer system. An experimental reduction tank constructed at the end of a private sewer on Central Avenue proved satisfactory, and plans were made for a general sewage system. The initial two trunk sewer districts installed in 1901 were expanded yearly by the addition of lateral sewers until the entire city was completed. Initially, sewage flowed directly into Lake Macatawa, but in 1927 a state-of-the-art sewage treatment plant went into operation. It would serve the needs of the city for the next 35 years until being replaced by a new wastewater treatment plant capable of processing 4.5 million gallons per day in 1962.

A long tradition of using its revenues for a variety of projects that benefit the community began in 1913 when the Board of Public Works invested surplus funds in city paving bonds, bonds for fire department apparatus, and other projects. City owned facilities also benefited from interest payments used for improvements. In time of need, the HBPW loaned money to the local school system. In 1919, it paid in part for the construction of a grandstand in the public baseball park and assumed maintenance of the park.

When citizens voted down three attempts at securing bonding for an urgently needed municipal hospital during the early 1920s, the Holland Board of Public Works made that life saving institution possible through its surplus funds.

The customer service area of the Department of Public Works in 1914.

The HBPW continued to expand its facilities. An odor control project at the Sewage Treatment Plant was completed in 1935, and two years later a new half-million gallon water tank stood complete at the 28th Street pumping station. Despite an upgrading in 1925, the original Fifth Street electric plant had become outmoded by 1938. That year construction began on a new generating station on a site west of Pine Avenue, adjacent to Lake Macatawa. Named after James DeYoung, the board's first full time superintendent, the station was completed in June 1940. The ready supply of low-cost electricity benefited Holland's downtown economic development in 1988 when the "snowmelt" system was installed in the central business district.

When the Michigan Department of Health declared Holland water wells unsafe in 1944, three new deep wells were drilled on the periphery of the city. In 1957 came the completion of a new water treatment plant near Tunnel Park. A concrete intake pipeline which extends nearly one mile out into Lake Michigan is capable of handling 40 million gallons per day. In 1978, a new water transmission main expanded service to the area, south of Lake Macatawa. A massive five million gallon water reservoir at the south side pumping station was erected in 1987. Three years later, an expansion to the Water Filtration Plant raised its capacity to 28 million gallons per day. Ensuring a safe and high quality water supply is a top priority of the Holland Board of Public Works, and the water that is treated by the HBPW Filtration Plant continues to meet or exceed all federal and state drinking water standards.

Efforts to make the electrical generating facilities more efficient and cheaper spurred the Holland Board of Public Works to begin construction of 9.1 miles of natural gas pipeline in 1996. The early 1990s also saw the installation of new instrumentation that allows for continuous monitoring of airborne pollutants.

Modernization and growth of the wastewater treatment facilities has kept pace with the city's burgeoning needs. In 1972 secondary treatment and phosphate removal facilities were added to the treatment plant. A state-of-the-art wastewater treatment plant addition, completed in September 1981, doubled its capacity. In 1995, the plant completed a major expansion which is capable of collecting and treating nearly 5.84 billion gallons of wastewater each year.

The Holland Board of Public Works has remained on the cutting edge of the new technology of the nineties. Following a feasibility study in September 1992, the HBPW began construction of a fiber optic backbone made up of a 48 fiber cable with node points located at various public works substations. Another technological advance that brought additional services to the community came in the form of a geographical information system (GIS). That comprehensive computer system enhanced the Board's ability to provide detailed descriptions of various utility delivery systems and continues to help the city and other units of government to map out areas of need.

Today, more than 20,000 electric customers, 10,000 wastewater customers and 10,000 water service customers depend on the Holland Board of Public Works to provide the electricity, water and wastewater treatment needed to run their homes and businesses.

The citizenry of Holland have long recognized the value of a municipally-owned utility. After more than a century, the Holland Board of Public Works remains proud of its unique relationship with the community it serves. By embodying the American values of hard work, efficient service, fiscal responsibility, continued growth, modernization and reinvestment into the community – the HBPW continues to enrich the quality of life in Holland.

Holland Charter Township

Wolves, wildcats and panthers far out-numbered people when the State Legislature created Holland Township nearly a century and a half ago. Now thousands of residents work in the many factories and businesses that dot the township, enjoy spectacular homes with modern water and sewage service, travel along mile after mile of smooth paved roads and recreate at numerous parks and bike paths - all made possible through the efforts of the Holland Township government.

Created on March 16, 1847, the township was named Holland at the request of the Rev. Albertus C. Van Raalte who earlier that year had led the vanguards of what would become a mighty exodus of colonists from the Netherlands. Despite inexperience in frontier survival those Hollanders set to work with a passion. A reporter from a Milwaukee newspaper who arrived the following year wrote: "When these people arrive, the first thing is to a buy a piece of land, the second to commence chopping, the third to plant and make fences, and lastly, build a house... This country is fast becoming a garden of the choicest kind. Truly, the wilderness is made to blossom like a rose."

By 1853 the township's population numbered 1,418. Seven years later 1,991 people called Holland Township home. Some dwelt in isolated farmsteads while others established settlements that are now little more than ghost towns.

A Dutch entrepreneur named Jan Rabbers was the guiding light behind the founding of Groningen in the spring of 1847. He opened a store, constructed a dam and sawmill nearby on Frenchman's Creek and launched a manufacturing enterprise that threatened to eclipse the City of Holland. That dream never quite worked out but during the 1850s others established grist mills, a tannery and a furniture factory. The most significant industry at Groningen came in 1851 when Jan Hendrick Veneklasen established his brickyard. By 1892, having been moved to Zeeland, it was manufacturing some 20 million bricks a year. When the road connecting Holland with Zeeland was relocated in 1856, most of Groningen's enterprises shifted to New Groningen about 3/4 mile to the north. Other settlements that once flourished in northern Holland Township include Norde Holland first settled by Jan Van Tongeren in the spring of 1848, and nearby Noordeloos, named in honor of a resident pastor's home province in the Netherlands.

On April 2, 1849, the first Holland Township meeting was held at Van Raalte's home. Henry D. Post, who had settled in the township prior to the arrival of the Dutch, was elected the township supervisor. Ten voters were all that could be mustered in the township, because the Dutch settlers were not yet naturalized as American citizens. Nevertheless, at that first meeting the newly elected township board ordered its first tax to be raised - $25 for the year's entire expenses!

In 1858, 337 voters turned out to elect John Roost as supervisor. Wiepke Diekema, the father of Holland's famous orator and politician Gerrit Diekema, was elected supervisor in 1870 and for the succeeding eleven annual elections.

Holland Township's geographical dimensions fluctuated throughout the 19th century. Originally it included all of present day Park, Holland and Zeeland townships. Zeeland Township left the fold in 1851. In 1915, with the creation of Park Township, the township assumed its permanent form. The township received its present charter in 1968.

The Bicentennial year of 1976 stands out as a milestone in the township's history with the dedication of the new Township Hall on 120th Avenue. The township also enacted a comprehensive land use plan that year in an effort to concentrate industrial development and provide for the best utilization of land for residential growth.

Burgeoning development was made possible by the extension of water and sewer lines throughout the township. The township also set high standards for new utility construction with all utilities to be buried. The township worked with HEDCOR to acquire land that made possible the Northside Industrial Park. The opening of West Shore Mall in 1988 spurred much additional commercial development along the U.S. 31 corridor.

The township's extensive network of bicycle paths and Dunton, Helder, Quincy and Beechwood parks offer unsurpassed recreational opportunities. Roads such as River Avenue, Lakewood Blvd., James St. and Butternut Dr. have been bettered year by year. During the previous 20 years Holland Charter Township also expanded and upgraded its volunteer fire department buildings and equipment. The immigrants of 1847 would be proud of their descendent's accomplishments.

Until it was replaced by the present facility in 1976, this structure served as the Holland Township Hall.

Holland Economic Development Corporation

Change is inevitable but growth is not. Without the careful planning, hard work and community leadership that characterized the era of the 1960s, Holland would be a far inferior place than it is today. The Holland Economic Development Corporation's (HEDCOR) role in transforming farmland to the south and north of the city into a diverse industrial mecca where some 16,500 people find employment stands as a model achievement that is the envy of many far larger communities.

Since its beginnings in the 1840s Holland's industrial base had passed through ongoing cycles of evolution. The city's economic vitality was in flux during the 1950s with the demise of the furniture industry and the once dominant Holland Furnace Company. In 1951 the Detroit based Parke-Davis Co. converted a former leather factory to production of pharmaceutical chemicals and five years later Holland lured a General Electric plant. Civic leaders pondered whether other factories could be attracted to the area to provide jobs for the upcoming generations.

In 1957 the Holland Area Chamber of Commerce embraced the challenge to provide leadership for the project. At its annual organizational meeting on September 16th, Marvin C. Lindeman, president of a local advertising agency, accepted the chairmanship of the Planning and Economic Committee. His committee composed of ten prominent business leaders worked with the Holland Planning Commission, Holland City Council, the Michigan Department of Economic Development and the Chesapeake and Ohio Railroad Industrial Department to conduct surveys and study the options. At a board meeting on July 8, 1958, the Chamber transferred $1,000 from its building fund to a new industrial fund. At the September 15, 1958, meeting came discussion about the possibility of forming an Industrial Development Corporation. The seeds for HEDCOR had been planted.

In 1959 and 1960 Clarence Jalving, president of the Peoples State Bank, reported to the Chamber about his discussions with the Michigan Department of Economic Development concerning use of land in the city's southside for industrial purposes. The year 1962 proved pivotal. The Fantus Co., a consulting firm hired by the city to conduct an industrial survey, issued its report that urged the city to move toward a more diverse manufacturing mix and for the acquisition and development of industrial sites that could be offered for immediate sale to prospective manufacturers. About that same time the Chamber of Commerce established a separate private non-profit corporation it called the Holland Economic Development Corporation (HEDCOR). While not officially a Chamber of Commerce entity, HEDCOR shared office space and an executive director with the chamber and the two organizations worked hand in hand. Over the succeeding decades HEDCOR would also use the Fantus recommendation as its blueprint for economic development.

HEDCOR's first task was to raise $100,000 from Chamber members to purchase a 100 acre tract of farmland in Fillmore Township for an industrial park. The local business community did not uniformly back the HEDCOR project because some considered it a threat to the downtown.

Despite the controversy HEDCOR moved ahead with its vision for the region's future. In 1965 it sold land to its first industrial client and soon hundreds of employees at the mammoth Lifesavers plant were making carloads of candy and gum. That coup proved the beginning of rapid growth at the southside park. Louis Hallacy, II, HEDCOR president since 1981, remembered: "Lifesavers made a tremendous impact at the time. After they moved here things just started to blossom." And blossom it did. By 1987 the park had expanded four times to 476 acres and 52 plants had located there.

That success and the scarcity of adjacent land spurred HEDCOR to open a 300 acre northside industrial center that year. Its first client, the Donnelly Corporation, soon constructed a 80,000 square-foot plant. By 1996 the northside park had grown to 535 acres occupied by 20 factories with 4,500 employees.

In addition to its active recruitment of new industry with an eye toward diversity, beginning in 1981 HEDCOR expanded its role to become involved in the commercial revitalization of downtown Holland. A major fund raising effort resulted in the purchase of eight acres of downtown property which HEDCOR later sold to the Riverview Development Limited Partnership. HEDCOR also took an active part in downtown planning activities.

As a result of HEDCOR's 35 year campaign to provide land for diversified industrial use, Holland continues to enjoy "one of the most prosperous economic climates in Michigan."

Holland Community Hospital

For Holland residents suffering illness or injury the "good old days" were not so good. As late as 1917 small pox, polio, diphtheria and other now conquered diseases annually took their deadly toll. Physicians made house calls but they also conducted "kitchen surgery" and doled out from their black medical bags a woefully inadequate array of medicine. Rare indeed was the infant not born at home. Patients requiring more sophisticated treatment and having the resources to do so traveled to medical facilities in Grand Rapids or Chicago - because Holland had no hospital.

During the early years of the century community leaders such as Dr. Henry Kremers, who served as one of the first city physicians, recognized the need for a hospital in Holland and campaigned to raise funds and encouraged citizens to support the concept. The first attempt to sustain a hospital - backed by local physicians, the churches and Adrian Henken, a graduate nurse from the Netherlands, - resulted in the opening of Bethesda Hospital in an 18-room

The Holland Hospital opened in the Dr. Henry Kremers Home in 1917.

house on the corner of 9th Street and Central Avenue in 1904. Unfortunately community patronage failed to materialize and Henken aborted the experiment after one month and fled the city for parts unknown.

Holland City News editor N.J. Whelan began editorializing for a hospital in 1911, chiding residents: "If smaller cities can do this thing, so can Holland." His continued agitation finally brought results in the summer of 1916 when the Holland Common Council voted unanimously to support a municipal hospital. By March, 1917, a special hospital committee had raised $12,000 for the project. The estate of Dr. Kremers, who had died three years before, offered his home, a brick carriage house and a tract of land along Central Avenue to the committee for $15,000 - the estate even offered to donate a third of the asking price in his memory.

Under the leadership of Holland Sugar Company Manager C.M. McLean the Holland Hospital Association moved quickly to secure the property. The Common Council encouraged the venture by pledging that the Park Board would care for the grounds and the Board of Public Works would pay the utility bills. Citizens labored to convert the mansion built in 1888 into a hospital. In the midst of remodeling, the first patient checked into the hospital in September 1917. With original rates as cheap as $2.50 per day, by the time the remodeling had been completed the hospital was full, with little room for visitors.

In January, 1919, Mabel Miller and Rena Boven, recent graduates of Butterworth Hospital's School of Nursing, arrived to take charge of the facility. Six additional nurses staffed the hospital around the clock. On February 24, 1919, the City of Holland officially accepted the property from the Hospital Board and the Holland Hospital became a public institution.

In an era when routine obstetric patients convalesced

from 10 to 14 days, the hospital was soon overburdened, being forced to turn away patients and crowd the halls with emergency cases on stretchers. By 1921, even with the addition of nine beds, patients faced a long waiting list for admission and only emergency surgery could be performed. But special elections held in 1921 and 1922 to secure bonding for a new municipal hospital failed largely because voters resented the use of local taxes to fund an institution that might be used by non-residents.

Newspaper editors continued to promote a new hospital and the Holland Chamber of Commerce picked up the banner by appointing a committee of community leaders to investigate the matter. Meaningful public discussions resulted but it became obvious that some method other than voter approval would be necessary.

In October, 1925, the Board of Public Works proposed to the City Council a plan to use utility profits to construct a new hospital. Enthusiastically endorsing the concept, the Council created a Hospital Planning Committee composed of representatives from the Board of Public Works, the existing Hospital Board, the City Council and the Chamber of Commerce. The committee acted quickly. By November it had decided to purchase a seven and one-half acre tract of land on Michigan Avenue.

The following spring, a team of Chicago architects had begun work on plans for the first unit. Designed in the fashionable Georgian Revival style of architecture, the brick structure trimmed with stone would feature a ground level service area, two floors containing 48 beds and a state-of-the-art laboratory and operating room. On January 19, 1928, the new hospital opened for a gala public reception as thousands of area residents surged through the building. The old hospital became the Netherlands Museum and now serves as a bed & breakfast.

The Depression of the 1930s brought substantial financial losses to the hospital and employees took pay cuts to help. Nevertheless the hospital stayed on the cutting edge of medical technology - an incubator for premature infants was donated in 1936 and three years later modern new x-ray equipment was added. World War II resulted in other problems as area doctors and nurses served in uniform. In 1942 the regular staff of 24 nurses had shrank to nine. Relief came through Red Cross nurses' aids and, beginning in 1944, senior nursing students from Detroit began training at the Holland Hospital.

Following the war, Holland's medical needs again exceeded the hospital's capacity. The city allocated funds for an addition in 1947 partially funded through a loan from the Department of Public Works. A 20-bed ward completed in 1951 brought the hospital bed count to 72.

Frederick S. Burd became hospital director in 1949 and over the next three decades he guided the hospital through a critical period of continued growth. Voters in Holland, Fillmore and Park townships joined with Holland residents to pass bond issues for a construction project in 1952. The four story addition built in 1955–1957 increased the bed count to 143 and brought additional space for ancillary departments. Another expansion project completed in 1969 added 55 more beds, a new emergency room, intensive care unit and other facilities. A spacious parking lot to the south of the hospital was added in 1970.

In 1976 Holland City and Holland, Laketown and Park township voters approved the creation of the Holland Community Hospital Authority. That key structural change provided funding and other benefits and relieved the City Council of involvement in the routine operation of the hospital. Additional construction made possible by that change came in 1976–1979, resulting in updated surgical facilities, the area's first 12-bed psychiatric unit and additional beds which then numbered 225. By 1979 the hospital medical staff included 80 physicians and 20 dentists.

The decade of the 1980s brought continuing growth and modernization. The hospital introduced computerized tomography (CT) scanning as a valuable diagnostic service in 1983. Two years later Prime Care, an urgent care center, opened on the hospital grounds. In 1986 the hospital developed Lakeshore HMO as an alternative health care delivery system for area businesses. It merged with Butterworth HMO in October 1992 to form Priority Health HMO. In 1987 the West Michigan Clinical Laboratory and Holland Community Hospital's laboratory consolidated.

The year 1988 proved particularly eventful when voters approved the hospital's change in corporate status to non-governmental, not for profit, in May. This freed the hospital from governmental restrictions in certain areas, allowing greater flexibility for new projects such as physicians networks and joint ventures.

Thanks in part to the greater freedom allowed by its new corporate status, the decade of the 1990s saw Holland Community Hospital participate in a variety of joint ventures with formerly competing institutions. In cooperation with Butterworth, North Ottawa and Zeeland hospitals, Holland Community Hospital opened a 10,400 square-foot Lakeshore Radiation Oncology Center on Riley Street in June 1993. Another collaborative venture with Butterworth and Zeeland hospitals - the Occupational Health Center -began providing Lakeshore area employees with health services in February 1994.

The Boven Birth Center, named in honor of one of the hospital's first nurses, opened in November, 1991. In 1994 in response to Fennville residents asking the hospital to assist with providing primary care, a 5,000 square-foot Health Center opened there. Adjacent the Holland Hospital Campus, the Community Health Center opened to service under insured or uninsured patients unnecessarily bogging down the hospital emergency room. With its start up funded by the hospital, the center treated over 1,000 patients during its first six months.

The hospital continues to stay on the cutting edge of technology. A $4.6 million investment in a new computer information system begun in 1993 went on-line on June 1, 1995 to improve patient documentation, provide quicker access to patient information and ultimately provide a paperless medical record system.

In July, 1996, hospital officials unveiled plans for an outpatient surgery addition, as well as expansion and renovation to ambulatory services such as Emergency, Prime Care and Radiology. The proposed $27 million project will improve accessibility, patient flow, efficiency of care and accommodate continued technology advancements. A planned two-tier parking deck will enhance accessibility for patients and visitors while maintaining green landscaping. A helicopter landing pad will be constructed to expedite transport of critical patients.

The Holland Community Hospital at 602 Michigan Avenue.

Holland Hitch Company

Holland Hitch's first customers were content with one-horsepower equipment - that is, they were powered by the strength of one real horse. Eighty-six years later the company manufactures products which harness the energy of roaring diesel rigs that zoom over mountain ranges and zip across deserts. From humble origins the company has grown to lead the world in the design and manufacture of fifth wheels, coupling devices, trailer suspensions and landing gear. Yet it continues a vital force in the Holland economy, a family owned operation with close ties to the community and its institutions.

The company began with a better idea. Gerrit Den Besten, Albert Hulsebos and Henry Ketel got together in the back of a record store in Corsica, South Dakota, in 1910, and designed the prototype for what they called the safety release clevis. An improvement over existing coupling devices, this innovation released when a plow hit a solid object, saving the horse from injury and the plow from damage. The Safety Release Clevis Co. prospered at first, but by 1920 with increasing use of tractors and automobiles the company realized it had hitched its future to the wrong market.

That year the company relocated to Holland to be closer to the automobile industry, moving into the former Holland City Brewery on West 10th Street. Total employment numbered ten. The firm changed its name to the Holland Hitch Company in 1921.

In the early 1930s Holland Hitch received its first fifth wheel patents. But the Great Depression of the 1930s forced the company into bankruptcy in 1935. Ketel teamed up with local businessman Henry A. Geerds and purchased the company's assets in an effort to save it. With Ketel as general manager, production continued with a mere three workers. But by the end of the year the company was back on its feet with a workforce of ten manufacturing plow hitches, couplers, and pintle hooks. Business grew as the company secured orders from leading farm implement manufacturers over the next five years.

Ketel had invented a pintle hook designed for heavy duty use, ideal for coupling field artillery to trucks. The U.S. Army remained uninterested, however, until Geerds won the gratitude of General Motors for his zeal in battling UAW workers as a National Guard officer during the Flint Sit-Down-Strike of 1937. General Motors helped Holland Hitch secure an Army contract for 1,600 hooks in 1940. By the end of the year the company employed 86 and annual sales reached $1 million.

The company grew rapidly during World War II. By May 1945 it had made one million hooks for the military. Also during the war the product line evolved to include fifth wheels, catering to the needs of the heavy truck industry. The company constructed and moved into a larger factory on Ottawa Avenue in 1945.

Geerds took over as general manager in 1946, facing lean years as government contracts dried up. In 1950, the Korean War brought a flurry of military business. Huge orders for civilian plow hitches followed and the company expanded its operations. A manufacturing facility opened in California in 1958. That year William F. Beebe succeeded his father-in-law as general manager.

Holland Hitch became an international manufacturer with construction of a facility in Woodstock, Ontario, in 1963. The company also expanded its Holland factory that year. Five years later a new facility was erected in the Southside Industrial Park.

The company purchased the former Westside Christian Elementary School in 1985 and after extensive renovations it became the Holland Hitch Corporate Offices. The following year the Training Center, which also houses the Research and Development departments,was constructed on the site of the old Hekman Rusk Bakery.

By 1996 the company, now part of the Holland Group, and in its third generation of family management, had grown to include 15 locations worldwide with 1,400 employees. Responding to changes in the global marketplace by placing facilities in areas such as the rapidly growing Pacific Rim, Holland Hitch also diversified into other aspects of the heavy duty commercial transportation market including components for tugs that pull airplanes, trailer landing gear, suspensions and kingpins.

Holland Hitch has actively supported numerous projects including the Holland Community Foundation, Hope College, Holland Public Schools, Holland Area Arts Council, Hospice, the Boys and Girls Club of Greater Holland and the Holland Historical Trust.

The Holland Hitch Company's corporate headquarters at 467 Ottawa Avenue.

Hope College

Business and industry have proved the backbone of Holland's vitality; its many churches its spirit. But the city would be far different were it not for its cultural heart - Hope College - that has made the community pulse with learning and academic tradition.

In 1850, the Rev. Albertus Van Raalte donated a five-acre tract of land as a site for "The Academy." Dissatisfied with the limited schooling available for their children, the colonists opened a "Pioneer School" in 1851 to provide secondary education. Van Raalte called that little school which would evolve into the college in 1866, "my anchor of hope for this people in the future."

As the community prepares to commemorate the sesquicentennial of the city Van Raalte and his followers founded, it is particularly fitting that Hope College anticipates playing a major role in the celebration. Much of the research behind the event will have been conducted in the Joint Archives of Holland, a major repository for documents, publications and photographs preserving the history of the community and Dutch immigration to the United States, housed in the Van Wylen Library, named for ninth President Gordon J. and Margaret D. Van Wylen. Among the books scheduled to appear during the sesquicentennial is a scholarly biography of Van Raalte published under the auspices of the A.C. Van Raalte Institute for Historical Studies established by the col-

---

The historic Dimnent Memorial Chapel and Pine Grove on the campus of Hope College.

---

lege in 1994. Hope College will offer another tribute to its founder when it accomplishes a project conceived in 1922 but never completed because of financial reasons, the placement of a statue of Van Raalte in Centennial Park.

Centennial Park had been laid out in 1876, the year of Van Raalte's death. The campus had survived the devastating fire of five years before that leveled most of Holland, but the decade of the 1870s brought serious financial problems. The college was officially opened to women in 1878 and two years later the student body numbered 121. Under the tenure of President Gerrit J. Kollen which began in 1893, Hope's financial picture brightened.

Graves Library and Winants Chapel were dedicated in 1894, Van Raalte Memorial Hall in 1903, Carnegie Gymnasium in 1906 and the Elizabeth R. Voorhees Girls Residence in 1907. When Kollen retired in 1911, Hope's enrollment stood at 317 students.

In 1913, Hope won accreditation by the North Central Association of Schools and Colleges. By 1916 the student body reflected a growing cosmopolitan nature with 15 states and three foreign countries represented. In 1929, the Memorial Chapel was dedicated - 30 years later it was renamed in honor of past president Edward D. Dimnent. In 1942, the Science Building, today's Lubbers Hall, was dedicated.

Following World War II, returning veterans took advantage of the GI Bill to swell college enrollments. Hope rose to the challenge of accommodating the increased numbers, following the vision of President Irwin J. Lubbers, who felt that colleges had a moral responsiblility to help those who had served their country.

A building campaign resulted in the Winifred Hackley Durfee Hall in 1950, Nykerk Music Hall and Kollen Hall in 1956, Phelps Hall in 1960 and Van Zoeren Library in 1961.

Two years later the Fraternity Dormitory Complex and Gilmore Hall opened. The Physics Mathematics Hall, later renamed VanderWerf Hall, in honor of Hope's eighth president, Calvin A. VanderWerf, opened in 1964, followed by Dykstra Hall in 1967, Brumler House in 1969 and the De Witt Student and Cultural Center in 1971.

Over the succeeding two decades Hope invested more than $75 million in the construction of new facilities, restoration of historic structures and campus beautification projects. The $15 million Haworth Learning and Conference Center, planned to open during the sesquicentennial year, capped the creation of a picturesque campus that offers a pleasant blend of old and new architecture.

Under President John H. Jacobson, Hope College has also played a significant role in the community's efforts to keep its central business core vital. It acquired the historic Knickerbocker Theatre on Eighth Street in 1988 and with two restoration projects produced an ideal setting to enjoy movies and live events such as concerts.

The decade of the 1990s also brought increasing national attention to Hope. The Carnegie Foundation designated Hope a national liberal arts college, and praise accorded the school has included being named one of only 42 "Best Buys" nationwide in the most recent editon of the highly-respected *Fiske Guide to Colleges*. Hope ranked in the top four percent in the nation in producing future Ph.D. holders in the sciences from 1920-1990.

During the 1995–96 school year, 2,919 students studied courses in 39 major fields. Hope College continues its mission "to offer with recognized excellence, academic programs in liberal arts, in the setting of a residential, undergraduate, coeducational college, and in the context of historic Christian faith."

J. B. Laboratories

J.B. Laboratories' new manufacturing facility at 13295 Reflections Drive.

Entrepreneurial opportunity comes in many ways, and in 1977, when the Chattem Co. bought the old DePree Chemical Co. on Central Avenue a pair of employees recognized opportunity's knock. One of DePree's products had been a line of bulk vitamins and mineral additives for the Keebler Company's "Pop-Tarts." When Chattem decided to drop that line, Bill Baker and John Otting, who had been involved in their manufacture, negotiated with Keebler and began production of those additives as a side venture in a little building on Spruce Street.

Baker and Otting had both grown up in the Holland area. Baker brought to the new company they had named J.B. Laboratories, after the initials of their first names, a background in accounting and finance. Otting had a masters degree in biology from Michigan State University. Before long Chattem closed its Holland plant and Baker and Otting's part time operation blossomed into a full time career change. In 1980 production had expanded from what was initially handled solely by the two founders into the need for increased space. The two made what they felt was a ridiculously low offer to the Chattem Co. for the plant on Central Avenue. To their surprise it was accepted and they relocated their company.

The early 1980s brought continued growth through the acquisition of the Hoppe Pharmaceutical Co. of Grand Haven which was consolidated to the Holland site. As the decade wore on J.B. Laboratories began manufacturing a wider variety of products for such leading pharmaceutical and food processing companies as Perrigo, Kellogg, Keebler and Upsher-Smith. By the decades end it produced over the counter drugs ranging from aspirin, allergy tablets, diet caplets, travel sickness tablets to women's laxatives. Its nutritional supplements included vitamins C and B, multivitamins, brewer's yeast, garlic tablets and bee pollen, as well as a variety of extended release products.

J.B. Laboratories' manufacturing capabilities grew to include blending, granulation, tablet compression, film coating, sugar coating, hard shell encapsulation, capsule banding, blister packaging and tablet bottle filling. A battery of chemists, microbiologists and research scientists staffed its quality control and research and development laboratories.

Beginning in 1984 Baker and Otting began offering select employees the opportunity to buy company stock. By 1992 when Otting retired J.B. Laboratories had become a unique company totally owned by its employees. After five years of seniority any employee could participate in the stock option plan. Currently the company consists of 59 stockholder employees and its total employment numbers 125.

Baker remains the company president, sharing duties in the executive management team with Frank Lamb, executive vice president, who joined the company in 1984. Patrick Mikula, vice president of operations, with a degree in biology has seven years of service with the company. Jon Baker, vice president of sales and marketing, arrived in 1993 after ten years with the Perrigo Co. of Allegan.

The company which believes if its employees have "stock in the company they have stock in its success" moved into its new 85,000 square foot state-of-the-art manufacturing facility at 13295 Reflections Drive in November 1995. There its skilled work force continues to enhance and diversify its contract pharmaceuticals product line, including the recent development of a variety of prescription vitamins.

Lake Michigan Contractors

Like many another Holland area business that grew from a dream into a prosperous reality, Lake Michigan Contractors, Inc. depended on quality products, hard work, adequate capital and timing. But timing, in particular - that of Mother Nature's cyclical rise in the level of Lake Michigan in conjunction with the start up of the company - proved critical.

Kemma J. Walsh, president, and husband Joseph Walsh, vice president, launched their company in April, 1980. He had gained experience working in the field of marine construction for a Muskegon contractor and having grown up in Holland with a love of the big lake and Lake Macatawa it seemed time to form a partnership with his wife and strike out on their own. Kemma who had grown up in Zeeland and gained business experience working at the Old Kent Bank and for her father in his beer delivery company also studied at Davenport Business College.

and salvage operations to their construction capabilities, and of course, additional employees and more equipment.

Another of the company's early successful projects was the stabilization of the waterfront before the historic Marigold Lodge at Macatawa with a natural breakwater of crushed limestone.

Yet another early project came close to proving a fiasco. A client wanted a good sized cottage moved from Waukazoo Woods across Lake Macatawa to Park Township. The Walshs successfully got it loaded on a barge but Park Township officials would not allow it to be landed because of a zoning technicality. The cottage sat on the barge for nearly three months. The story ultimately had a happy ending and "the little house that made it" was towed up the lake to Beaver Island where it reposes as a summer cottage.

Lake Michigan Contractors branched into marine con-

The Lake Michigan Contractors, Inc., newly refinished headquarters at 265 Kollen Park Drive, originally housed the Superior Ice Company.

Many individuals who learned of the Walshs' intent to follow the dream of forging their own company "said they were crazy." Nevertheless, the two convinced Kemma's father to advance them a loan. They bought a used barge and a 20 foot work boat, rented a crane and went to work constructing pilings, sea walls and docks. During their first job, building a steel seawall, Joe taught his wife how to weld. The successful completion of that project so pleased the client that he provided many references which landed them additional customers.

During their first three or four years of business the Walshs operated their office out of their bedroom and then in a 10 by 50-foot tool trailer. Hard work, references by other satisfied clients and Lake Michigan's rise to record levels coupled with the booming growth of lakeside residential construction paid off. They eventually added dredging, towing

struction in Florida in 1989, working on projects on the Atlantic Ocean side of the peninsula as far south as Miami and north into Alabama. Ultimately such southern jobs would comprise 50% of their work.

In September 1995, the company moved into its new headquarters at 265 Kollen Park Drive, a beautifully refinished example of historic adaptation of an old factory originally constructed to house the Superior Ice Company at the turn-of-the-century. Their company has grown from an original work force of only the Walshs to 54 employees, 16 tug boats, 2 hydraulic dredges and 52 barges ranging from 80 to 200 feet in length.

Pleased with her company's American success story achieved through hard work, Kemma Walsh is also proud of her Potawatomi ancestry, a heritage that predates the settlement of Holland.

Metal Flow Corporation

Curtis H. Brown often told his son Marc, "The mark of your life is not what you take, it's what you leave." And while many men leave little more than fading memories and a granite tombstone, the thriving company that the Browns founded in 1978 stands as a memorial to Curtis Brown's hard work, perseverance and the philosophy he imparted to the other family members who now guide the business.

The Brown family saga began in 1946 when Curtis Brown was discharged from the Army Air Corps at the end of World War II. He got a job as a machine operator in the deep drawn metal stamping business. Rising through the ranks, he became general manager of a large Detroit manufacturer. During the late 1950s and early 1960s he flexed his entrepreneurial muscles when he developed a profitable business as a side line. He later sold that operation to his employer.

Marc, the third oldest of Brown's five children, followed in his father's footsteps, starting as an apprentice machine operator after graduation from high school in 1971. He became particularly adept at the delicate art of machine set up. A job at the recently opened Drawform Co. brought him to Holland in 1978. But when that position did not work out he struggled with the decision to return to Detroit and leave the Holland area, a prime environment to raise his family.

Marc talked to his father and together they decided to make their long cherished dream of building their own company a reality. The elder Brown then took a risk that might have proved disastrous for a less confident person. He resigned his position of more than 30 years, sold his Detroit home and sunk the proceeds and his entire retirement into the fledgling Metal Flow Corporation, so named because during the deep draw process the metal actually flows between the punches and dies.

After moving into his son's house, the two purchased a Waterbury Farrel 108 eyelet transfer press which they set up in a 1,500 square-foot facility rented for $300 a month in a century old factory on 19th Street. The father and son team worked feverishly. Eighteen hour days were commonplace.

But the Browns had more than drive and a strong work ethic, traits common enough in the Holland area - they had a special relationship of being good friends and trusted business partners. And they were able to combine the vigor of youth and the priceless wisdom of age. With that wisdom came a philosophy that the senior Brown had evolved over the decades – "An unrelenting desire for excellence in everything you do, treating people fair with honesty." That ideal, coupled with an old fashioned financial policy, pay as you go, brought results. When the company began in the winter of 1978, a notably bad economic slump, the Browns went out and secured orders by knocking on doors, by competitive pricing and by sheer perseverance. Once they got orders they accomplished that work in a manner that would insure repeat business.

Curt Brown long remembered the day when the first check came in. "It was only for $1,200, but it was the first real evidence that we were a viable concern." Other orders and bigger checks followed. By year's end total sales had reached $49,000. In the meantime, to keep up with the growing orders the Browns had expanded by leasing and later buying three additional machines. Rather than borrow money from a bank at a high rate of interest which would have made competitive pricing of their product more difficult, the two plowed profits back into the company.

In 1980, the company moved into a 10,000 square-foot facility at Ottawa and 22nd Street and began hiring more employees. That is where another aspect of Curt Brown's wisdom came into play. Through 30 years of management experience he had learned to quickly size up a person's character in the course of a short interview and separate the potential sluggards from the hard workers. Furthermore, he believed in "hiring bright young people and giving them their heads, to let their talents carry them as far as their limits."

In addition to developing a hard working and efficient team of employees, the company spurred continuing growth by developing and redesigning products for customers and thereby creating a bigger market. For example, in 1983 *Precision Metal* magazine carried an article about Metal Flow's ingenious redesign of a front plate for a door lock assembly that lowered the customer's cost to one quarter the price that was being paid for a screw machined plate. Two years later the company won a prestigious AMSA-Higgins Design

The Metal Flow Corporation's headquarters at 11694 James Street.

Award for another process it perfected to reduce the cost and vastly improve a product's performance.

In 1984, Metal Flow's 23 employees had again outgrown their plant and the company built a new 20,000 square-foot factory at 259 Hedcor Street in the Southside Industrial Park. The following year Metal Flow invested nearly a half million dollars in state-of-the-art machinery and employment had grown to 37 people.

Marc's older brother C. Michael Brown joined the company in November 1985. Following graduation from Eastern Michigan University with a degree in physics, he had worked for the Ford Motor Co. as a mechanical engineer for nine years. From his original position with Metal Flow as director of engineering and quality control he rose to the rank of vice president and executive vice president. In January 1995 he was named company president. In the meantime, other family members accepted positions with Metal Flow. Brother Kevin Brown serves as human resources director, sister Kate is customer services administrator and another sister Karen works on a consulting basis.

The year 1986 witnessed construction of a 15,000 square-foot addition to the plant. By 1987 the work force had expanded to 77 employees and sales had increased more than twenty fold over the previous seven years. The following year Metal Flow was ranked by *Michigan Business Magazine* among the state's 100 fastest growing privately held companies.

Curtis Brown retired in 1990, continuing as chairman of the board. The company celebrated its first $1 million sales month in August, 1992. It duplicated the feat in October and finished the year with $11 million in sales, a 25% increase over 1991. That year also, Metal Flow made headlines with its $750 cash incentive to employees to buy American made vehicles. That offer highlighted the Browns' long time faith in American industry and its ability to compete in the world market – a sense of patriotism reflected by the stars and stripes that wave from the company flag pole and the little U.S. flags sewn on uniforms issued to employees.

Curtis Brown died in January 1993. That same month he

and his company were awarded a U.S. patent for a threaded sheet metal decorative cap he had jointly invented. In his honor the Metal Flow Corporation became Curtis H., Brown Industries. In October 1993, Marc Brown was named Holland Area Chamber of Commerce's Small Businessperson of the Year. Accepting the award in his father's name, Brown articulated what his father would have thought of the honor: "Remember who made this possible for you – the people out in the plant."

In June 1994, the company moved into its new 65,000 square-foot plant on 14 acres of land on the corner of James Street and 120th Avenue. By that time the company's product line had grown to include stainless steel parts for anti-lock brake systems, air bags and fuel systems as well as other products made from the deep draw process. About 70% of the company's business went to automotive suppliers, in particular to those manufacturing products for emerging markets like air bags.

As the decade of the 1990s wore on, to reduce its dependance on the cyclical automotive market the company increasingly diversified its product line to include parts for the recreation industry such as camping equipment and bicycles. Metal Flow also began producing more complex pieces made up of various components that reduced the customer's assembling cost. By responding to changing times, including the developing international marketplace, the company sought to create new markets and to offer a wider range of products.

Another diversification came through the formation of a joint venture with stamping firm JMS, a manufacturer of smaller sized drawn metal components. The Browns supplied funding and expertise which made possible the opening of a new JMS plant at 101 East Roosevelt Avenue in Zeeland in 1995.

The following year Metal Flow received the Ulbrick Award for excellence in product development for its work in developing a stainless steel connector body that replaced a less efficient plastic design. In 1996 the company also earned the prestigious QS-9000 certification. A work force of 105 people utilizing state-of-the-art machinery produced in excess of $20 million worth of products during the year.

Representative of the type of parts produced by Metal Flow are these examples produced on a transfer press with deep draw capability.

Lithibar Matik

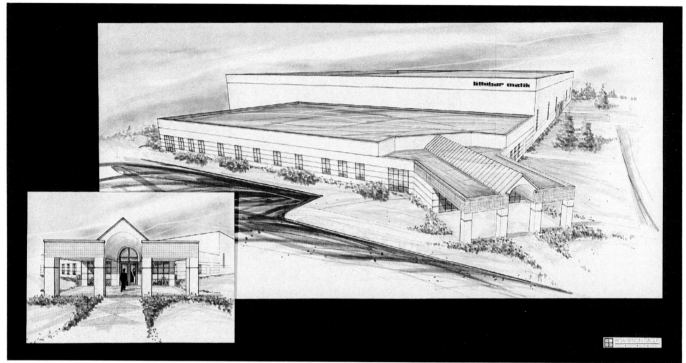

Lithibar Matik's new 92,000 square-foot manufacturing and office facility currently under construction on Shoreline Drive

Lithibar Matik, Inc., traces it origins to 1929, the year that ushered in the dark days of the Great Depression. A number of prominent Kalamazoo entrepreneurs had established the firm to produce machinery to manufacture reinforced concrete joists for heavy construction. Howard F. Young, an architect's and manufacturer's agent, served as first president of the firm whose name stems from the Greek word for stone - "Lithibar" meaning literally - stone bar. The first product, an ingenious piece of machinery that produced reinforced concrete joists up to 40 feet in length and eight to 14 inches wide enabled the company to weather the Depression.

In 1946, Frank Mileski, formerly a salesman for the Holland-based Dunn Brick Co., relocated Lithibar to Holland. He teamed up with Ralph Samuelson of Traverse City, who had developed concrete brick making machinery. Lithibar first used the facilities of IXL Machinery to produce its products but in 1948 Mileski launched his own production department in an old sugar beet plant.

Charles Sligh, Jr., and Bill Lowry of local furniture fame headed the Lithibar Co. from 1953-1957. Under their leadership the company advanced from an air powered to hydraulic powered source for its concrete block machinery. Lithibar also added accessories such as cement mixers and ship hoists to its product line.

Leonard Zick, formerly an officer of the Allen Electrical & Equipment Co. of Kalamazoo, moved to Holland to serve as Lithibar president from 1957-1962. Zick was succeeded by Bernard Donnelly, an officer of the Holland mirror company that continues to honor his family name. Donnelly guided the company from 1962-1985. Under his tenure Lithibar diversified into manufacture of palletizing machinery for concrete products in 1967. The company also entered international markets with shipments to Mexico, Australia and the United Arab Emirates.

The early 1970s saw increased efforts to further diversify the company's markets. Lithibar applied its engineering resources to development of automatic bag palletizing systems for feed and grain mills, cement and limestone producers, chemical manufacturers and for other products that required special handling due to size, weight or load shape. The company also developed automatic case palletizers widely used by paper mills, beverage bottlers and manufacturers of household products.

The decade of the 1980s proved important for company development. On November 1, 1985, Lithibar Matik was established as a new company, taking over the assets of the original firm. Lithibar moved the Stearns Equipment line from Kansas to Holland in 1988 and three years later added Beco block curing equipment and Quikstak® palletizers.

Larry B. Hilldore, who had grown up in Holland prior to joining the company in 1977 as a shop laborer, worked his way up the ladder to become vice president of sales in 1987 and president in 1989. Under his leadership the firm expanded its international markets, placing its equipment in Ireland, Spain, Greece, Central and South America, India, Russia, Korea, Thailand and China. In 1996, Hilldore could proudly cite that 95% of Lithibar's concrete palletizing equipment produced since 1967 was still in operation. Furthermore, half of all U.S. block producing plants utilized Lithibar machinery.

By April 1995, Hilldore had become owner of the company. That month he sold the firm to the Besser Co. of Alpena, while continuing to serve as the president of the 33,000 square-foot facility employing 140 people and with a dozen sales and service locations across the nation.

In 1996, Lithibar Matik began construction of a new manufacturing and office facility. The 92,000 square-foot building on Shoreline Drive features specialty masonry products produced for Lithibar Matik customers. The 11 acre site allows for future expansion to accommodate the growing worldwide demands for specialized handling machinery.

Michigan Gas Company

Back in 1903 when the Holland Gas Works opened for business on East 8th Street, nine employees shoveled coal and huge retorts distilled "coal gas" with coke as a byproduct. About the only use for that manufactured gas then was for household illumination and with a plentiful supply of cheap electricity being supplied by the Holland Board of Public Works the gas company found but few customers. Times would change and over the decades as the Holland operation became affiliated with increasingly larger companies it would grow to provide steady dependable service to more than 35,000 customers in the Holland area.

The Michigan Gas Company traces its origins to 1904 when the Portage Lake Gas and Coke Co. was organized to produce and distribute illuminating gas in the Houghton-Hancock area of the Upper Peninsula's rugged Keweenaw Peninsula. Two years later it was renamed the Houghton Gas and Coke Co. As a result of its campaign to acquire smaller gas companies it was incorporated as the Michigan Gas and Electric Company in 1917, with headquarters in Ashland, Wisconsin.

The same year that witnessed the U.S. enter World War I brought the acquisition of the Marquette County Gas and Electric Co., the Cassopolis Milling and Power Company, the Constantine Hydraulic Co., the Three Rivers Light and Power Co, and the Three Rivers Gas Co. The year 1928 brought expansion into the Niles-Buchanan region with purchase of the manufacturing plants and distribution system of the Niles Gas Light Co., followed by the Dowagiac Light and Power Co. and the Klinger Lake Light and Power Co. in 1930.

In 1930, also, the firm that had evolved into the Holland City Gas Co. by 1910 and later became the Holland Gas Co. joined Michigan Gas and Electric. In 1938 the company operated two sites in Holland, general offices, with William C. Blanchard as president, near the original location on 8th Street and a retail appliance outlet managed by Marshall W. Berg at 215 River Avenue. Company advertising that year promised "If it's done with heat – You can do it better with gas."

Natural gas was introduced into the Holland-Zeeland and the Niles, Buchanan and Dowagiac areas in 1950. At that time, dramatic changes in the gas and electric industry brought about the relocation of the corporate offices from Ashland, Wisconsin, to Three Rivers. As part of that restructuring Ralph Casperson was transferred from Ashland to begin a memorable 20 year stint as manager of the Niles District. By 1958, Charles W. Madison served as the Holland district manager.

Michigan Gas and Electric was acquired by the American Electric Power Co. (AEP) in 1967 and operated as Michigan Power Co. Michigan Power Co. continued to supply both natural gas and electric energy to its customers until the gas division was sold by AEP in 1987 to the Southeastern Michigan Gas Enterprises, Inc. of Port Huron, Michigan.

That corporation began in 1950 with the acquisition of the Marysville, Michigan, manufactured gas plant from Detroit Edison. The Battle Creek Gas Company which traces it origins to 1870, joined the Enterprises group in 1985 . A year later SEMCO Energy Services, the fourth of the corporation's gas systems, was incorporated in Port Huron to efficiently purchase natural gas at the wellhead and sell it directly to such large volume users as the Ford Motor Co., the Kellogg Co. and the Michigan Sugar Co. in Croswell.

When the Michigan Gas Company was acquired by Enterprises in 1987 it served 77,000 customers. The following year the company initiated a major upgrading of its distribution and service lines both in the Upper and Lower Peninsulas. It constructed new offices, remodeled existing structures and adopted a precise computerized information system to better serve customer needs. In 1989 the company expanded its merchandise program in Holland, Three Rivers, Niles and Negaunee to stock a full line of appliances including washers, dryers, ranges, grills, refrigerators and water heaters. By 1996 Michigan Gas Co. serviced an additional 20,000 plus customers.

The Michigan Gas Co. and its affiliated partners are justifiably proud of its current project to expand the use of compressed natural gas for vehicles and forklifts. Since 1980 the corporation has demonstrated its practicality by converting its own cars, trucks and vans to that fuel. Cheaper than gasoline, safer and cleaner burning, this fuel source will become increasingly important in preserving the Holland area's air quality for many years to come.

A 1927 view of the Holland gas plant adjacent the Pere Marquette Railroad tracks.

Old Kent Bank – Holland

The first financial institution in Holland that joined the Old Kent family traces its origins back to September 9, 1905 when the People's State Bank opened at 29 East 8th Street. Arend Visscher, an attorney, served as the bank's first president.

In 1909 its advertising urged "Do it now - Today is the time to start a savings account - Bring your dollar and we will put other dollars with it and make it work for you." By 1910 enough Holland residents had heeded that advice to bring the bank's deposits to $331,000.

By 1928 the bank's total assets had reached more than $3 million. That year the People's State Bank erected a handsome new structure at 36-38 East 8th Street, sparing no expense at a time when the majesty of a bank's facade was an important symbol of its strength. But when the following year's stock market crash ushered in the Great Depression the People's Bank, like many other banks, was in trouble. Forced to close its doors, the bank was in the process of reorganizing and liquidating frozen assets to pay off depositors in 1933. That's when a young man destined to make his mark in the annals of Holland's banking history entered the picture.

Born in Holland in 1906, Laverne "Curly" Dalman was the eldest of the seven children of George Dalman, a skilled woodworker at the Holland Furniture Company. Young Dalman had started his working career at the age of 12, hawking *Holland Sentinel* newspapers for two cents each. Following attendance at Hope College and the Holland Business College he got a job in the office of the Bush and Lane Piano Co. on 24th Street. That factory fell on hard times during the late 1920s and Dalman spent two years prior to its closing in the fall of 1930 liquidating its assets. In July 1933 he was hired as assistant cashier of the People's Bank of Holland to help it liquidate assets.

Thanks in part to Dalman's perseverance, the bank reopened. It grew stronger as the Depression ended in the late 1930s. During World War II the bank focused on home front activities such as liberty loan drives. After the war, the People's Bank helped many returning G.I's to start homes and families and establish successful businesses.

Dalman served as president of the Chamber of Commerce in 1961 and 1962. The banker who earned a remarkable reputation in the area in part by following his principle of "never making a promise I couldn't keep" ultimately rose to the presidency of the bank.

On January 1, 1974, People's State Bank joined the Old Kent Financial Corporation. Dalman remained president until April when he became a director of the Old Kent Bank of Holland until his retirement five years later.

Jerrald H. Redeker, a native of Waupun, Wisconsin, succeeded Dalman as president of the bank. Following graduation from Hope College in 1956, Redeker cast his lot with the Wolverine State. Following a stint in the U.S. Army, he joined the Old Kent Bank in 1960, working his way up the corporate ladder.

One of Redeker's first campaigns was to convince Hollanders the People's Bank would continue to be run as a local bank. By persistent and gentle persuasion he got that message across and during the next 20 years the bank continued to grow while undergoing the pressures brought about by changing times.

This growth necessitated the establishment of several branches, beginning with the Northside Office in 1960. The Main Office was also expanded with the purchase of properties to its west. By 1984, assets had reached $200 million and the name was changed to Old Kent Bank of Holland. Richard N. Lievense succeeded Redeker as president in 1994. Lievense, who had graduated from Alma College, was pivotal in guiding the Holland bank through a period of reorganization. C. William Whitlock, a graduate of Cornell University and University of Denver Law School who had joined Old Kent in 1976, became president of Old Kent Bank–Holland in 1996.

Now nine branches and 140 employees strong, Old Kent Bank–Holland reports assets of over $400 million. It remains a true community bank, sensitive to the economic, cultural and social changes of its market. Old Kent people are actively involved in civic, public and private agencies, committed to the success of these organizations and the community they serve.

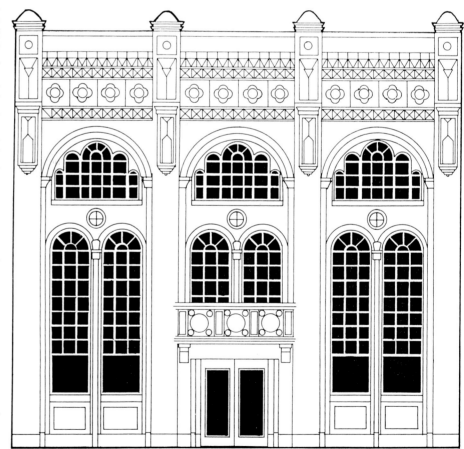

The graceful art deco facade of the Old Kent Bank - Holland Building at 36 East 8th Street.

Parke-Davis

Industrial evolution has long been a factor in Holland's economic vitality. When industries fell by the wayside other young businesses, often of a different nature, again made abandoned factories hum with production.

One of the area's first industries, the tanning of leather, dates back to the 1850s. By the late 1940s the last plant in Holland, the Armour Company Tannery along the north bank of the Macatawa River, stood vacant. In 1951 Parke-Davis and Co., a long established Detroit pharmaceutical firm, purchased the 30-acre site, remodeled the buildings and launched production of the drug chloromycetin. Discovered during World War II, chloromycetin, the first broad-spectrum antibiotic that could be synthetically manufactured on a large scale, had been thoroughly tested and released for general use in 1949. Soon production at the Holland plant was up and running with more than 300 employees.

Parke-Davis traces its origins back to 1866, when Detroit druggist Dr. Samuel P. Duffield founded a partnership with Hervey C. Parke. The following year a young promotional genius named Solomon Davis joined the firm. Soon Duffield left the business and the firm became Parke-Davis and Co. Over the decades, as the plant grew into a huge brick complex on the Detroit River, Parke-Davis pioneered with medical accomplishments, including the first machine manufactured hard gelatin capsules in the 1870s; Dilantin, a treatment for epilepsy in 1930; and the first antihistamine marketed in the U.S., Benadryl, in 1946. A decade later the company established a new research laboratory located close to the North Campus of the University of Michigan at Ann Arbor.

The role of this multi-disciplinary team, that grew to number 80 skilled scientists, is to further the development of promising new compounds of potential therapeutic value discovered at the Ann Arbor research facilities. They accomplish their work by using state-of-the-art equipment and techniques to enhance the chemical structure of former compounds to make them safer and environment friendly, while developing production processes that will be used for full scale production.

By 1975 Parke-Davis had enlarged the Holland plant to include a chemical manufacturing building, and a process development building that housed seven laboratories. Some of the leading products then produced included, Benzophenone, a chemical used to make food service plastic containers biodegradable, P-Aminobenzoic Acid, a sun screening agent that filters out ultraviolet light, a variety of nasal decongestants antihistamines, antibiotics such as chloromycetin, anti-convulsants and pain relievers. Most of the facility's final products were in the form of fine powders produced by eliminating unwanted liquids created during chemical reactions and vacuum or air drying the desirable residue.

A merger with Warner-Lambert started in 1971. By the late 1970s Parke-Davis had become part of that Fortune 500 international giant, one of the world's largest marketers of consumer health care products, chewing gums, breath mints, razor blades and pharmaceuticals. Corporate sales of Warner-Lambert reached $7 billion in 1995.

Meanwhile sales and facilities to keep pace with new products continued to grow in Holland. By 1996 some 350 employees at the 426,000 square-foot-factory manufactured more than 20 active ingredients for shipment to Parke-Davis plants around the world. The Chemical "B" complex, distinguished by its unique honey-combed plastic windows designed to pop out without shattering in the event of undue pressure created within the structure, is the facility's primary manufacturing center. The cholesterol regulator Lopid, the first drug proven to reduce the risk of coronary heart disease, is the plant's leading product. Other noteworthy products include Accupril, Neurontin and Dilantin.

A hallmark of the Parke-Davis Holland plant continued to be concern for the environment. State-of-the-art equipment includes a Thermal Oxidizer that destroys air pollutants at 1,800 °F, an above ground tank farm to safeguard ground water and a new chemical waste water treatment facility designed at a cost of over $6 million.

An Aerial view of the massive Parke-Davis facilities taken in 1994.

Prince Corporation

Business entrepreneur, benefactor, family man, hard worker, visionary, fantastic steward, friend – those were the words used to describe Ed Prince following his sudden death on March 2, 1995. But when the shock and grief of his passing had lessened, some of his friends, the 4,500 employees who owed their livelihood to the company he founded and the many thousands more who benefitted from his philanthropic endeavors that made Holland a better place to live, would realize that those traits were not a eulogy but a legacy to the community he loved.

A child of the Great Depression, Edgar Prince was born on May 3, 1931. His father Peter struggled to make ends meet at the produce market he operated in Holland while his mother Edith cared for their three children at the West 17th Street home. Despite the bleak times that left a psychological scar on all who experienced the Depression, young Edgar absorbed some valuable lessons from his parents that would influence his subsequent philosophy. He learned "the value and dignity of hard work, the importance of trying no matter how tough the challenge, and the power of faith."

World War II brought an end to the Depression, but halfway through it the Prince family suffered the personal tragedy of the loss of its father and breadwinner. Twelve-year-old Edgar suddenly had the demands and responsibilities of adulthood thrust on his shoulders. While that pain and trauma might have broken the spirit of some, it only made Edgar all the stronger and more determined to succeed – to make a mark in the world.

Following graduation from Holland High School in 1949, Prince studied mechanical engineering at Michigan Tech. in Sault Ste. Marie for two years and earned his BSME degree at the University of Michigan in 1954. He then married his long-time sweetheart Elsa Zwiep, who had also grown up in Holland before earning an education and sociology degree from Calvin College. Enlisting in the Air Force and serving at bases in Colorado and South Carolina, Prince rose to the rank of lieutenant.

After his discharge, the Princes returned to Holland where Ed took a position as engineer with the Buss Machine Works on West 8th Street. Over the next nine years he earned promotion to chief engineer. But that success was not satisfying enough. As Prince remembered 20 years later, "I looked back at the management direction of Buss Machine Co. as well as the future management direction. I wanted to be a part of an organization that shared its profits with charitable causes."

In 1965, Prince decided to establish his own company in Holland to manufacture die-cast machinery. The fact that he had no start-up capital did not deter him. He simply got a second mortgage on his home, purchased a plat of land with no down payment, and erected a 8,500 square-foot plant at the present site of Prince Machine. His original office was a bare room with a couple of chairs and a flimsy cardboard table for a desk. Thirty years later, Bill Van Appledorn remembered his first assignment when he reported for work – go to Pete Yff's, a local butcher, and ask for some meat wrapping paper. When he returned, the paper was spread out on the card table and they went to work drawing machinery layouts on it.

Even before the first building had been completed, a young machinery salesman named John Spoelhof arrived and sold Prince a lathe and drill press. He needed to get his employer to co-sign the bank note to finance the purchase. As Prince later recalled, "it was a time of starting from the bottom."

What the company lacked in capital it more than made up for in vision, determination to succeed, and hard work. Long time employee Jim Hoeve remembered: "Often during my first years at Prince, we started working at 5:00 a.m. Sometimes when we started early, Mr. Prince would be operating a boring mill, machining parts. When 7:00 a.m. came, the regular machinist would take over. Shortly afterward you would see Ed walking through the shop tying his tie and getting ready for a day in the office."

The first two years are a critical time for new businesses. Most do not survive. But Prince's company did, because as its founder remembered, it had "a good product, a good market, tight cost controls, friendly banks, customers who paid their bills on time, close attention to every detail, 12–20 hour a day efforts, and a prevailing can-do attitude." Those factors paid-off when the company received orders at crucial times – three machines bought by Shelby Die Cast and an order for 20 machines from Honeywell.

But even as his company struggled through the tough start-up phase, Prince placed in operation a series of uncompromisable core values to guide employees in their work, at home, and in relationship to customers: "honesty – integrity – trust – individual responsibility – teamwork – caring and sharing – high expectations – open communication – balance in work, faith and family commitments – a positive attitude

A young Ed Prince (right) confers with a customer, ca. 1968.

A view of the Prince Corporation's 700,000 square-foot Technical Campus.

– active involvement in work and the community." Thirty years later, those concepts continue to pervade Prince's corporate culture.

A milestone in company annals came in 1969 when John Spoelhof, the machinery salesman who had become acquainted with the company before it had even started production four years before, decided to cast his lot with Prince. Born and raised in Grand Rapids, Spoelhof had become a journeyman tool and die maker at the Grand Rapids Fisher Body plant before owning a machine tool sales organization. A devoutly religious man who also believed in the company's core business values, Spoelhof would become a close confidant and best friend to Prince while rising from salesman to company president in 1980. Spoelhof and Prince, with the help of many others, would be the architects of the tremendous growth of the company.

During the early 1970s the company sought diversified products to offset the cyclical nature of the machine tool market. Not all experiments proved successful. A notable example was the venture into producing and marketing a ham deboning machine. But the year 1972 brought results when the company entered the automotive market with the industry's first lighted vanity visor. Prior to July of that year, only a few prototypes, each one taking hours, had been made. But upon receiving a massive order from Cadillac, the company went into feverish production, developing processes and pulling a plant together with little time, money, and resources. Working around the clock, teamwork paid off with customer satisfaction.

The year 1973 brought $11 million in sales of automotive products. Five years later, Prince began shipping its new floor consoles to Ford and Cadillac. A new assembly plant, Lakewood, was opened to handle the floor console business.

Prince suffered a serious heart attack in 1974, an illness that caused him to move forward with his many goals with a renewed sense of urgency. In 1980, he relinquished daily business operations of his burgeoning company to Spoelhof, while remaining chairman of the board, and expanded his philanthropic work in the Holland community. Working closely with Elsa, they pushed to revitalize the downtown area. The Princes loved their hometown and their leadership and generous financial support furthered numerous

causes including Evergreen Commons Senior Center, Hope College, Ridge Point Community Church, Freedom Village and the Holland Area Arts Center.

In 1983, sales, engineering and purchasing were brought together in the newly constructed Corporate Center on Waverly Road. By 1984, employment at the corporation had reached 1,000 and sales topped $100 million. Chrysler installed the first overhead console from the Prince Corporation in the New Yorker sedan in 1985 and the following year that product appeared in the popular Chrysler minivans.

In 1986, the 500,000 square-foot Southview Campus opened to increase manufacturing space for the rapidly growing interior trim production. The Beechwood facility followed in 1987 to handle production of new overhead consoles and map lamps. A year later, Prince Corporation concentrated its product development functions, industrial design, engineering, modeling, and electronics in a new Technical Center.

During the decade of the 1980s the corporation's employment had grown from 600 to 2,000. The 1990s would usher in an even greater rate of expansion. The Interior Technology facility was opened in 1990. In 1991, came the opening of the Peoples Center to house Human Resources, the Training and Development Group, classrooms, meeting rooms and a world class fitness complex for all employees.

In 1994, the corporation expanded its international operations with the start-up of manufacturing in England and Mexico. Growth in sales of door panels, introduced in 1994, and overhead systems resulted in the opening of the Maplewood Plant in 1995 and Meadowbrook in 1996. In 1995 the corporation also brought together all groups involved in creating a new product under one roof at a new state-of-the-art, 700,000 square-foot Technical Campus.

In 1996 the corporation employed 4,500 team members at its ten facilities in Holland and Mexico City, and sales and technical offices in Detroit, Japan, the United Kingdom and Europe. Those employees remain committed to the success of customers at every level of the organization by continuing to honor the ideals and values that have proved critical in the Prince Corporation's development from its origins in 1965 – a common spirit of trust, teamwork, individual responsibility, personal integrity and charitable activity.

The Parsonage 1908 Bed & Breakfast

From the moment you enter the front door of the Parsonage 1908 Bed and Breakfast it is a trip into the past – but with the benefit of all the modern amenities. Finely finished oak woodwork and the carved spindles of the stairway gleam from the light of original leaded glass and stained glass windows. Everywhere you glance are museum quality furnishings, an ornate pump organ, a curved glass china cabinet crammed with pattern glass heirlooms, a massive walnut sideboard and dining table lined with high back chairs, a stately grandfather clock that solemnly ticks out its task, marble and bronze statuary, dozens of beautifully bound gilt edged Victorian books, an oak pocket door flanked by tiger oak pillars that once graced the Marigold Lodge. No mere museum stiff with formality and "do not touch" signs, this is a residence that exudes the warmth and nostalgia of forgotten time - that invites a visitor to relax and enjoy.

The story behind the stately Colonial-Revival structure at 6 East 24th Street began in May 1907 when 29 families from the Ninth Street and Central Avenue Christian Reformed churches organized the Prospect Park Christian Reformed Church. They first worshiped in a former schoolhouse that had been moved to the corner of Central Avenue and 25th Street. Church services were entirely in Dutch and not until 1934 would English entirely supplant that language

In 1908, the Rev. J. Bolt and family moved into the new parsonage the congregation had constructed for its pastor's use. The Rev. H. J. Kuiper succeeded Bolt in 1910, serving until 1913. He was followed by the Rev. A. F. Rus. In his honor the congregation had the church and parsonage spruced up with a new coat of paint – although the cost, $123.65, seemed a bit high to them. The Rev. R. Veldman served from 1917-1920, followed by the Rev. J.C. Schaap in 1921-1925. Schaap's arrival coincided with the construction of a new church built at a cost of $31,000. In 1994, 70 years after he had been born in the parsonage, one of Schaap's nine children, Ward Schaap and his wife Mary Nelle, returned to Holland and enjoyed a memorable stay in the bed and breakfast. Schaap explained why the structure was so big - "most parsonages were large because the Dutch families tended to be large."

The Rev. I. Van Laar followed Schaap as pastor from 1926-1939. Beginning in 1940 J.T. Hoogstra would guide the congregation. In 1962, the Prospect Park Church sold the parsonage and built a new one. Twelve years later Bonnie Verwys bought the structure and it became her family's residence over the succeeding 10 years.

A Michigander through and through, Bonnie was born in Lansing within the shadow of the stately Capital Building. Her grandmother came from the Upper Peninsula and her parents had settled in East Grand Rapids. Her maiden name - McVoy - and her dancing dark eyes reveal her Irish heritage. As a teenager, her family moved to Douglas. In 1951 she was voted Pancake Queen in nearby Glenn's beauty pageant and she became runner up in the Blossom Queen contest. Following graduation from Saugatuck High School and marriage she resided in Douglas until moving to Holland in 1962.

An avid antique collector, Bonnie combed dimly lit shops, estate sales and auctions to assemble the eclectic furnishing that crowd her home. In 1984 she opened Holland's first bed and breakfast there, and she later was awarded a U.S. trademark for Bed and Breakfast flags. Her hostelry's gaily decorated rooms, named in honor of some of her children, portray themes. Heather's room contains framed examples of her prize childhood art work. Brian's room features a patriotic theme, with stenciled soldiers tumbling down the wall. Raggedy Ann dolls accent Kimberly's room. A massive walnut burl bed that towers to the ceiling dominates the Pastor's room. The upstairs bathroom features a grand old cast-iron bathtub with ball and claw feet and a unique shaving stand.

In 1992 the 1908 Parsonage was awarded the prestigious Triple AAA approval. The bed and breakfast was also rated highly by *Fodor's Guide* in 1993 and in *Country Extra Magazine* in 1995. A retired California judge who spent nine days there in 1996 wrote: "Having been gone from Holland for 57 years, it was a delight to find such an outstanding bed and breakfast, the 1908 Parsonage."

Not the least of the delight of a stay with hostess Verwys is her culinary skill. Guests rave about her sausages, cheeses, fresh juice and strong black coffee. A specialty, "silky smooth and softly sweet" baked custard is her grandmother's recipe. And, oh yes, the former Pancake Queen still serves her prize winning baked pancakes.

The Parsonage 1908 Bed & Breakfast, Holland's first such establishment, was gaily decked out for Independence Day, 1996.

Progressive Architecture Engineering Planning

When the Holland-based KSV Architects merged with Progressive Engineering Consultants in 1985 and moved to Grand Rapids, both companies had a well developed sense of their individual heritages.

They really became one in 1993 when all 120 Progressive Architecture Engineering Planning employees moved into their award winning new headquarters on Four Mile Road. As one company they shared the experience of designing the structure to satisfy the firm's specific needs while maintaining the integrity of the site's environment. All had input into the selection of everything from the structural tubular steel tree that mirrored the exterior forest setting, the layout of the building that reflected the nonhierarchical organiza-

tion of the workplace to the design of the office chairs which were the same type for everyone. The building represented the architectural and engineering talents of the entire staff - the move unified the force of architects, engineers and planners seeking to design and deliver diverse projects to delight their clients.

Progressive traces its roots to the year 1956 when Howard Kammeraad and Rodger Stroop opened an architectural engineer office at 788 Columbia Avenue in Holland. Five years later Paul van der Leek joined the firm of Kammeraad and Stroop that was rapidly achieving local fame through its designs for churches, schools, banks and office buildings. In 1963 the American Institute of Architects honored the firm with an award for its design of the new Hart & Cooley Co. corporate offices. Stroop retired in the 1970s. Phillip Lundwall, a principal in a Grand Haven-based firm and who had also designed many similar area structures, joined Kammeraad and van der Leek in 1979. The office was then located on the corner of 16th Street and US 31. Lundwall remembers his colleagues "as fine, community service oriented professionals who practiced the art of interactive communication with clients to mutually solve design problems." The firm had grown to 28 employees by the late 1970s but with the harsh economic times of the early 1980s it shrank to a dozen.

Kammeraad retired in 1984. The following year Kathleen Ponitz joined KSV as its marketing director so van der Leek

and Lundwall could devote more time to clients and projects. Eventually she became vice president of marketing and the firm's first female officer. Later in 1985 came the merger with Progressive Engineering Consultants - as a result of the realization that both firms could provide a fuller service to clients by combining their mechanical, electrical, civil engineering, surveying, community planning, landscape and interior design functions. Soon environmental and water resources were added. At the time of the merger Progressive Architecture Engineering Planning had grown to 65 employees. Three years later the firm totaled 100 people.

The Progressive Engineering Consultants branch of the firm dates to 1960 when four former Daverman Co. employees, mechanical engineers Bernie Bauer and Sam Feravich, electrical engineer Fred Bagey and chemical engineer Earl Goozen formed a firm with an office at the corner of Burton and Kalamazoo in

---

Visitors to the new headquarters of Progressive Architecture Engineering Planning at 1811 Four Mile Road, N.E., in Grand Rapids enjoy this vista.

Grand Rapids. The company grew rapidly with the majority of work coming from architects. In 1964 Progressive Engineering Consultants moved to larger quarters at Michigan and Lafayette and four years later to Fuller Avenue. Major projects during the 1960s included Eastbrook Mall, Woodland Mall and Calder Plaza.

Company founder Feravich retired but remains active in the firm. van der Leek served as president until his death in 1993. Ray Fix, a registered civil engineer and attorney who had joined Progressive in the 1970s, succeeded him as president. Lundwall, vice president, became director of design and was inducted into the prestigious AIA College of Fellows in 1995. The Progressive Architecture Engineering Planning management group also includes Charles L. Swanson, Charles D. Guikema, Brian K. Craig, Ronald J. Kadelsik and John K. Martin.

By the summer of 1994 Progressive Architecture Engineering Planning had been involved in the design of over 400 churches as well as diverse projects in both Michigan peninsulas ranging from the Sault Ste. Marie Tribal Hotel and Casino, Lake Superior State University Library, Butterworth Hospital expansion, Kent Intermediate School District, Old Kent Bank and Meijers.

Notable recent Ottawa County projects include the Holland Christian Junior High School and the expansion, the award winning Christ Memorial Reformed Church in Holland, the Sandpiper Restaurant with its views of Lake Macatawa, the Coast Guard Station in Grand Haven and Holland's majestic new post office. In 1995 Progressive Architecture Engineering Planning with 140 employees had grown to a $13 million a year company.

Request Foods

The key to success in many a business venture is a timely response to opportunity. Jack DeWitt and Roger Draft heard opportunity knocking loud and clear over the sound of kitchen clatter in 1987 and the result was the development of one of Holland's premier young companies.

DeWitt, the son of Borculo-based turkey processing giant Bil Mar's co-founder Marvin DeWitt, had worked for that firm for 30 years, rising to the rank of executive vice president. Draft was Bil Mar's director of engineering. In 1987 the Sara Lee Corporation of Chicago purchased Bil Mar. That is when the opportunity developed because Sara Lee was not particularly interested in the convenience food division of Bil Mar which then accounted for 10% of its sales.

But DeWitt had followed closely the development of the frozen food aspect of Bil Mar since its origin in 1971 and thought there was a good prospect for continued growth. Furthermore, he wanted the personal challenge of running an operation of his own, apart from the family business. Sara Lee responded favorably to the buy out offer proposed by DeWitt, Draft and several others and in November 1989, Request Foods, Inc., was born.

The first challenge to be surmounted involved the relocation of all the equipment involved in the $25 million a year food production lines from the Bil Mar plant to Request Food's new 94,000 square-foot facility in the Northside Industrial Center. The transfer began on July 12, 1990, and two weeks later Request had two chicken lines in production at the new site. The final lines to be moved started up the week of September 17th.

Request Foods' product lines included prepared entrees, chicken specialties, crepes and pancakes, airline entrees and custom processing. Some of the more popular foods were breast of chicken a la Kiev, rock Cornish game hens, veal cordon bleu, lasagna, deep dish burritos, beef chow mein and stuffed cabbage. In 1990 airline meals comprised 20% of the volume, food service for restaurants 30% and contract packaging for customers ranging from Weight Watchers and On Cor Frozen Foods to Wal-Mart the remainder.

Initially approximately 240 employees, half of them former Bil Mar employees, operated the plant in two shifts on every day except Sunday and holidays. The focal point of the Request Foods plant was a well lit state-of-the-art kitchen containing an enormous walk-in oven capable of cooking 10,000 steak patties at a time, immense 5,000 pound capacity ribbon mixers and a battery of huge steam jacketed cooking kettles set in a pit to control spills and make loading easier on employee backs. After preparation in the kitchen the various meats, sauces, vegetables and pastas flowed to the packaging line where employees adroitly placed them in containers, sealed and sleeved them in containers prior to their passage through a two hour freezing process.

DeWitt management style reflected the age old values expressed in the Bible as well as such modern approaches as "Quality Circles" and "Total Quality Management." The company's people oriented approach is summed up in its corporate creed: "We're devoted to offering people those opportunities which will enable them to fully develop their God given skills so that they can enhance the quality of their lives as well as that of our customers, their fellow employees, and all mankind."

Each year brought continued growth for Request Foods despite a shift in focus away from the airline industry which was increasingly offering fliers little more than a soft drink and a pack of peanuts. The company celebrated its fifth anniversary with record sales of $50 million and annual shipments of 50 million pounds of prepared foods. A 47,000 square-foot addition in 1995 and another 12,000 square-foot refrigeration and warehouse facility in the summer of 1996 increased the plant to a total of 165,000 square feet.

There, approximately 340 employees practice the "golden rule" while preparing mouth watering manna for the nation's dinner tables.

The Request Foods, Inc., 165,000 square-foot facility at 3460 John F. Donnelly Drive.

S-2 Yachts

Sooner or later most companies encounter a critical period that will determine their future. It may come in the form of their response to changing consumer needs, the development of new products and marketing strategies, diversification attempts, loss of market shares to competitors, wartime's military or home front requirements, the timing of physical growth patterns or any of the multitude of other factors that have proved a boon to some and spelled doom for others.

In the case of S-2 Yachts, events out of its control in the early 1990s would pose the greatest challenge to company survival in five decades of existence. In January 1991, in an effort to reduce the federal deficit, the U.S. Congress imposed a 10% luxury tax on select items including boats priced at $100,000 or more. This seemingly sensible plan to place a greater tax burden on the wealthy backfired because Congress failed to take into account that citizens, even rich ones, have choices. Overwhelmingly the choice was not to buy expensive boats. Within the first six months of the tax the boat industry suffered a 75% business loss. Nationwide, approximately 40,000 manufacturing jobs were lost. The employment level at S-2 Yachts dropped from 800 to 290 in less than two years.

S-2 Yachts traces its origin to the early 1950s when Leon Slikkers began building 14-foot runabouts in his garage during his spare time. He had learned well the art of boat building through his employment at Chris-Craft in Holland beginning as a teenager in 1946. Slikkers' beautifully built, mahogany hulled boats were popular. In 1955, he sold his home to raise capital and went into production of Slickcraft wooden boats in a workshop under an apartment on Washington Avenue.

The following year Slikkers experimented with fiberglass hulls and in 1961 he discontinued wooden models. The company expanded in 1962 and four years later booming sales, in particular of the popular SS235 deep V-bottom, trailered, cuddy cabin style boat, necessitated construction of a new plant on Brooks Avenue.

In 1969, the 40-year-old entrepreneur sold his thriving business to AMF Inc., staying on as president for four years. In 1974 he started up another business - S-2 Yachts, Inc.,

"Slikkers the second time around," and went into production of sailboats in a 72,000 square foot facility with 53 employees. David Slikkers and his younger brother Bob who had both learned the boat business from the ground up at Slickcraft, joined their father in his new venture.

S-2 Yachts began with a flourish - sales reached 1.6 million the first year. In 1976, S-2 reentered the powerboat market with the Tiara powerboat line, followed by the Pursuit series of fishing boats in 1977. It expanded product lines and doubled its Holland plant capacity in 1979. Four years later the company moved production of the Pursuit line to a new 75,000 square-foot factory in Ft. Pierce, Florida.

David Slikkers succeeded to the presidency in 1984. His father became chairman of the board and CEO. That year a 200,000 square-foot fiberglass technology plant on East 40th Street pushed total manufacturing and engineering space to nearly half a million square feet.

Tom Slikkers, a third son, became product manager of the new Slickcraft division in 1986. By 1987 company employment had risen to 600. That year S-2 decided to narrow its focus and eliminate production of sailboats. In 1991, the company narrowed its focus again by dropping the sport boat line.

That's when the government bombshell, in the form of the luxury tax, rocked the industry. David Slikkers fought for the company's survival, campaigning with congressional representatives via personal appearances in Washington, to make the misguided tax a jobs issue. In August 1993, Congress quietly allowed the luxury tax to die. Pent up demand spurred S-2 Yachts sales during the following 18 months and by 1996 both the Tiara Division in Holland and Pursuit Division in Ft. Pierce had reached the same level of sales as before the tax - but with less units produced by fewer employees.

David Slikkers knows full well that the luxury tax was a painful experience for the company but it also proved a mixed blessing by causing company management to carefully rethink its strategies. Before, the company was mostly product driven. Now it has become more sensitive to consumer wants - listening more to what buyers' perceive as important features. That has placed S-2 Yachts in a better position for future growth.

In 1996, Leon Slikkers, CEO, remains as active and passionately involved with the success of the company as he was when he founded it half a century ago.

The S-2 Yachts 200,000 square foot fiberglass technology plant at 725 East 40th Street.

Sligh Furniture Company

Three generations of Sligh Furniture Company presidents in 1993.
(left to right) Charles R. Sligh, Jr., Robert L. Sligh and Robert L. Sligh., Jr.

The year was 1933, the nadir of the Great Depression that would stifle the nation's economic vitality for an entire decade - not a very propitious time to revitalize a business. Yet that is exactly what 27-year-old Charles R. Sligh, Jr., did. But that kind of courage displayed in the face of adversity had long been a family tradition.

Sligh's grandfather, Capt. James W. Sligh, and his uncle, Capt. James M. Sligh, had volunteered to preserve the Union as members of the First Michigan Engineers and Mechanics. His grandfather was killed as a result of a guerrilla ambush in Tennessee in 1863. Sligh's father, Charles R. Sligh, had been too young to serve in the Civil War but he later compiled a history of his relatives' famous regiment.

Charles R. Sligh had dropped out of school at the age of 12 to help support his family following the death of his father. Despite his lack of formal education, hard work and perseverance brought him success. In 1874 he joined the prestigious Grand Rapids-based Berkey and Gay Furniture Company. Following an apprenticeship in the factory, he traveled the frontier selling the company's furniture. Saving his money, he established his own Sligh Furniture Company in 1880.

The company, which specialized in bedroom furniture, prospered, due largely to what Sligh later remembered as "incessant toil and sacrifice." The company added chairs, desks and other furniture to its line and by 1910 it employed 409 craftsmen. The company enjoyed continued growth until a depression struck the furniture industry in 1926. Its effects, acerbated by the Great Depression that began three years later, forced the Sligh Company, "the largest factory in the world devoted exclusively to the manufacture of chamber furniture," to stop its manufacturing operations in 1932. Unlike many another victim of those hard times the company liquidated some of its assets and honorably paid off all creditors.

In 1933, Charles R. Sligh, Jr., acquired the name and other assets of his father's company. Forming a partnership with Bill Lowry, formerly the Sligh plant manager, he moved the business to Holland. Initially 45 woodworkers produced quality maple bedroom furniture and desks. The company prospered due largely to the popularity of those desks which became the chief product line.

Expansion continued in the decade of the 1940s. Sligh and Lowry bought a plant in Zeeland in 1940 and formed the Sligh Lowry Furniture Company. The acquisition of the Grand Rapids Chair Company followed in 1945. Three years later the Ply Curves subsidiary corporation was established. It supplied curved plywood parts to the Grand Rapids, Holland and Zeeland plants.

In 1957, Charles R. Sligh, Jr., became Executive Vice President of the National Association of Manufacturers while remaining chairman of the board of the furniture company over the succeeding 31 years. In 1957, also, Lowery was elected President of Sligh-Lowry and the Grand Rapids Chair Company was sold. Sligh-Lowry absorbed the furniture operations of Charles R. Sligh Company, Ply Curves was sold to Bill Lowry, Jr. and the Sligh-Lowry Furniture subsidiary of Sligh-Lowry was established to market student dormitory furniture.

The year 1968 proved a milestone in company history. The Sligh-Lowry Furniture Company bought Lowry's shares and the company name reverted to the original Sligh Furniture Co., with 40-year-old Robert L. Sligh as president. Charles R. Sligh III, 41, was elected president of the Sligh Contract Furniture subsidiary. The Sligh Furniture Co. purchased Trend Clock Company of Zeeland.

Following the consolidation of the Contract Furniture and Trend Clock operations into the Sligh Furniture Co. in 1975, desks and clocks became the main product lines. To honor the company's founder, the Charles R. Sligh line of high end clocks was introduced in 1983. The following year Trend Clocks became Sligh Clocks. Thirty-six-year-old Robert L. Sligh, Jr., who had joined the company in 1983, rose to the rank of president in 1990 and chairman of the board in 1993.

In 1996, Sligh Furniture Co., whose heritage as a centennial business had been honored by the Historical Society of Michigan in 1980, employed more than 325 people. The majority of products manufactured in its Holland and Zeeland plants are used in homes and business offices. The company remains a privately held family business where "your name doesn't have to be on the door to be part of the family."

Summit Properties

Much of the entrepreneurial history of the Holland area has been made by men and women who focused their energies on filling a need - an innovation that made life better, safer or easier. In the case of Summit Properties, founder Tom Speet perceived the need for services not being offered by other area Realtors - direct contact by the most knowledgeable agent with clients and potential clients. His company's efforts to satisfy that need through techniques as varied as including the names of listing agents in all advertising and lawn signs and making those agents available to potential clients 24 hours a day through beepers, like doctors use, has spelled success for his organization.

Speet, born and raised in the Holland area, started his professional career as a mechanical engineer. He worked for the Donnelly Corporation for 11 years, eventually serving as facilities engineer responsible for buying and selling properties for the company. He enjoyed that occupation so well that he switched to a career in real estate, working for a Holland area firm for the succeeding 15 years. He picked up valuable on-the-job skills and training and capped his knowledge of the industry with CRS and CRB certification, both requiring lengthy and demanding studies.

In 1990, Speet felt that he could do a better job as his own boss when he launched Summit Properties. It wasn't long before he was joined by Beth Foley, Realtor, Associate Broker for the firm. Foley, who had grown up in Ohio and graduated from Ohio State University, worked in different sections of the country before settling in Holland in 1983. Active involvement in the Newcomers Club, which made the transition of becoming acquainted with Holland's many facilities easier for new residents, stimulated her to enter the real estate field. For nine years she worked closely with Speet in the same firms. In 1996, Foley was awarded the prestigious Certified Real Estate Brokerage Manager (CRB) designation by the National Association of Realtors, the only woman of the more than 300 members of the Holland Board of Realtors to be so honored.

As opposed to general practitioners of the profession, Summit Properties specialized in waterfront and distinctive homes, many of them on the higher end of the market, and emphatically "all good clean homes." The company has handled the sales of lake front homes in excess of $1 million and is particularly proud of its work in marketing Tunnel Breeze,(an upscale development just south of Tunnel Park) and Horner's Woods on Lake Macatawa. One of Summit's successful mar-keting techniques has been to commission a local artist to render a water color painting of each home to better highlight its attractions.

Summit Properties also recognized a need for making available additional services in the area of corporate relocation. That service proved very popular with several Holland area companies interested in an efficient transfer of new executives and their families into the area. Dee Barney, Summit Properties director of corporate relocation, has also served as president of the Lakeshore Human Resources Management Association.

Perhaps most effective in terms of Summit's success in satisfying both buyer and seller has been the emphasis on 24 hour availability of knowledgeable agents. Agents frequently respond to late evening or weekend contacts from potential clients calling from car phones at the site of the available property. And, as Foley confides, more than one early morning call from a European client on a different time zone has proved difficult but productive.

In May of 1996, Summit Properties moved its sales offices from the Paragon Bank Building on Hoover Blvd. to a completely refurbished office building at the intersection of Division and Ottawa Beach Road. At the time of its move to this larger office facility the company had just added three new licensed Realtor/Sales Associates, and a licensed Realtor, Relocation Director.

The area's leader in sales of waterfront and distinctive homes, Summit Properties anticipates continued growth in volume of business and staffing.

**Summit Properties'
new sales office at
691 Ottawa Beach Road.**

185

Tectron

Tectron, whose name signifies the integration of technology with electronics, received some well deserved recognition in 1993 when Outstate Business Magazine rated it as one of the top 19 fastest growing privately-held companies in Michigan outside of Detroit. The author of the article about that honor noted that each of the 50 diverse companies that were ranked "brought something special to its marketplace - a better idea, pricing, more responsive service or especially savvy management."

The management and employees of Tectron feel they know what their "secret of success" is and it is reflected in their mission statement - "to help our customers to become more productive and profitable by providing innovative automation solutions to the challenges presented in today's industrial manufacturing environment."

Tectron traces its origins to 1987 when Kim Grotenhuis and a partner founded the company. Five years later Grotenhuis bought out his partner's interest in the firm. Grotenhuis had grown up in Zeeland and worked at the Prince Corporation, Capital Engineering and various other companies before striking out as an entrepreneur. The initial Tectron workforce consisted only of the two founders, a panel builder and a secretary. They located their company in a small building on the south side of Holland, later moving to 13261 Riley Street.

Tectron is an electrical control systems integrator which designs software and hardware used for industrial processes including programmable controls and computer number controls. It tailor designs controls for customers' applications. It offers quality installation service after installation and can provide "turn key" systems to design, build, program, install and start up the system at the customer's site. It can also furnish complete documentation of electrical schematics and drawings.

Over the nine years since its establishment Tectron has specialized in offering solutions in two major areas of industrial need - CNC machine tools and material handling. In a relatively short time it has compiled a diverse roster of satisfied customers - mostly from western Michigan. Tectron increased the efficiency of wood routers at Howard Miller's clock factory and installed controls on a dual purpose lathe that simultaneously cuts the inside and outside diameters of parts at the Lowell based Metric Manufacturing Company. It successfully set up a control system for Stephenson & Lawyer, Inc., of Grand Rapids, that guides water jet cutting machines which manufacture styrofoam components with a fine stream of water. It has also improved operations at the Donnelly Corporation for cutting out automobile mirrors from sheets of glass as well as controls for a Grand Rapids firm's cookie cutter machinery. In the realm of material handling, Tectron has solved the rapid conveyor movement of products ranging from bottle caps and baby food to juice bottles and groceries.

In recent years, even more emphasis has been placed on quality control with the growing demand for global standards and ISO 9000. Tectron has been involved in the development of many test fixtures as well as custom software for quality verification processes. From logging production information to a data-base, to full load testing automobile wiring harnesses, Tectron has developed high quality systems for its clients.

The company's volume of growth rate has averaged 20% a year since its beginnings in 1987. Its work force, consisting of engineers and production staff, has grown from four to 19. And whether the company is involved in projects utilizing new machinery or the refitting of old machinery with state-of-the-art controls its goal is to "design a bullet proof system that goes in and runs without problems."

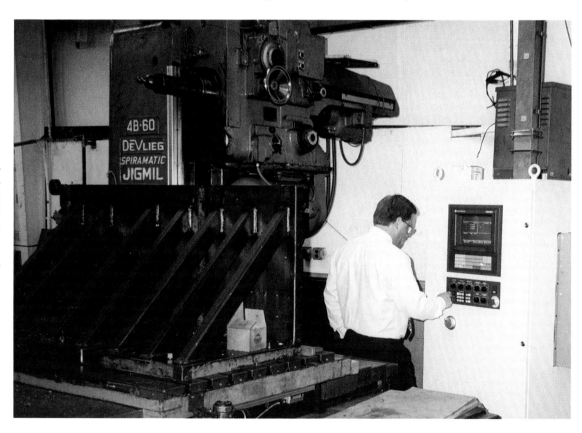

Tectron founder Kim Grotenhuis final programming a CNC machine - tool.

Thermotron Industries

"It was the best of times, it was the worst of times." So Charles Dickens began his immortal novel centered around the French Revolution of the 1790s. Two centuries later the fall of Communist Russia, the end of the Cold War and the subsequent reduction in the U.S. military brought about the best of times and the worst of times for Thermotron whose products had been primarily focused on the defense industry. The company reacted by redirecting its energies and shifting rapidly into a new area of opportunity, resulting in a stronger organization and cycle of even greater growth.

Thermotron had been founded by Charles Conrad in 1962. Conrad, an inventor who had operated a refrigeration business in Holland since 1948, began marketing low temperature test chambers four years later. The name Thermotron reflected his firm's interest in thermoelectric heating/cooling devices. By 1977 Conrad's initial $1,000 investment had grown to a company with five plants in Holland and service offices nationwide with 250 employees. Three years later Thermotron had become the world's largest manufacturer of environmental simulation equipment, with 370 employees.

Conrad retired in 1980, selling Thermotron to the Milwaukee-based Wehr Corporation. The following year the company consolidated its six Holland plants and 500 employees into two facilities totaling 240,000 square-feet. Growth continued as the company developed innovative environmental test chambers, vibration test systems, control instrumentation and stress screening systems. In 1987 when the Wehr Corporation was sold to Venturedyne, Thermotron was twice as large as its nearest competitor.

Conrad died in 1995 and the company he founded perpetuates his memory by a plaque at its entrance that reads: "We fondly remember him as an entrepreneur, inventor, innovator and philanthropist. He was tireless in his efforts to improve environmental testing technology and the equipment and services provided by Thermotron. He taught us the true meaning of customer satisfaction and wove those concepts into the fabric of Thermotron. We are grateful for his efforts and the legacy he has left us."

In the meantime Thermotron faced the challenge of finding new markets. Company management recognized that need and developed a strategy to accomplish a shift in energies into the automotive, telecommunications, computers and life sciences fields. One technique that proved helpful was to conduct seminars to actively promote the application of the environmental simulation and stress screening lessons learned from the military to the commercial market. Cost conscious commercial customers motivated Thermotron to develop procedures and equipment to simultaneously test multiple products. Thermotron also became much more active in the international arena, establishing marketing and service branches throughout Europe, the Far East, Canada, Israel and Brazil.

Thermotron hired numerous engineers in emerging fields and developed new talents in its existing staff. The company responded to the 1990 Clean Air Act by developing its solvent vapor recovery systems, a clean, economical and environmentally safe method to reduce volatile organic compounds emissions to within the new federal limits.

Based on customer needs ranging from testing anti-lock brakes, packaging for food products, building materials, windows, or the viability of coolant fluids under differing environments, Thermotron designed and built testing chambers as large as 35 feet tall to as small as one cubic foot, capable of testing factors such as high and low temperatures, sand, dust, humidity, vibrations and stress. The new SE-Series of environmental testing chambers are equipped with larger compressors that allow the testing of bigger products, faster performance of temperature transitions and increased precision in detecting product stress and failure points. The revolutionary chamber instrumentation the company developed - the 7800 programmer/controller - added memory capacity and increased operating speed.

The decade of the 1990s also saw Thermotron move into the life sciences market with new products including laboratory freezers for reliable ultra low temperature storage of biological specimens, walk-in environmental rooms for medical or scientific labs, clinics and commercial research operations and cytogenetic drying chambers developed in cooperation with the Mayo Clinic for laboratory analysis of tissue and chromosomes.

By 1996 Thermotron's response to these new areas of opportunity had placed it in the enviable position of being three times as large as its nearest American competitor.

Thermotron's manufacturing plant at 836 Brooks Avenue.

Trendway Corporation

Trendway's master plan (estimated completion 2000), with over 750,000 square-feet of manufacturing and office space, houses all products the company makes. The inset black and white photograph shows how the company has changed from its modest beginnings.

Like so many of modern Holland's successful corporations Trendway rose from humble beginnings to become a world class company. The story began in 1968 when Justin Busscher, an experienced floor-to-ceiling panel designer and sales representative, founded a company to manufacture his better idea, a gypsum-based panel that offered higher fire resistance and better sound rating than the existing partitions then available. With the help of approximately 100 investors he started up in a tiny office in the rear of the Mode-O-Day ladies' dress shop on the corner of Eighth Street and Central Avenue. Sadly, Busscher died three years later, leaving a promising operation struggling without his leadership or sufficient capital.

That's when the Heeringas came to the rescue. George Heeringa, a Holland native who had spent his entire working career with Hart & Cooley, rising to the rank of president, learned of Trendway's problems and its potential. In 1973, in partnership with his sons, Jim, who had been a sales manager in San Francisco, and Don, then working in the commercial real estate business in Phoenix, Arizona, Heeringa purchased 85 percent of the outstanding stock in Trendway (later the family acquired the remainder).

Despite the fresh working capital, energy and renewed leadership the Heeringas brought to the venture, the first years proved tough. The business numbered but 13 employees who worked in a 24,000-square-foot facility. The company lost money in 1973, broke even in 1974 and, triumphantly, the following year, the long hours and diligent work paid off with a profitable bottom line. After three years Trendway not only was financially stable but with a strengthened product line and the addition of key people to its management team the future boded well.

The year 1976 proved pivotal when Trendway purchased the partition line of Modern Partitions (now Haworth). This new product not only meshed well with the existing line but it brought with it additional clients (many of which continue as major accounts) and a steady backlog of orders. That year, also, the company finished the first of a series of five additions to its Quincy Street manufacturing facility that

would increase it in size to 415,000 square feet by 1996. Trendway finished the American Bicentennial year with $3 million in sales and a solid profit.

Three years later the company began development of its own line of open office furniture, the Space Management System, which allowed it to compete directly with the industry leaders. By 1983 nearly 200 employees worked at the Quincy Street plant and others operated out of its new Xpress quick ship facility in Zeeland where 109 line items and 206 product types were available for shipment ranging from same day to three days. A year later Trendway's Chicago showroom opened.

During the 1980s Trendway capitalized on rapid delivery of orders, thus securing an enviable industry niche. At a time when competitors averaged 12-16 weeks for delivery of orders, Trendway established a delivery lead time of four weeks or less.

Trendway celebrated its 20th anniversary by opening its second national showroom in New York City and another in Washington, D.C. It also entered the Canadian market with a showroom in Toronto. Five years later, with a work force of 300, the company further branched into office furnishings with its Prelude seating group. Continuing to emphasize fast shipment, Trendway expanded its product offerings to include 342 line items and 1,481 product types available for shipments in three days or less via its company owned fleet of trucks.

In the meantime Don Heeringa succeeded his father as president. His brother Jim held the title of executive vice president in charge of sales prior to his retirement in January 1995. George Heeringa continued as the corporation's chairman of the board until his death in 1991.

Since 1982 Trendway has grown at an average rate of an amazing 24% each year, a record that won it recognition three times as one of the "State's One Hundred Fastest Growing Privately Held Businesses" by *Michigan Business Magazine*. In 1996, Trendway President Don Heeringa and his nearly 400 employees continue to emphasize the factors that they feel brought prior success - quality products, quality customer service and lightning fast delivery!

Tulip Time Festival, Inc.

Ah, Tulip Time in May - how it assaults the senses. The eye is gladdened by millions of tulips, in all the hues of the rainbow, lining streets and parks. The ear is greeted by the rhythmic clack of thousands of colorfully costumed klompen dancers, the blare of marching high school bands, the whir of automobiles and roar of tour buses carrying wide-eyed visitors and the crackle of applause of crowds that swell 8th Street sidewalks. The air is redolent with sizzling ollie bollen, bratwurst and elephant ears.

On a par with national festivals such as the Washington, D.C., Cherry Blossom Festival and Mardi Gras, the event staged each May by the relatively small community of Holland is a cross between a carnival with class and a celebration of ethnic heritage. Hosted by some 7,000 local volunteers, Tulip Time draws an estimated one million visitors who generate an economic impact of $6 million in the Holland area and $11 million in west Michigan. Operated by an independent, non-profit operation, based entirely on "earned" income with the exception of City of Holland support via purchase and planting of tulip lanes, police and traffic control and the setting up of bleachers, the festival raises roughly $1 million through

One of the many youngsters who enjoyed the Tulip Time Festival 1996.
(photo from Tulip Time Festival Office)

sales and sponsorship. After the bills are paid an amazing 75% of the profit of each year's festival is returned to the community. Beyond the bustle and pageantry of the festival, as Mary Duistermars, Tulip Time executive director, notes, "Tulip Time has become one of the largest fund raising opportunities of the year for Holland's churches, schools, civic and arts organizations." And that is one of Tulip Times "best kept secrets."

In a city that traditionally boasted that 90% of its residents were of Dutch origin, Holland area business and industry had long utilized Dutch themes, windmills, tulips and peasant costumes in advertising. But the idea for an official celebration of that heritage dates back to 1927 when Lida Rogers, a high school biology teacher, suggested the planting of tulips as a civic project to beautify the city. The following year the Holland Common Council bought 100,000 bulbs imported from the Netherlands and planted them throughout the parks and along street curbs. That spring articles about the tulips in bloom in area newspapers brought thousands of visitors. The following year more tulips were planted and in 1930 the city promoted its first annual Tulip Time Festival featuring a week of parades, concerts, street scrubbing and other ethnic activities and a flower show. Fifty thousand visitors showed up that year. In 1931 the crowds had swelled to 175,000. In 1932, two million tulips were in bloom and the first annual parade of school children in Dutch costumes was held.

Despite the Depression the festival continued to grow during the 1930s. A skilled wood carver practiced the art of making klompen. High school girls were taught authentic Dutch dances to demonstrate to the growing audiences. A

miniature Little Netherlands, became a leading attraction. Next came the Netherlands Museum under the leadership of Willard Wichers. By 1938 the festival had grown to a nine day event with three million tulips that drew a half million tourists. The following year, the old AAA traveler touted Tulip Time as "undoubtedly the most brilliant spectacle in all these United States."

In 1938-1941, the famous Holland Furnace Co. promoted Tulip Time through Hollywood celebrities including Dorothy Lamour, Pat O'Brien and King Kong's sweetheart Fay Wray. Tulip Time was suspended when America entered World War II. In 1946 the city planted bulbs along eight miles of streets and the festival, shortened to four days, was back in business.

In 1965, the reconstruction of the authentic 200-year-old "De Zwaan" on Windmill Island added another tourist attraction. The first grand marshal was named for the Saturday Parade of Bands in 1966 and in 1974 grand marshals were added to the Volksparade and Children's Parade. The annual Tulip Time Poster program originated in 1981 with the first poster in the series available for Tulip Time '82. In 1989 Tulip Time was lengthened from four to six days and in 1991 it became a ten day event.

By 1996 only about 1/3 of Holland's population still boasted Dutch ancestry, yet that fall 800 area high school students and 700 veteran "alumni," including those of Spanish and Oriental heritage, were practicing the intricacies of "klompen dancing." And 1997's Tulip Time, marking the sesquicentennial of the city, will begin as always with the town crier announcing in Dutch: "The mayor declares the streets are dirty and therefore they must be scrubbed!"

Vito Palmisano Photography

Holland was built upon the dreams of immigrants who sought a better life for their families in the land of the free. One-hundred and fifty years later that same American dream beckons to those who want a fair chance to achieve their potential while benefiting society through the fruits of their talent. One of the area's newer residents, photographer Vito Palmisano, is living proof that that dream is alive and well in Holland, Michigan. With artistic eye and technical skill he practices his craft, photographically capturing nuances of the region's beauty in ways that make the hearts of even long time residents beat with renewed pride.

He is the son of Maria and Giuseppe Palmisano, immigrants who fled the poverty of World War II ravaged Bari, Italy, near the "Achilles Heel." Born in Chicago, Palmisano grew up in the downtown area prior to his family moving to suburban Noridge. A family vacation in Italy when he was 13-years-old opened his eyes to the beauty of the Old Country as well as to the blessing that his parents had bestowed on him by leaving that rural society which offered little opportunity.

Following graduation from high school in 1973, Palmisano attended Triton Junior College where he earned an Associates Degree in architectural drafting. But he soon found the long hours sitting at a drafting board little to his liking. Another trip with his family to Italy proved fateful. Like other tourists, an instamatic camera dangled from his neck. And the many photographs he snapped hooked him on the mystique of the frozen image.

Returning to America, Palmisano bought his first 35mm camera and took some photographic courses at Triton Junior College. Next came a stint working his way through Chicago's prestigious Darkroom Workshop. There he ran the dark room while studying under such masters of the photographic art as Ansel Adams.

By 1978 Palmisano had decided on a career as a *National Geographic Magazine* photographer. Enrolling in the Maine Photographic Workshop, he studied under Pete Turner, Jay Maisel and Dick Durrance II, a former *National Geographic* photographer. Working with those experts had a profound influence on his shooting style. But Palmisano also learned from Durrance that to be a *National Geographic* photographer required six month absences, too long away from family for him.

Instead, returning to Chicago, Palmisano launched his own full time photography company, specializing in corporate communications and advertising. As he built an impressive stock file from his travels and work for some of the Windy City's major advertising agencies, he found himself increasingly performing aerial work, in airplanes, helicopters and while precariously dangling from skyscrapers, daredevil techniques for which he developed an affinity.

Black Monday's 1987 stock market crash brought a temporary hiatus to Palmisano's spiraling career when corporate customers slashed their advertising budgets. But he rolled with the punches as he had been taught while earning his black belt in Tae Kwon Do, packed his bag and set out on some adventurous travels that further enhanced his photographic skills.

In 1991, while working for a Chicago client he met Mary Procopio from St. Clair Shores, Michigan, and two years later they were married. In 1994, the Palmisanos moved to Holland where Mary took a position with the BilMar Foods. Like many others who have fallen under the sway of the Holland area's life style, the Palmisano have decided to spend their life in Michigan. And Holland is an ideal site for Palmisano's headquarters, halfway between Detroit and Chicago where he does much of his work as well as New York City, Boston and other cities.

Since moving to Holland Palmisano's photography has been featured on the covers of two Holland Area Chamber of Commerce directories and ten of his works were picked to decorate the Chamber's office. In 1996 he was selected the official Tulip Time photographer. Other local clients include S-2 Yachts, Bruischat Environmental, Inc., Lithibar Matik and Drawform.

In partnership with wife Mary, the Palmisano's have also developed a separate enterprise, Great Lakes Fine Art Photography. His fine art prints are represented at the Moynihan Gallery in Holland. The contemporary color images that illustrate this book further document the artistic skill of Vito Palmisano, photographer.

Vito Palmisano, photographer, on the job while dangling 1,200 feet high off Chicago's John Hancock Building.

Wolbrink-Lievense Insurance

The Wolbrink-Lievense Insurance Agency, an amalgam of two of the Holland area's oldest and well established agencies, prides itself on its heritage of providing a high level of service and of continuing to demonstrate its concern with making Holland a fine place to work, live and raise a family.

Ironically, the Wolbrink Agency which has provided automobile insurance to thousands of drivers over the decades traces its origins to an automobile accident. In 1917, Orrin A. Wolbrink experienced a minor accident with another driver who happened to be insured by the Citizen's Mutual Insurance Co. that had begun selling insurance in Michigan two years before. Wolbrink was so impressed by the company's service that he soon added the selling of Citizen's Insurance to the thousand and one other goods he stocked in the general store and post office combination he had operated since 1906 in the Allegan County hamlet of Ganges.

Automobile insurance policies were far simpler in those less hectic days of Tin Lizzie's and rumble seats. A surviving policy from 1919 consists of one page with no options as to limits or deductibles available. The cost per year was 25 cents per horse power plus a $1.00 policy fee.

In 1926, at the urging of the insurance company, Wolbrink sold the store in Ganges and he and wife Grace moved to Holland and opened an agency. Gradually the firm evolved into handling a general line of insurance. By the 1930s the agency was located at 68 W. 8th Street and with the addition of Orrin's son Irving, it became the O.A. Wolbrink & Sons Agency. Later Orrin's daughter Evelyn Wolbrink Allen also joined the firm as a bookkeeper.

The business continued to grow and following service in World War II as an Army Air Corps pilot, Irving's son Bob entered the business. As he developed more experience he took over management of the company. In 1966 the firm relocated west on the block to a new office at 86 W. 8th Street. Bob Wolbrink retired in 1986 to be succeeded by his son Bob Jr., who following graduation from Michigan State University and several other jobs had joined the firm in 1978. In 1993 Robert Frieling purchased the Wolbrink Agency.

Frank M. Lievense founded the agency that bore his name in 1922. Originally specializing in Auto-Owners Insurance, Lievense's firm soon became a general agency. By the 1930s his office was located at 215 Central Ave., part of the big brick structure that also housed his relatives' Battery and Car Storage Co. and bowling alley.

Frank Lievense's son Don joined the agency in 1944, followed by son Frank, Jr., nine years later. The firm moved to the Temple Building at 17 W. 10th Street. During the 1950s it operated from above the old Woolworth's Store at 2 E. 8th Street. In 1981 continued growth spurred the construction of a new building at 1061 W. Washington Avenue.

Four years later a third generation of the Lievense family bought the business. Don Lievense had repeatedly told his son Jim while growing up that "he could do anything he wanted to do and be anyone he wanted to be but don't go into the insurance business." Jim heeded that advice and graduated from Ferris College with a degree in pharmacy. After working for several years at drug stores in the Holland area he realized he hated counting pills. So in 1978, he started at the family agency and soon "he loved his work."

In 1985, Jim and Frank M. Lievense III bought the agency. Six years later Jim became sole owner. The firm then numbered nine employees.

Then in 1994 the Lievense and Wolbrink agencies, which had nurtured a mutual respect and friendship for each other over the generations, made what seemed a logical move by merging. Economies of scale and the joining of forces of the various insurers that each represented placed the combined agency in a position for even greater growth.

In 1995 Robert Frieling added the Galien Agency to his firm. By that year the agency had grown to employ more than 40 professionals who served the insurance needs of more than 10,000 families and 2,000 businesses throughout the Great Lakes region.

Frank M. Lievense's Insurance Agency shared a building with a automobile battery dealer and a bowling alley at 215 Central Avenue ca. 1930.

Woodland Realty

When Jack Bouman and four other shareholders bought Woodland Realty in 1981 the economy was at its lowest ebb in 30 years. Interest rates stood at 18-20%, the building industry was at a standstill and Realtors were dropping like flies. But Bouman was not in the least worried because he knew that in tough times the type of quality services and creativity Woodland had to offer would grow even more in demand. Fifteen years later the record speaks for Bouman's confidence. With annual sales in excess of $135 million, the 51 associate Realtors who make up Woodland Realty command 38% of the area real estate market with their nearest competitor holding only 12% with more staff.

In 1972 Bouman joined Woodland Realty, an organization that had been founded earlier in the year by a group of five local businessmen and Realtors. At that time the firm's office was located at the corner of 16th Street and U.S. 31. From the start Woodland Realty was committed to developing a higher caliber real estate organization than was available in the Holland area - setting the tone for the subsequent evolution of even higher levels of service, commitment to the area and professional expertise.

By 1979 Woodland had 11 sales associates. With the onset of the recession the firm went through restructuring. In 1981 when Jim Jurries decided to sell Woodland to concentrate on land development projects, Bouman and his associates bought the firm to continue the excellent working environment that had evolved.

Woodland weathered the economic climate of the early 1980s in part by working with clients to utilize every conceivable type of creative financing. By the mid 1980s the Holland area was enjoying a real estate boom fueled by the success of area industry. As Woodland participated in that strengthened market its associates rose to greater levels of professionalism. Traditional sales techniques gave way to the philosophy of building long term relationships with clients, by being sensitive to their needs, counseling them, solving problems and serving people. The resultant customer loyalty brought sustained growth.

In 1987 Woodland moved into its architectural award winning office. Residential in character, the building was designed to make a statement of Woodland's long term commitment to the community. The following year Woodland opened a commercial/industrial department, with three associates, devoted to the west Michigan region.

A relocation division followed in 1989 to offer free service for people transferred into the area, making that transition easier by helping them decide on housing, selecting schools, babysitting services and other aspects of adjustment to the Holland area. Woodland opened a branch office in Saugatuck in 1990 and it soon dominated that market. In 1996 another satellite office opened to service the rapidly expanding Hudsonville, Jenison and Jamestown region.

Woodland remains a company composed of self-employed sales associates who make their individual salaries based on their success in selling real estate. Business decisions are made jointly for the benefit of customers and the sales staff. This results in much more of a team approach than is common with realty organizations. There is an understanding among the team members that by working collectively they can achieve greater success more efficiently. Woodland assists its agents with literature, handouts and publishes its own trade magazine.

A full service company, Woodland Realty dominates the Holland area in every price range of real estate. Woodland's president Bouman and his 51 sales associates and staff of 10 support people are equally proud of their record of community involvement, participating in numerous social welfare organizations and fund raising activities.

The Woodland Realty sales staff gathered for a photo in front of the Woodland Building. President Jack Bouman is in the back, second to the left from the sign.

Sources Consulted

Alberts, Robert C. *The Good Provider: H.J. Heinz and His 57 Varieties.* Boston, 1973.

Alward, Dennis E. and Pierce, Charles S., compilers. *Index to the Local and Special Acts of the State of Michigan 1803-1927.* Lansing, 1928.

American Graphic. Vol. 18. No. 8. Chicago, Aug. 25, 1899.

Armstrong, Joe, and Pahl, John. *River and Lake: A Sesquicentennial History of Allegan County, Michigan.* N.P. 1985.

Baker Book House Story: 1839-1989. N.D., [1989].

Baum, Frank Joslyn, and MacFall, Russell *P. To Please a Child.* Chicago, 1961.

Blackbird, Andrew, *History of the Ottawa and Chippewa Indians.* Ypsilanti, 1887.

Blouin, Francis X. *100 Years: A Great Beginning: Sligh Furniture Co.* N.P., 1979.

A Book of Remembrance: Pillar Christian Reformed Church. N.P., 1984.

Boer, William H. *The Holland Furnace Company Tragedy,* N.P., [1995].

Bozich, Stanley J. compiler. *Michigan's Own. The Medal of Honor Civil War to Vietnam War.* [Frankenmuth, 1987].

Brinks, Herbert J., ed. *Dutch American Voices. Letters From the United States, 1850-1930.* Ithaca, N.Y., [1995].

Bruins, Elton J. "Albertus C. Van Raalte and His Colony." *The Reformed Review.* Vol. 29, 1976. _____. *The Americanization of a Congregation.* Grand Rapids, [1970].

_____. "Holocaust in Holland: 1871." *Michigan History.* Vol. 55, No. 4, (Winter 1971).

_____. *Isaac Cappon, Holland's "Foremost Citizen."* Holland, 1987.

_____. *The Netherlands Museum, Holland, Michigan 1937-1987.* Holland, 1987.

Business Directory of Holland, Mich. N.P., ca. 1894

The City of Holland, Michigan. N.P., ca. 1891.

[Butler, William and Strode, William, eds] *Hope College.* [Prospect, Kentucky, 1991].

Caplan, Ralph. *The Design of Herman Miller.* New York, [1976].

Carefree Days in West Michigan. [Grand Rapids, 1957].

Casperson, Ralph. *A Northern Boyhood.* [Decatur], 1993.

Census and Statistics of the State of Michigan. Lansing, 1854.

Clifton, James A., Cornell, George L. and McClurken, James M. *People of the Three Fires . . .* Grand Rapids, 1986.

Cocks, J. Fraser, III. "George N. Smith: Reformer On the Frontier." *Michigan History.* Vol. 52, No. 1. (Spring, 1968).

Cohen Stuart M. *Zes Maanden In Amerika.* 2 vols. Haarlem, Netherlands, 1875 (partial unpublished translation by Harry Boonstra).

Cole, Maurice F. *Voices From the Wilderness.* Ann Arbor, 1961.

Cooke, John Estes (Lyman Frank Baum). *Tamawaca Folks.* N.P., 1907.

Daugherty, Nina. "Incidents of Early Days in Allegan County." *Michigan Pioneer and Historical Collections.* Vol. 38, 1912.

De Jong, Gerald F. *The Dutch in America, 1669-1974.* Boston, [1975].

De Kruif, Paul. *The Sweeping Wind.* New York, 1962.

Den Herder, Marguerite *T. Bankers' Hours—A History of First Michigan Bank and Trust Company 1878-1978.* Zeeland, 1978.

Directory of Allegan County, Michigan. Philadelphia, 1916.

Downing, Elliot Rowland. *A Naturalist in the Great Lakes Region.* Chicago, [1922].

Duke, Basil W. *Morgan's Cavalry.* New York, 1906.

Dunbar, Willis F. *All Aboard: A History of Railroads in Michigan.* Grand Rapids, 1969.

_____. *The Michigan Record in Higher Education.* Detroit, 1963.

[Durant, Samuel]. *History of Kalamazoo County.* Philadelphia, 1880.

Everett Franklin. *Memorials of the Grand River Valley.* Chicago, 1878.

Ewing, Wallace K. *The American Red Cross in Ottawa County.* N.P., 1996.

Fafnir Folks. Holland. Vol. 1. No. 1. [July 1943]. — Vol. 3. No. 2. [August, 1945].

Fairman, Leroy. *The Growth of a Great Industry. H.J. Heinz.* Pittsburg, [1910].

Gitchel, Pauline Hall. *The Early History of Jamestown Township, Ottawa County, Michigan.* N.P., 1925.

Goodspeed, E.J. *History of the Great Fires in Chicago and the West.* New York, [1871].

Greenwood, John O. *Namesakes 1920-1929*. Cleveland, [1984].

Haan, Gilbert G. *My Life in Vriesland Michigan*. (unpublished manuscript).

Historical and Business Compendium of Ottawa County, Michigan. Grand Haven, 1892.

Historical Souvenir of the Celebration of the Sixtieth Anniversary of the Colonization of the Hollanders in Western Michigan. Grand Rapids, 1908.

History of Allegan and Barry Counties, Michigan. Philadelphia, 1880.

History of the Holland Board of Public Works. (unpublished manuscript), 1972.

History of Ottawa County, Michigan . . . Chicago, 1882.

Hodge, Frederick Webb. *Handbook of American Indians North of Mexico*. 2 vols. Washington, 1912.

Holland Chamber News. Vol VlII, 1984.

Holland City Directory. Holland, 1901.

Holland Evening Sentinel. Centennial Edition. 16 Aug. 1947.

Holland Human Relations Commission. *The Hispanic Population in Holland, Michigan, Based on the U.S. Census*. N.P., March 1988.

Holland: The Gateway of Western Michigan For Chicago and the Great West. Holland, [ca. 1912].

Hubbard, Gurdon Saltonstall. *The Autobiography of Gurdon Saltonstall Hubbard*. Chicago, 1911.

Hyma, Albert. *Albertus C. Van Raalte and His Dutch Settlements in the United States*. Grand Rapids, 1947.

Illustrated Souvenir Edition of Holland, Mich. Lansing, July 1901.

James, Ben. "The Way of the Dutch." *The Country Home*. Vol. 8, No. 7. [July 1934].

The Kalamazoo Valley Family Newsletter. Vol. 8, No. 1. [1978].

Keppel, Anna K. *The Immigration and Early History of the People of Zeeland...* Zeeland, [1922].

Keppel, Ruth. *Trees to Tulips*. N.P., [1947].

Kuiper, R.T. *A Voice From America About America*. Grand Rapids, 1970.

Kunitz, Stanley J., and Haycraft, Howard. *Twentieth Century Authors*. New York, 1942.

Kunst, Scott G. "Holland's Centennial Park: A Victorian Survivor." *Michigan History*. Vol. 70, No. 4. (July/August 1986).

Lafitau, P. *Moeurs des Sauvages Ameriquains*. 2 vols. Paris, 1724.

Lane, Kit. *Buried Singapore: Michigan's Imaginary Pompeii*. Douglas, MI., [1994].

_____. ed. T*he History of Western Allegan County*. [Dallas, Texas, 1988].

_____. *Some Stories of Holland Harbo*r. Saugatuck, 1975.

Lanman, Charles. *The Red Book of Michigan*. Detroit, 1871.

Leenhouts, Abraham. *From the Crest of the Hill*. N.P., ca. 1951.

Lillie, Leo C. *Historic Grand Haven and Ottawa County*. Grand Haven, 1931.

Lorenz, Charles. *The Early History of the Black Lake Region 1835-1850*. (unpublished manuscript).

_____. *The Early History of Saugatuck and Singapore, Michigan 1830-1840*. N.P., [1983].

Lozon, Michael. *Vision On Main Street*. Holland, 1994.

Lucas, Henry S. *Dutch Immigrant Memoirs and Related Writings*. 2 vols. Assen,The Netherlands,1955.

Lucas, Henry S. *Netherlanders in America*. Ann Arbor, 1955.

[Maday, Eileen T.] *Squirt & Company*. N.P. [1984].

McClurken, James M. *Gah-Baeh-Jhagwah-Buk: The Way It Happened*. East Lansing, [1991].

McCoy, Patrick T. [Cornelius Van Putten]. *Kiltie McCoy...* Indianapolis, [1918].

McGee, John W. *The Catholic Church in the Grand River Valley 1833-1950*. Grand Rapids, 1950.

McGeehan, Albert H., ed. *My Country and Cross: The Civil War Letters of John Anthony Wilterdink, Company I, 25th Michigan Infantry*. Dallas, Texas [1982].

McKenney, Thomas L. and Hall, James. *History of the Indian Tribes... 2 vols*. Philadelphia, N.D.

Michel, Sara. *With This Inheritance. Holland, Michigan the Early Years*. [Spring Lake, 1984].

Michigan: A Guide to theWolverine State. New York, [1941].

Michigan Biographies. 2 vols. Lansing, 1924.

Michigan Bureau of Labor and Industrial Statistics. Annual Reports. Lansing: 1884-1920. Title varies.

Miller, Randall M. "Pilgrimage to Paradox: The Holland Harbor Question." *Inland Seas*. Vol. 23, Winter 1968.

Moceri, Peggy S. *History of an Institution: Davenport College*. N.P., [1990].

Moore, Raylyn. *Wonderful Wizard Marvelous Land*. Bowling Green, 1974.

[Nyhuis, Jeanne], compiler. *75 Years; The Story Behind Our Success 1920-1995 HFB*. [Holland, 1995].

100 Years Parke-Davis. [Detroit, 1966].

Pare, George. *The Catholic Church in Detroit 1701-1888*. Detroit, 1951.

Parke-Davis 1866-1966 A Backward Glance. [Detroit, 1966].

Parke-Davis Review: Perspective. Vol. 32. No. 1 [January 1975].

Pieters, Aleida J. *A Dutch Settlement in Michigan*. Grand Rapids, 1923.

Portrait and Biographical Record of Muskegon and Ottawa Counties, Michigan... Chicago, 1893.

Postma, Charles Henry. *Isaac Fairbanks: An American In a Dutch Community*. (unpublished master's thesis). Ball State University, 21 August 1969.

Prakke, H.J. *Drenth in Michigan*. Grand Rapids, [1983].

Quimby, George Irving. *Indian Life in the Upper Great Lakes 11,000 B.C. to A.D. 1800*. Chicago, [1960].

Receipt Book Published by the Ladies Aid Society of Hope Church. Holland, 1896.

Record of Service of Michigan Volunteers in the Civil War: Twenty-fifth Michigan Infantry. [Kalamazoo, 1903].

Renner, Thomas L., ed. *Hope College 1992 Alumni Directory*. 8th Edition. [Holland, 1992].

Revised Statutes of the State of Michigan. Detroit, 1838.

Robertson, John. *Michigan In the War*. Lansing, 1882.

Rural Directory of Ottawa County, Michigan. Philadelphia, 1918.

Schrier, William. *Gerritt J. Diekema, Orator*. Grand Rapids, 1950.

Semi-Centennial Reminiscences . . . N.P. 1897.

Seventy-fifth Anniversary of the Central Avenue Christian Reformed Church 1865-1940. [Holland, 1940].

Sligh, Charles R. *History of the Services of the First Regiment Michigan Engineers and Mechanics*. Grand Rapids, 1921.

Smith, Arvilla . *A Pioneer Woman*. Lansing,1981.

Standard Atlas of Ottawa County, Michigan. Chicago, 1897.

The Story of the Dutch Windmill De Zwaan. Holland, 1965.

Swierenga, Robert P. "The Dutch Transplanting in Michigan and the Midwest." Clarence M. Burton Memorial Lecture. 1985.

Ten Zythoff, Gerrit J. "The Americanization of Albertus C. Van Raalte: A Preliminary Inquiry." *The Reformed Review*. Vol. 29, 1976.

Ter Nagedachtenis van Rev. Cornelius van der Meulen. Grand Rapids, 1876.

The Traverse Region, Historical and Descriptive . . . Chicago, 1884.

Travis, B.F. *The Story of the Twenty-Fifth Michigan*. Kalamazoo, 1897.

Tulip Time, Holland, Michigan. Holland: J. Klaasen Printing Co., 1941.

Tulip Time, Holland, Michigan. 1987 Souvenir Program.

Urban, Matt. *The Matt Urban Story*. Holland, [1989].

Vander Hill, C. Warren. *Gerrit J. Diekema*. Grand Rapids, [1970].

Vanderveen, Engbertus. *Life History and Reminiscences*. [Holland, ca. 1917].

Vande Vusse, Raymond L. *A Short History of the Holland, Michigan Post Office*. [Holland, 1987].

Vande Vusse, Robert. "Last On the Lakes A Brief History of the Georgian Bay Lines." *Holland Historical Trust Review*. Vol. 1, No. 2. [Spring, 1988].

Vande Water, Randall P. "Heinz in Holland A Century of History. Illustrated Story 1896-1996." (unpublished manuscript).

_____. *On the Way to Today*. Holland, 1992.

Van Eyck, William O. *Landmarks of the Reformed Fathers*. Grand Rapids, [1922].

van Hartesveldt Fred. "Decorative Brick, A Gift to Michigan From the Dutch." *Michigan History*. Vol. 71, No. 3, [May/June 1987].

Van Hinte, Jacob. *Netherlanders in America*. 2 vols. Grand Rapids, 1985.

Van Koevering, Adrian. *Legends of the Dutch*. Zeeland, Inc., 1960.

van Reken, Donald. L. "Early Printing and Publishing in Holland, Michigan." Occasional Paper #1, Holland Bicentennial Committee. N.D.

_____ *The Farm That Was a Zoo*. Holland, 1983.

_____. *The Holland Fire of October 8, 1871*. Holland, 1982.

_____. *The Interurban Era in Holland, Michigan.* N.P. [1981].

_____. *Macatawa Park A Chronicle.* N.P., [1991].

_____. *Ottawa Beach & Waukazoo A History.* N.P., [1987].

_____. *A Window to the Past.* N.P., [1988].

van Reken, Donald L. and Vande Water, Randall P. *Holland Furnance Company. 1906-1966.* N.P., [1993].

VanSchelven, Gerrit. "The Burning of Holland, October 9, 1871." *Michigan Pioneer and Historical Collections.* Vol. 9, 1886.

_____. "Early Settlement of Holland," *Michigan Pioneer and Historical Collections.* Vol. 26, 1896.

_____. "Michigan and the Holland Immigration of 1847," *Michigan History Magazine.* Vol. 1, No. 2. (October, 1917).

Van'T Lindenhout, J. *Zes Weken Tusschen de Wielen of De Hollanders in Amerika.* Nijmegen, N.D.

Victory Fair Premium List. Holland, 1919.

Vlekke, Bernard H.M., and Beets, Henry. *Hollanders Who Helped Build America.* New York, 1942.

Wabeke, Bertus H. *Dutch Emigration to North America.* New York, 1944.

Wendell, Emory. *History of Banking and Banks and Bankers of Michigan.* 2 Vols. Detroit, [1902].

Whelan, Nicholas J. *Ten Days in Cuba.* [Holland, 1908].

White, George H. "Sketch of the Life of Hon. Rix Robinson... *Michigan Pioneer Collections.* Vol. 11, (1887). p. 186.

Wichers, Willard, ed. *The Hope Milestone of 1930: Alumni Number.* Zeeland, 1930.

Wichers, Wynand. A *Century of Hope.* Grand Rapids, 1968.

_____. *The Dutch Churches in Michigan During the Civil War.* Lansing, 1965.

Williams, Mentor L. ed. *Schoolcraft's Indian Legends...* East Lansing, 1991.

Wilson, Etta Smith. "Life and Work of the Late Rev. George N. Smith, A Pioneer Missionary." *Michigan Pioneer and Historical Collections.* Vol. 30, 1906.

Woods, Francis Henry. "Deluge" in *Encyclopedia of Religion and Ethics.* edited by James Hastings. Vol. IV. New York, 1922.

Youngstrand, C.O., compiler. *Our Michgian Friends "As We See 'Em."* [Detroit, 1905].

This Macatawa resorter failed to heed her mother's warning about making faces. So, now, nearly a century later she's stuck with it.

196

Index